Fast Track to Real Estate Wealth

Accelerate Your Wealth with Property Investments in Just 6 Months—Even If You're Starting From Scratch. Sidestep the Usual Roadblocks with Ease

About the Author

Bishara Andonie's passion for real estate began in high school, learning from his father and grandfather who established a family legacy in the business. This early exposure deepened his interest, especially after assisting in his first property sale.

He has helped turn many people's dreams into reality. Over the years, he has managed significant projects, such as renovating a historical building and overseeing a large-scale commercial development, showcasing his hands-on expertise. Bishara has adapted to market changes, embracing digital marketing and sustainable building practices.

His curiosity drives him to explore emerging market trends and investment strategies, regularly attending industry workshops and engaging in self-learning to stay updated on the latest developments in real estate.

FREE GOODIES FOR OUR DEAR READERS

Congratulations! You are eligible for free worksheets, real estate journals, planners and many more gifts.

Get Free Goodies, workbooks and many more surprises by connecting with us.

Visit us at Andonierealty.com

Or scan the QR code here:

Table of Content

Introduction

Welcome to the gateway of real estate success! This book is your compass in the dynamic world of property business and investments. Explore tried-and-tested methods that have been carefully crafted to help you reach long-term growth. Whether you're a seasoned investor or a budding enthusiast, this journey promises to unlock the secrets of thriving in the ever-evolving realm of real estate.

"While life renews itself endlessly in animals and plants, the land remains a finite and irreplaceable resource. In a world of constant reproduction, it is the scarcity of land that defines its true value."

- **Bishara Andonie**

There aren't many paths to wealth development with the same proven attraction, stability, and potential for significant expansion as the real estate industry. Strategic ideas, business acumen, and measured risk-taking create, nurture, and sustain fortunes here. This book is an all-encompassing manual created to help novice and experienced investors find their way through the maze of real estate investing.

Fundamentally, real estate represents a unique fusion of science and art, where clever financial computations collide with a gut feeling of market dynamics. But the world of real estate investing and business is not picture-perfect; rather, it is a place full of challenges, uncertainties, and constantly changing trends. This book is your go-to guide for understanding the subtleties, tactics, and procedures that support profitable projects in this booming sector.

In the following chapters, we explore the fundamentals of real estate investing in-depth, revealing layers of information and insight gleaned from market experiences, successful businesses, and industry pioneers. Every chapter serves as a pillar in the construction of real estate expertise, from providing the basic knowledge of real estate markets to dissecting the intricacies of financial principles, property selection, negotiating techniques, and legal issues.

This guide's structure is intentionally created to accommodate a range of skill levels and interests. The first few chapters provide a solid foundation for those new to the real estate industry by explaining basic ideas and giving them a broad market overview. Experienced investors, however, will uncover cutting-edge tactics, methods for adjusting to changing markets, and perspectives on building long-term wealth that go beyond traditional thinking.

Essentially, this book serves as a detailed guide tailored to assist you in achieving success in real estate investment. It's not merely a compilation of ideas and methods; rather, it's a blueprint meticulously crafted to aid you in your journey towards financial prosperity through real estate. Through real-life examples, interviews with experts, and actionable strategies, it demonstrates that thriving in real estate isn't limited to the affluent and influential. Anyone equipped with the appropriate knowledge, determination, and strategic mindset can attain such goals.

"Landlords grow rich in their sleep."

- *John Stuart Mill*

Our research extends beyond mere acquisition of assets; it transcends the pursuit of gains and profits. It looks at the morality of building wealth wisely, moral problems, and the lasting effects that real estate can have. It acknowledges that social duty and making money go hand in hand and are mutually beneficial. It discusses how real estate assets can be used for personal gain and to help the community.

Let's work together to discover the mysteries, overcome the obstacles, and mold our destiny within the colorful world of real estate so that we may emerge as wise investors and stewards of long-term success and sustainable progress.

Our ultimate goal? Achieving mastery in the realm of real estate wealth awaits us!

|1|

Understanding Real Estate Investment

Real estate investing is like opening a door to a world full of opportunities to make money and build wealth. If you're ready to jump in, you could go far! In this chapter, we will explore the foundational concepts, strategies, and essential knowledge that pave the way for success in this dynamic and rewarding industry. Welcome to the world where real estate turns into avenues for achieving financial success, regardless of your level of experience as an investor.

For the relevant case studies, articles , worksheets and free resources, you can visit: andonierealty.com

"Ninety percent of all millionaires become so through owning real estate."

- *Andrew Carnegie*

1.1 Definition and Evolution

Fundamentally, real estate investing is the art and science of using physical assets, such as land, buildings, and projects, to produce revenue and meet long-term financial goals. Its origins may be found in prehistoric societies when possessing land symbolized wealth and authority. The idea changed throughout millennia, blending with social, cultural, and economic forces to influence how real estate investing is understood and done today.

The Old Foundations

The ancient civilizations of Mesopotamia, Egypt, and Rome are the origins of real estate investing. Agriculture was the main economic activity, and owning land was a sign of power and prosperity. Real estate transactions began with landlords leasing their homes and collecting rent differently.

The feudal institutions of medieval Europe first introduced the idea of property rights and tenures, which laid the groundwork for modern land ownership. Large swathes of land were given to vassals by feudal lords in return for labor or money. The foundation for the current legal system controlling property ownership and transactions was established during this time.

The beginning of the Industrial Revolution caused a profound change in real estate dynamics. Urbanization increased as more people moved from rural to rapidly growing cities in pursuit of work. Residential communities and business districts developed due to the growing housing and commercial space demand. Real estate investing became a recognized asset class in the late 19th and early 20th centuries. The emergence of real estate firms and investment trusts allowed people to invest in real estate without taking direct ownership. During this time, contemporary financial instruments and real estate markets emerged, opening new avenues for investment possibilities and diverse portfolios.

Innovations in Technology and Globalization

Technological improvements and globalization transformed Real estate investments in the late 20th and early 21st centuries. While technology advancements transformed property management, market research, and investment strategies, the interconnection of economies made cross-border investments easier. The emergence of digital technologies and internet platforms facilitated the democratization of real estate investing options by streamlining procedures. This type of investing crosses conventional borders in today's environment.

It includes various industries, including mixed-use, commercial, industrial, and residential complexes. Investors use a variety of tactics to achieve their financial goals and diversify their portfolios, ranging from long-term buy-and-hold methods to short-term property flipping. Real estate investment has evolved throughout time, a story that is continuously being told and influenced by cultural trends, technology advancements, regulatory changes, and economic cycles. Sustainability concerns mark a new chapter in developing this dynamic business, integrating proptech (property technology) solutions and ESG (environmental, social, and governance) considerations.

Knowing the history of real estate investing offers a comprehensive viewpoint, embracing the potential and complexity of the modern day and understanding its historical foundations. This information is a foundation for navigating the complex world of real estate investing and business to build wealth and achieve sustainable growth.

1.2 Historic Triumphs in Wealth Creation

One only needs to study history to fully appreciate real estate's strength and potential as a means of earning riches. People and visionaries have used the mechanics of real estate to accumulate money over time, changing the face of wealth creation forever. These past successes serve as lights that show how smart real estate investments may alter circumstances.

1. **Florence during the Renaissance: The Medici Family**

The Medici family, located in the center of Renaissance Florence, is a prime example of how wise real estate decisions can spark social, political, and cultural revolutions. Renowned art collectors and powerful politicians, the Medici, carefully bought and developed excellent estates. Their vision improved their financial situation and significantly contributed to the creative and cultural revival that characterized the time.

The Medici family became famous for the banking empire. They used bank gains to buy valuable properties in Florence and Tuscany, such as houses and castles. These properties would earn them steady income from rents and leases, and their values would rise over time. Having real estate not only kept them financially stable, but it also gave them more power over Florence's politics and economy.

2. **John D. Rockefeller's Investments in Manhattan**

The American oil business magnate John D. Rockefeller made strategic real estate decisions that had lasting effects in the early 20th century. In addition to positioning him as an industrial mogul, his investments in Manhattan's finest real estate, such as purchasing the Equitable Building, also made him a real estate visionary.

3. **The Ascent of Real Estate Tycoons in Hong Kong**

Tycoons such as Li Ka-Shing and the Kwok family dominated the real estate scene in Hong Kong in the second half of the 20th century, making the city a breeding ground for real estate wealth creation. Often regarded as one of Asia's wealthiest people, Li Ka-shing made astute investments in residential and commercial real estate and skillfully managed market swings. The Kwok family enhanced Hong Kong's skyline with Sun Hung Kai Properties, demonstrating the possibility of generating riches via real estate development over generations.

4. The Pioneers of Silicon Valley Real Estate

Real estate became essential to Silicon Valley's prosperity as the technology industry flourished there. Entrepreneurs such as Mark Zuckerberg, the creator of Facebook, and Larry Ellison, co-founder of Oracle, not only transformed the IT sector but also made calculated investments in large tracts of real estate. The purchase of whole Hawaiian islands by Ellison and Zuckerberg's Palo Alto home demonstrates how real estate can serve as a financial asset and a symbol of a person's legacy.

5. The Andonie Family

Luis Andonie Siman, the man who started it all, stands as a visionary figure who transformed San Pedro Garza Garcia, next door to Monterrey, into one of Mexico's most affluent and secure municipalities. He pioneered the development of the Moll del Valle and erected the city's inaugural 14-story skyscraper in 1982. This marked the inception of Monterrey's trajectory toward a landscape rich with growth opportunities and burgeoning commercial ventures.

Andonie Family can be approached easily at **andonierealty.com**

Today, our family remains deeply involved in numerous ventures across Mexico, including Monterrey, Tampico, Saltillo, Cancun, and Tulum. Our headquarters are situated in San Pedro Garza Garcia, specifically in "El Centrito," where my grandfather established the first residence in the center.

These historical real estate wealth creation success stories have one thing in common: they all had a vision, made smart decisions, and recognized the mutually beneficial link between real estate and larger economic and cultural factors. They demonstrate how real estate is a dynamic stage where fortunes are crafted by a combination of vision, timing, and measured risk-taking rather than just a background for wealth development.

Exploring the domains of past real estate successes reveals that prosperous investors were not constrained by the conventions of their day; rather, they were innovators who saw the revolutionary possibilities of well-timed real estate ventures. These stories provide:

- Motivation, discipline and priceless insights for modern investors.
- Highlighting the significance of research and flexibility.
- A forward-thinking perspective in negotiating the always-changing terrain of real estate wealth development.

We break down these lessons in the following pages, bringing to light ideas and tactics that have stood the test of time and providing direction to those looking to make their mark in the fast-paced world of real estate investing.

1.3 The Current Landscape

When navigating real estate investments, it's crucial to consider the dynamic environment shaped by sociological, technical, and economic factors. Real estate investing in the modern era is characterized by continuity and quick change, offering investors never-before-seen possibilities and difficulties. The capacity of real estate to withstand swings in the world economy has shown its durability as an investment class. Property has shown a resilient ability to recover and flourish even in the face of the COVID-19 epidemic and the shocks of the 2008 financial crisis. The material qualities of real estate assets have comforted investors as they seek stability in the face of financial market turbulence.

Technology-Driven Shifts: The digital revolution has impacted every aspect of our lives, and real estate is no different. Proptech, a combination of property and technology, has become a key player in the industry's transformation. Incorporating technology has improved transparency, shortened procedures, and broadened the potential of real estate investments. Examples of this include virtual property tours, online property listings, blockchain-powered transactions, and smart home technologies.

The democratization of real estate investment access is one of the most significant changes in the contemporary environment. Previously, high-net-worth individuals and institutional investors often used real estate as their playground. However, more types of investors may now participate thanks to the introduction of real estate investment trusts (REITs) and crowdfunding platforms. With reduced capital requirements, individuals may now engage in real estate projects, creating a more diverse investing environment.

Punta Loma

Tampico, Mexico

Changes in Preferences for Properties: Alongside social developments, property searchers' and investors' choices have also changed. The sorts of assets that attract attention have changed due to urbanization, increased distant employment, and a greater emphasis on sustainability. Mixed-use complexes, including commercial, residential, and recreational areas, are becoming increasingly popular as people seek convenient and all-encompassing living spaces.

Real estate investing is undergoing a paradigm shift due to the threat of climate change and growing public awareness of environmental problems. Eco-friendly and sustainable methods are becoming more than just catchphrases; they are essential to investment and real estate development plans. Investors try to match their financial aims with more general societal and environmental objectives by including environmental, social, and governance (ESG) considerations in their decision-making processes.

The modern environment is full of challenges. The intricacies of regulations, which differ across different regions, provide a significant obstacle for investors managing international transactions. In addition, a complex and flexible strategy for real estate investing is required due to the risk introduced by shifting interest rates, geopolitical unpredictability, and the possibility of economic downturns.

Flexible Investment Approaches: Investors are embracing adaptive methods beyond conventional models in response to the changing scenario. One important thing to consider is the contrast between short-term profits and long-term stability. Hybrid investing techniques are becoming more popular since they include buy-and-hold and property flipping aspects. Furthermore, the investigation of novel investment vehicles like syndication and crowdfunding for real estate shows a quick reaction to the shifting market conditions.

The rise in cross-border real estate investments may be attributed to the interdependence of the world's economy. Investors are searching for possibilities outside of their home markets in various locations. The pursuit of better returns, portfolio diversification, and an awareness of developing nations' potential are driving this trend of globalization. But it also requires thoroughly comprehending every target market's unique legal, cultural, and economic characteristics.

The following data can help investors make informed decisions based on their risk tolerance, capital availability, and investment timeline preferences.

Investment Approach	Expected Annual Return	Risk Level	Investment Horizon
Buy and Hold	8-12%	Low	Long-term (10+ years)
Fix and Flip	10-30%	High	Short-term (1-2 years)
Real Estate Investment Trusts (REITs)	4-10%	Medium	Medium-term (5-10 years)
Commercial Real Estate	6-12%	Medium	Medium to Long-term (5+ years)

Vacation Rentals	8-15%	Medium to High	Medium to Long-term (3+ years)
Real Estate Crowdfunding	8-20%	Med-High	Variable (depends on project)
Land Development	15-40%	Very High	Long-term (10+ years)

Handling the Changing Terrain: Navigating this changing terrain becomes critical when we find ourselves at the intersection of tradition and change in the real estate investing sector. The setting of the modern environment is characterized by the democratization of investment access, imperatives of sustainability, and the linkages of technology. It also needs an investor who is flexible. This investor should be open to looking at opportunities in other countries and understand that laws and economies are always changing.

It will be a difficult but exciting journey to grasp the complexities of sustainable practices, global market dynamics, and technology. Given the complexity of modern real estate investing, the present environment calls on investors to not only adapt but also to lead and to see possibilities and dangers.

1.4 Government Organizations

Several parts of the U.S. government are involved in the real estate business. You can check official site here: Buying from the U.S. government | USAGov

1. **GSA**

The General Services Administration (GSA) is in charge of the government's property. They help people rent out properties, sell properties, choose sites, and do other real estate-related things. Through GSA Auctions, the GSA sells land, homes, and other things that belong to the government. You can visit it here: Real estate | GSA

2. **HUD**

Through its HUD Homes program, the U.S. Department of Housing and Urban Development (HUD) buys homes that have been taken back by banks. HUD puts homes all over the U.S. up for sale. You can visit it here:

3. **Agriculture Department**

Land, fields, and homes that belong to the government are sold by the U.S. Department of Agriculture, either at sale or by offer.

4. **FDIC**

The Federal Deposit Insurance Corporation (FDIC) buys homes and business property from banks that have gone out of business.

5. **U.S Treasury**

Homes, land, businesses, and other things that owners gave up because they broke Treasury law are sold at sale by the U.S. Treasury.

6. **U.S Marshals**

In the U.S. and the Caribbean, the U.S. Marshals Service sells houses, condos, business property, and land that they have taken at auction.

7. **BLM**

The Bureau of Land Management (BLM) sells federally owned public lands that haven't been built on.

1.5 Potential Risks and Challenges

Starting out in real estate is like going on a big journey. It's exciting but can be tricky. Even though making money and owning property is tempting, it's smart to understand and lessen the risks. We'll talk about the problems you might face and help you navigate the real estate world.

Market turbulence and fluctuations in the economy

The real estate asset class is not impervious to the rippling waves of economic shifts. Real estate prices and rental earnings may be affected by market volatility, which is driven by variables including interest rates, GDP growth, and employment rates. Economic downturns, such as the one that occurred during the 2008 financial crisis, may cause a drop in demand and property values, which can be difficult for investors who depend on cash flow and property appreciation.

One of the main characteristics of real estate investing is the strategic use of finance, which enables investors to leverage their funds for greater property purchases. However, there are hazards associated with this leverage. Interest rate fluctuations affect borrowing costs, which may affect investment profitability. Furthermore, over-leveraging—a situation in which debt levels exceed the property's ability to generate income—presents a serious concern, especially in recessionary times when cash flow may be limited.

Risks Particular to a Property

1. **Location and Quality:** The proverb "location, location, location" captures a basic fact about real estate: a property's geographic setting significantly impacts its value and attractiveness. Returns may be compromised when investing in places vulnerable to economic downturns or lacking basic services. Furthermore, dangers may be introduced by a property's quality

and condition. Unexpected costs arise from overlooked structural problems, environmental hazards, or poor maintenance, which lowers the investment's overall profitability.

Older doesn't always mean cheaper and newer doesn't always mean better. For example: In California, a house that's over 50 years old can be for sale for more than $500,000. It might have 2 bedrooms and 1 bathroom. The house might not be well maintained. Because of the location, it's expensive. You could possibly find a buyer, but the quality is bad and maintenance is required.

Compared to a new home in Texas with the same price, this home has 4 bedrooms and 4 bathrooms. It also has a nice backyard. However, it is located by the border. The quality of the home is good, but the location is something to consider.

2. **Challenges in Regulation and Law:** A crucial component of real estate endeavors is navigating the maze of legal and regulatory requirements. Different jurisdictions have

different zoning rules, land use laws, and property tax policies, necessitating a thorough awareness of local legal environments. Infractions of these rules may result in penalties, hold-ups, or even an involuntary property sale. Legal conflicts involving renters, neighbors, or other stakeholders may pose possible difficulties, highlighting the need for careful due diligence and legal advice. Best thing is to do your due diligence.

3. **Competition and Market Saturation:** The desire for profit may cause market saturation and increased competitiveness in developing real estate markets. Inflated housing prices brought on by overcrowding might reduce prospective returns on investment. Investors must manage these circumstances by identifying specialized possibilities, keeping up with market trends, and using creative tactics to set their initiatives apart from rivals. An example is that as of 2020 and up, realty companies have brought more than 1,000,000+ new apartments in the USA and it's still expanding, changing the market for renters.

4. **The Risks of Interest Rates and Inflation:** Interest rate variations may affect the cost of financing and the availability of mortgages

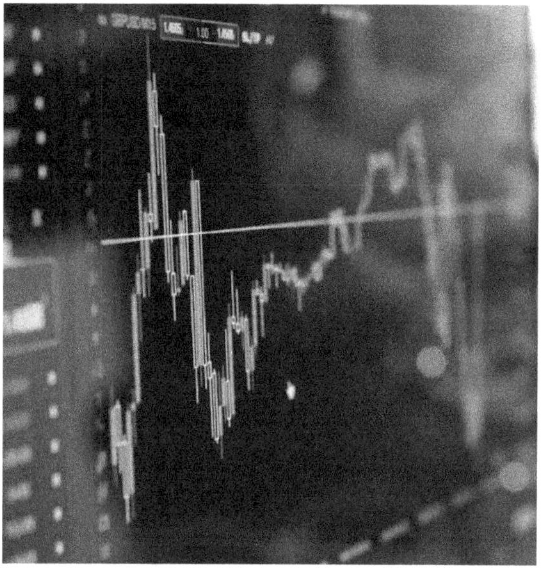

since real estate investments are closely linked to these fluctuations.

A rise in borrowing expenses due to rising interest rates may make refinancing and property purchases less feasible. Furthermore, although the property is sometimes seen as a hedge against inflation, unanticipated increases may pressure running expenses and lower the buying power of rental revenues. As of 2020, anyone living in the USA knows that inflation has skyrocketed and has increased the price of everything.

5. **Hazards of Natural and Environmental Disasters:** The growing emphasis on sustainability pushes environmental factors to the forefront of real estate projects. There are dangers associated with owning property in a region vulnerable to natural catastrophes like hurricanes, earthquakes, or floods. Concerns about climate change make it more important to evaluate a property's vulnerability to environmental elements. These factors may affect insurance rates and property values. This is due to changes in regulations and increased public awareness of environmental impact.

6. **Operational and Management Risks:** Reaching the maximum return on real estate investments requires efficient property management. Inadequate management may result in greater vacancy rates, lower property values, and more maintenance costs—whether it is done in-house or by

hiring outside experts. Strong management procedures are essential given the difficulties in monitoring renters, taking quick action on maintenance concerns, and guaranteeing legal compliance.

7. **Unexpected Developments and Black Swan Hazards:** A "black swan" is an unexpected event that goes beyond what people usually expect from a situation and could have very bad results. People usually say that black swan events were clear after they occurred because they happen so rarely and have such a big effect.

   Events like international pandemics, terrorist strikes, or financial crises may significantly alter market dynamics and property prices. Even if it's hard to forecast these things, investors may strengthen their portfolios using risk management and diversification techniques. I'm guessing most of you reading this book are from the USA, thankfully there aren't many terrorists but a pandemic happened four years ago that changed the game, making prices skyrocket and people needing to rent because they can't afford a home, this is something to just consider.

Wrapping Up: Handling the Facts

You as an investor need to understand that managing the always-changing real estate market requires careful due diligence, flexible approaches, and a resilient outlook. As an example, when the economy goes bad, what is the one real estate investment that has a good chance to succeed? It's Residential Investments.

People will always need somewhere to sleep, renting apartments, condos or homes can help in this type of economy. The next chapters deconstruct the approaches and perspectives critical for reducing risks, grabbing hold of possibilities, and guaranteeing a strong basis for long-term success in the ever-changing realm of real estate endeavors.

Here is a short Activity for you related to your Business:

Business Overview

Business Name		Opportunity Horizon
Tag Line		
		Mission
Website:		

Social Media Usernames	Business Goals
	3 Months
	6 Months
	1 Year
	2 Years
	5 Years
	10 Years

Main Business Focus	Target Customer

YOUR Unique Selling Point

|2|

Understanding Real Estate Markets

Welcome to the gateway of real estate dynamics! You will understand the intricate world of real estate markets in this chapter, where we unravel the complexities and nuances that define their pulse. From trends to intricacies, in unraveling the keys to comprehending and navigating these ever-evolving landscapes. I will also provide you with some projects that my family is building to give you an idea of how it looks.

For the relevant case studies, worksheets and free resources you can visit: andonierealty.com

"Buy land, they're not making it anymore."

- Mark Twain

2.1 Types of Real Estate Markets

The real estate market is a dynamic and varied landscape with many sectors, each with its attributes, concerns, and investment dynamics. Comprehending the several categories of real estate marketplaces is fundamental for any investor aiming for prosperity and durability in this diverse industry. We will examine three main real estate markets: residential, commercial, and industrial.

Residential Property: The Foundation of Ownership

The foundation of the real estate market is residential real estate, which is made up of homes used by single people and families. This category includes many properties, including apartment buildings, multifamily dwellings, single-family homes, and condos. The residential market allows people to invest in a place they can call home, closely linked to homeownership. This is usually where most investors start.

Important Features of Residential Property:

- ***Single-family homes:*** are stand-alone buildings intended for only one family. They are a popular option for homeowners since they provide privacy and freedom.
- ***Multifamily residences:*** These include apartment complexes, duplexes, triplexes, and other constructions that house many families. For investors, they provide potential for rental revenue.
- ***Condominium:*** These are often called condos i.e. "units within a larger complex," privately owned residences. Owning a condo combines aspects of community living with proprietorship. (San Francisco Plaza and Condos, wel.mx)
- ***Townhouses:*** These are usually two or more stories with common walls. Townhouses provide a compromise between single-family homes and condos.

Investors often prioritize long-term wealth growth, property appreciation, and rental income when investing in residential real estate. Elements, including community amenities, school districts, and location, heavily influence property prices. Residential real estate is a dynamic and flexible market that reacts to macroeconomic variables, lifestyle choices, and demographic trends.

Commercial Real Estate: The Confluence of Property and Business

Properties intended for use in a business context are referred to as commercial real estate. This category includes various buildings, including hotels, medical institutions, retail stores, office buildings, and more. Commercial buildings serve as locations for various economic operations, in contrast to residential real estate, which is largely focused on living areas.

Principal attributes of commercial real estate include:

- ***Office Buildings:*** Areas created to house corporate activities. They range in size from multi-story office buildings to single-tenant offices.
    - Plaza Santa Isabel, (wel.mx) and Torre Vetro, (wel.mx)
- ***Retail Spaces:*** These are places where companies directly provide their products or services to customers. This covers freestanding retail establishments as well as strip malls and shopping centers.
    - Punta Loma, (puntaloma.com.mx) and Olivos261, (olivos261.com.mx)
- ***Hotels and Hospitality:*** Real estate that offers short-term lodging, such as resorts, hotels, and motels.
- ***Healthcare Facilities:*** Buildings like clinics, hospitals, and doctor's offices intended to provide medical and healthcare services.

The two main goals of commercial real estate investing are maximizing property value and earning rental revenue. Commercial ventures' success heavily depends on location, accessibility, and the local economy. Several factors influence commercial assets' stability and profitability, including lease agreements, tenant creditworthiness, and general economic conditions.

Industrial Property: Enabling Manufacturing and Distribution

Properties designed for product manufacture, distribution, and manufacturing are the focal point of the industrial real estate sector. It provides the infrastructure required to create and move goods from producers to consumers, acting as the logistical foundation of economies.

Important Features of In Real Estate:

- ***Warehouses:*** Serve as expansive storage facilities crucial for housing various commodities. Within the supply chain they play a pivotal role in facilitating the swift movement of goods, contributing significantly to efficient logistics and distribution.
    - Wel Parks, (wel.mx)
- ***Distribution:*** These centers are strategically located hubs designed to streamline the flow of commodities, ensuring optimized delivery to merchants or end users. Their positioning is key in enhancing the efficiency and speed of the distribution process.
- ***Manufacturing Plants:*** Encompass real estate dedicated to hosting specialized equipment and facilities essential for conducting manufacturing operations. These plants are the operational core where goods

are produced and processed. ***Flex Spaces:*** Offer adaptable solutions for enterprises, providing versatile areas that can be utilized for diverse industrial applications. These spaces are designed to accommodate changing needs and offer businesses the agility to adjust their operations as required, allowing for increased adaptability and innovation within the industrial landscape.

Investors in industrial real estate often consider the effectiveness of logistics, accessibility to major transportation hubs, and the general need for manufacturing and distribution services. The growth of e-commerce has especially impacted the need for strategically positioned distribution centers and warehouses. The industrial real estate investment environment is shaped, as it is in other industries, by global supply chain dynamics, technology breakthroughs, and economic trends.

Building a Diverse Portfolio

It's like learning the many instruments in a symphony when you understand the subtleties of the residential, commercial, and industrial real estate markets. Wealthy investors often create diverse portfolios that maximize each segment's advantages while reducing hazards. Every market type contributes a different melody to the overall composition of a real estate investment plan, whether due to the stability of residential real estate, the opportunity for profit on commercial buildings, or the practical significance of industrial spaces.

The nuances of each market type will be further explored in the next chapters, along with risk management, sustainable development, and success techniques in the dynamic world of real estate businesses.

2.2 Real Estate Economics

Numerous variables affect property prices, investment possibilities, and general market dynamics in the intricate and dynamic interaction between real estate markets and the larger economic environment. Real estate markets and the status of the economy are interdependent, and investors, developers, and other stakeholders must negotiate this complex relationship. This investigation examines the economic forces that profoundly influence and sculpt the real estate landscape.

Dynamics of the Mortgage Market and Interest Rates: The cost of borrowing, closely related to current interest rates, is at the center of real estate transactions. Interest rate fluctuations significantly affect mortgage affordability, affecting investors' and purchasers' buying power. Low-interest rates make borrowing more affordable, which increases demand for real estate and may raise property prices. On the other hand, increased interest rates have the potential to reduce demand, which might affect real estate prices and cause a downturn in the industry. The availability and design of mortgage products can impact the real estate market. The dynamics of real estate transactions are further shaped by innovations in the mortgage market, such as fixed-rate mortgages and adjustable-rate mortgages (ARMs), which provide different degrees of flexibility and risk to borrowers.

Here is one key formula related to the dynamics of the mortgage market and interest rates:

Effective Annual Interest Rate (EAR):

$$\text{EAR} = \left(1 + \frac{r}{k}\right)^k - 1$$

- r: Nominal interest rate
- k: Number of compounding periods per year

This formula adjusts the nominal interest rate for the number of compounding periods to determine the effective annual interest rate.

Employment and Income Distribution: The status of people's finances as individuals and families significantly influences the real estate markets. Employment levels, salary growth, and general income distribution significantly impact housing demand. Demand for residential properties is fueled by people entering the housing market, whether as homeowners or renters, during periods of economic success and substantial employment. On the other hand, dips in the economy, job losses, or stagnating income levels may cause the demand for homes to decline. Delays in homeownership by renters and difficulties in mortgage payments by current homeowners might result in a rise in rental market vacancies and a decrease in property prices.

Here is a quick table for you:

Category	Statistic
Employment Statistics	
Real Median Earnings (2021-2022)	Decreased by 2.2% (U.S. Census Bureau)
Median Weekly Personal Income (Q1 2022)	$1,037 for full-time workers (U.S. Bureau of Labor Statistics)
Income Distribution Statistics	
Incomes Over $1 (2022)	88.07% of individuals over age 15 (U.S. Census Bureau)

Median Income (2022)	$40,480 (U.S. Census Bureau)
Mean Income (2022)	$59,430 (U.S. Census Bureau)
Income Below $30,000 (2015)	50% of individuals over age 15
Top 10% Income (2015)	Over $95,000
Income Disparities	Men > Women, Asians/Whites > African Americans/Hispanics

Consumer Spending Trends and Confidence: Consumer psychology, often captured in consumer confidence metrics, is a powerful factor influencing real estate markets. A strong sense of consumer confidence is often correlated with higher levels of investment and consumption, especially in real estate transactions. Optimistic investors are more inclined to make large financial investments, such as buying houses or commercial real estate. Conversely, a lack of consumer confidence may cause people to be frugal with their money. Prospective homeowners may postpone purchases during uncertain economic times, while companies may be reluctant to grow or invest in new commercial locations. It becomes essential to comprehend and keep an eye on consumer mood to predict changes in the real estate market dynamics.

Dynamics of Supply and Demand: Real estate markets are governed by the laws of supply and demand, which have significantly impacted prices. Prices and rental rates are significantly influenced by the relative availability or scarcity of available property demand in a particular market. Economic variables such as migration patterns, urbanization trends, and population expansion influence the dynamics of supply and demand. Demand for housing and commercial space may exceed availability in quickly urbanizing areas, resulting in price rises and competitive marketplaces. Conversely, an overabundance of homes may lead to falling prices and more competition among sellers in areas facing economic difficulties or a population reduction.

Preservation of Asset Value and Inflation: Property values have traditionally shown some tenacity in the face of increasing costs, making real estate a popular choice for those looking to hedge against inflation. Tangible assets, such as real estate, tend to hold or even grow in value during inflationary times, providing a buffer against the declining purchase power of money. In inflationary times, investors often see real estate as a way to protect and even increase their wealth. This viewpoint is especially important when contrasting conventional financial assets, which could be more vulnerable to the effects of inflation, with real estate.

Here is a concise table:

Category	**Statistic**
Inflation Rate	3.7% (September 2023), consistent with previous month

Wage Growth	4.7% (March 2024), outpacing 3.5% inflation rate
Interest Rates	Federal Reserve rate at 5.33% (September 2023)
Consumer Price Index (CPI)	Measures change in prices of household goods/services
Asset Value	BLS provides data on inflation and consumer spending

The regulatory environment and government policies: The regulatory framework and governmental policies significantly impact real estate markets. Tax laws, zoning ordinances, housing programs, and fiscal policies strongly impact the cost, accessibility, and allure of real estate investments.

For example, zoning laws may influence the construction and usage of commercial and industrial assets, while tax incentives for homeownership might increase demand in the residential market. To predict market dynamics and investment possibilities, real estate players must thoroughly understand the changing regulatory environment.

International Economics: Global economic issues significantly influence local real estate markets in an increasingly linked world. Global economic events that impact property prices and investment patterns include trade agreements, financial crises, and geopolitical conflicts.

Cross-border real estate investors need to be aware of changes in the world economy. Because economies are intertwined, incidents in one region may impact real estate markets, affecting risk assessments and investment plans. In short, the economic variables influencing real estate markets are like a symphony of interwoven parts, each adding a unique note to the overall composition. Investors and stakeholders must pay close attention to economic indicators and comprehend the subtleties associated with interest rates, job patterns, consumer attitudes, and governmental regulations.

2.3 Geographic Influences and Market Dynamics

Through the intricate web of real estate markets, geography plays the role of a silent master. The location of a property affects its value, market dynamics, and appeal in addition to being just a question of coordinates.

This is true for both tranquil suburban landscapes and expansive metropolitan skylines. In this investigation, we explore how geographic factors shape the characteristics of residential, commercial, and industrial landscapes and orchestrate the subtleties of real estate markets.

❖ City Dynamics and Urbanization

Cities are the throbbing heartbeat of real estate markets, pulsing with energy, possibilities, and problems. The movement of people from rural to urban regions, or urbanization, is a revolutionary force that is influencing demand for real estate, both residential and commercial. Cities develop into hubs of social interaction, cultural vitality, and economic activity that attract people and companies looking for the ease and energy of city life.

Residential real estate in urban locations often favors high-density living, with townhouses, apartments, and condos making up most of the architecture. Cities with limited space have more expensive real estate and more competitive marketplaces. Tall buildings that house offices, retail stores, and cultural institutions are the hallmarks of commercial real estate in metropolitan environments. The demand for excellent properties in busy metropolitan centers drives the vitality of urban real estate markets.

On the other hand, suburban neighborhoods have a distinct charm that emphasizes openness, peace, and a feeling of community. Suburban residential properties often consist of single-family houses with bigger yards and an emphasis on family-friendly features. Suburban business districts provide neighborhood shops, educational institutions, and community services. Personal preferences, lifestyle choices, and accessibility to facilities and places of employment often influence the decision to live in an urban or suburban area.

❖ Agricultural Dynamics and Rural Real Estate

Outside the urban-suburban divide, rural real estate is a separate market driven by recreational, natural, and agricultural factors. Ranches, farms, and agricultural property are essential elements of rural real estate that support agribusiness and agricultural output. A farm's worth is related to climate, water availability, and soil quality. The worldwide demand for agricultural goods, crop prices, and government regulations influence the changes in agricultural real estate markets. The tenacity and flexibility of farmers and agribusiness owners significantly shape the characteristics of the rural real estate market.

In addition to agriculture, those looking for a slower pace of life, second homes, or recreational properties sometimes choose to live in rural regions. There may be a desire for vacation rentals or rural getaways near lakes, woods, and other natural features. The idea of rural-urban interaction emerges when people try to strike a balance between their metropolitan jobs and their country vacations, impacting the residential and recreational real estate markets.

❖ Properties by the Sea and the Waterfront

Living by the water on a riverbank, a lakeside, or a coastline has always been appealing. Particularly around the coast, distinctive elements like easy access to the ocean, beautiful scenery, and recreational options influence real estate markets. Due to the limited availability of waterfront homes and the high demand for riverfront living, coastal properties often fetch premium rates. Fortunately, there are still beautiful beaches outside of the USA that allow investors to get a good deal and a beautiful sight in other countries.

The thriving tourist and hospitality sectors further influence the dynamics of residential and commercial real estate in coastal locations. The combination of natural beauty and real estate generates a unique market niche for anything from beachside houses and resorts to waterfront business buildings. However, these markets have an additional element of risk since coastal properties are also susceptible to natural causes, including erosion, storms, and rising sea levels.

❖ Mountainous and Grassy Settings

Homes tucked away in picturesque or mountainous settings are another aspect of geography's impact on real estate. The allure of tranquil landscapes, mountain vistas, and easy access to outdoor activities shapes these places' residential and recreational real estate markets. Mountainous areas are often visited by those looking for getaways from the hustle and bustle of the city, second houses, or cottages.

Resorts, ski lodges, and vacation rentals flourish in mountainous areas, serving seasonal travelers and recreational lovers. The distinct experiences provided by the natural surroundings, such as skiing in the winter, hiking in the summer, or just taking in the peace of the mountains, are often the driving force behind the demand for real estate in these places.

❖ International Trade

With the increasing interconnectedness of the globe, geographic effects transcend local limits. Due to the effects of globalization, cross-border real estate transactions add another level of complexity to the market dynamics. Investors look for chances in various places, looking for advantageous regulatory frameworks, economic circumstances, and development prospects.

Global cities, often centers of finance and culture, draw foreign investors searching for luxury real estate and great commercial assets. Cross-border real estate dynamics include considering legal frameworks, cultural quirks, and currency exchange. Furthermore, the stability and attractiveness of real estate investments in various locations may be influenced by geopolitical considerations.

❖ Sustainability and Environmental Aspects

Environmental awareness has recently been a major issue affecting real estate markets. Properties in ecologically sensitive areas—such as wetlands, greenbelts, or regions vulnerable to natural disasters—may be subject to additional regulations or inspection. On the other hand, a niche industry centered on energy-efficient houses, green construction techniques, and ecologically sensitive projects has emerged in response to the growing demand for sustainable and eco-friendly buildings.

To combine development with environmental preservation, towns and developers consider geographic factors and sustainability issues. The emergence of eco-friendly construction techniques, sustainable urban design, and green infrastructure represents a changing real estate paradigm where environmental stewardship and geography meet. In essence, the fundamental characteristics of a site impact the nature of properties and the dynamics of investment, and the geographic effects on real estate markets provide a varied and complex picture. The symphony of real estate markets is enhanced by the distinct melodies contributed by urban, suburban, rural, coastal, and mountainous regions.

The next chapters will provide tactics for negotiating this complex terrain. A keen awareness of the geographic factors that shape the always-changing landscape of properties is essential for anybody venturing into the real estate market, whether it is to capitalize on the attraction of waterfront living, comprehend the dynamics of urbanization, or investigate chances in international markets.

2.4 Identifying Emerging vs. Mature Markets

The difference between developing and mature markets is an important topic in the world of real estate investment. Every part of the real estate market has its own opportunities and challenges. To succeed, you need to understand these differences and know how to deal with them. In this topic, we examine the essential traits, financial factors, and tactics for recognizing and prospering in both developed and developing real estate markets.

Rapidly developing real estate markets are known as emerging ones, often defined by expanding economies, rising urbanization rates, and rising property demand. These markets, which are still undergoing significant change, entice investors with the prospect of enormous profits and unrealized potential. However, hazards are associated with enormous potential, so taking a calculated strategy to seize chances and minimize obstacles is necessary.

Important Emerging Market Features:

Economic Growth: Strong economic growth is usually linked to emerging markets. These economies are becoming more appealing due to growing GDP, rising income levels, and expanded employment prospects.

Infrastructure Development and Urbanization: Emerging markets are characterized by the urbanization process. Demand for residential and commercial real estate rises as more people move into metropolitan regions. This tendency is often accompanied by infrastructure growth, including public services, utilities, and transportation.

Population Growth and Demographic Changes: In developing economies, there is a growing demand for residential and commercial real estate due to high population growth rates and demographic changes, including the emergence of a middle class. These markets' youthful and vibrant populations support consumer-driven businesses and provide various investment possibilities.

Investor Interest and Foreign Direct Investment (FDI): Investors looking for high-growth possibilities pay close attention to emerging economies. The infusion of cash, knowledge, and international views that foreign direct investment provides is essential for the growth of the real estate industry.

Name:

Date:

Important Emerging Market Features

Infrastructure Development and Urbanization

Population Growth and Demographic Changes

Investor Interest and Foreign Direct Investment (FDI):

Economic Growth

How did the character solve the problem?

Taking Into Account Investment in Developing Markets:

High Growth Possibility: The possibility for large returns on investment is the main attraction of developing economies. Particularly in quickly expanding metropolitan areas, the early phases of development can provide chances for property appreciation and profitable returns.

Risk management: Emerging markets have higher risks even when there is a clear chance for large gains. Investors may face difficulties due to political unpredictability, regulatory uncertainty, and inadequate legal frameworks. It is crucial to use risk management techniques and complete due diligence.

Market cycles and timing: In developing markets, timing is crucial. Investors must know economic indicators, market cycles, and possible turning moments. While investments made at the wrong moment may encounter difficulties, entering the market at the correct time may increase rewards.

Establishing Local Partnerships and Knowing Cultural Subtleties: Success in developing markets requires establishing local partnerships and comprehending cultural subtleties—connections with stakeholders, local knowledge, and a thorough understanding of the regulatory landscape aid effective decision-making.

Mature Markets: Consistency and Well-Guided Investment

A history of consistent economic development, well-established infrastructure, and a clear regulatory environment distinguishes these markets. Mature economies provide stability, liquidity, and a distinct range of investment possibilities, even if their growth rates may be more modest than those of developing markets.

Important Features of Mature Markets:

Stable economic circumstances and a well-established infrastructure characterize mature markets. These marketplaces are often more stable when existing utilities, public services, and transportation networks exist.

Variable Property Kinds and Specializations: Residential, commercial, and industrial property kinds are among the many that may be found in a mature market. Niche investment possibilities may be available in specialized industries like healthcare, hotels, and elder living. These industries may flourish. High levels of both liquidity and market depth are characteristics of mature markets. Efficient property acquisition and sales provide investors flexibility and the chance to make timely portfolio modifications.

Investors in developed markets often place a high priority on predictable returns and stable income. An established property's rental revenue may be a dependable source of cash flow, drawing in investors looking for assets with an income stream.

A Look at Investing in Mature Markets

Reliable Cash Flow: In developed economies, reliable cash flow is often prioritized. Properties with a track record of reliable rental revenue and long-term lease agreements could be given priority by investors. Finding a balance between revenue production and appreciation is the aim.

Market research and local trends: Although established markets provide stability, it's still important to keep up with changes in the local economy, demographics, and market trends. Making strategic decisions is aided by knowledge about shifting customer wants, developing communities, and shifting tastes.

Adaptability to Changes in the Market: Trends and changes might affect mature markets. In these dynamic marketplaces, investors need to keep on top by being flexible and sensitive to changes in the economy, technology, and consumer behavior. Risk reduction and portfolio diversification are important, even in mature markets where stability is guaranteed. Portfolio diversification across various property kinds, regions, and industries improves resistance to market swings and risk management.

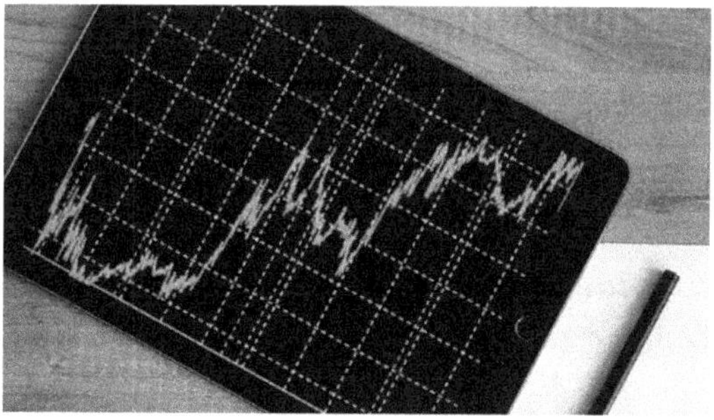

Techniques for Recognizing and Handling Both Markets:

Portfolio Diversification: Properties from both mature and developing areas are often included in a well-balanced real estate portfolio. By distributing risk, diversification enables you to take advantage of various real estate cycle phases.

A simple formula to calculate the return of a portfolio is:

$$R_p = \sum_{i=1}^{n} w_i R_i$$

where:

- R_p = portfolio return
- w_i = weight of asset i in the portfolio
- R_i = return of asset i
- n = number of assets in the portfolio

Let's consider a portfolio with two assets: Stock A and Stock B.

- Stock A has a return of 8%.

- Stock B has a return of 12%.

Suppose the portfolio is allocated 60% to Stock A and 40% to Stock B.

Using the formula:

$$R_p = (0.6 \times 0.08) + (0.4 \times 0.12)$$

$$R_p = 0.048 + 0.048$$

$$R_p = 0.096$$

So, the portfolio return is 9.6%.

Adaptive methods: Investors must have adaptable methods considering every market's distinctive qualities. When applied to mature markets prioritizing income stability, strategies like opportunistic investments and ground-up development that perform well in developing economies could need modifications.

Global Views: Global investors may take advantage of their viewpoints by taking a calculated risk in both established and developing markets. A real estate investment plan may be improved by being aware of how intertwined the world's economy is and by taking advantage of chances for cross-border investments.

Extensive Due Diligence: Extensive due diligence is essential, regardless of the kind of market. This entails being aware of local laws and ordinances, researching the market thoroughly, and keeping up with the economic factors that affect real estate.

Final Thought: A Harmonious Symphony of Investments

Investing in real estate is like conducting an orchestra. You need skill to find the right places to invest and guide your investments as they grow. While investors enjoy the steady melody of income and liquidity in established markets, they must also listen to the different notes of opportunity and risk in developing economies.

The techniques for creating a harmonic symphony of investments are further unveiled in the next chapters. The path through real estate projects requires a comprehensive strategy that resonates with the different characteristics of both developing and established economies, from recognizing market cycles to changing investment methods.

2.5 Strategies for Analyzing Market Trends and Forecasts

Understanding market trends and predictions is like having a compass in a constantly changing environment in the real estate industry. Successful real estate investors and stakeholders need a deep grasp of economic data, market dynamics, and predictive analytics to make wise judgments. In this investigation, we explore the methodologies that serve as the foundation for evaluating market trends and projections, enabling investors to take advantage of favorable opportunities and reduce the dangers associated with real estate ventures.

Recognizing Economic Indicators: The Market's Pulse

Real estate markets are driven by economic indicators that show the general health and vibrancy of the economy. The ability to analyze important economic indicators, which have a direct impact on real estate trends, must be developed by investors. Among these indications are:

Factors	Description
GDP	GDP growth rates provide valuable information about a region's economic well-being. As companies flourish and consumers gain confidence, a positive correlation exists between positive GDP growth and higher demand for real estate.
Employment Rates	Changes in employment affect both commercial and residential real estate. Strong demand for commercial space and a thriving housing market result from low unemployment and job growth.
Interest Rates	Shifts in interest rates directly impact borrowing costs and mortgage rates. Investors frequently watch interest rate trends because they impact affordability, real estate demand generally, and property prices.
Rates of Inflation	Inflation reduces buying power and affects real estate prices. Since real estate has long been considered an inflation hedge, investors must evaluate inflation patterns.

Housin g Starts	The number of building permits granted and the number of housing starts show how quickly new development progresses. Comprehension of the dynamics of supply and demand in the real estate market requires comprehending this data.

Using Technology and Data Analytics

Technological and data analytics developments have completely changed how real estate agents assess market trends. Understanding market dynamics more thoroughly and proactively is possible using big data, predictive analytics, and machine learning algorithms. Among the strategies are:

Big Data Analysis: By examining huge datasets, analysts may see trends, correlations, and patterns that conventional approaches might miss. Analyzing demographic information, purchasing patterns, and real estate transaction histories are all part of this.

Predictive analytics: Based on past performance and present indications, investors may estimate future market patterns using predictive modeling. This makes risk reduction and proactive decision-making possible.

Machine Learning Algorithms: These algorithms can sift through enormous volumes of data to find trends and patterns that can be predicted. These algorithms provide real-time insights into market dynamics, which are constantly learning and adapting.

Real Estate Technology Platforms: The analytical process may be streamlined using technology platforms and solutions specifically for real estate professionals. These systems often integrate predictive technologies, property analytics, and market data.

Tracking the Dynamics of Supply and Demand: Equilibrium Management

The basic law of supply and demand shapes real estate markets. Among the methods for examining the dynamics of supply and demand are:

Factors	Description
Inventory Levels	It's critical to evaluate the properties that are currently in stock. Excess inventory creates a buyer's market, while low inventory shows strong demand and price rise.

Absorption Rates	Absorption rates indicate the speed at which available real estate is sold. Low absorption rates indicate a slowing demand, while high rates point to a healthy market.
Rental Market Trends	Keeping an eye on changes in tenant preferences, rental prices, and vacancy rates may provide investors in the rental market with important information about demand and prospective rental revenue.
Leasing Activity of Commercial Property	Understanding market trends in the commercial sector requires examining leasing activity, tenant turnover, and the absorption of office or retail premises.

Local Market Analysis:

While macroeconomic statistics provide a broad overview, local market research explores the particular possibilities and problems on a micro level. Among the methods used in local market research are:

Community Analysis: It's critical to comprehend the traits and patterns of a certain community. Variables, including distance to amenities, safety, and the caliber of the school, influence property prices.

Demographic Studies: Target markets may be identified, and the interests of possible renters or purchasers can be understood by analyzing demographic data. This covers lifestyle preferences, income brackets, and age groupings.

- From 2024 to 2028, the US real estate market is expected to grow by 4.51%, reaching US$142.90 trillion.

- The National Association of Realtors (NAR) keeps track of sales and costs of current single-family houses across the United States. Every month around the 25th, this information comes out.

These numbers give us a look at the growth and trends in the US real estate market. This is useful for studying demographics and making business decisions.

Zoning and regulatory considerations: Zoning laws and local regulations directly impact real estate development and usage. Investors need to be informed about any changes to the law that can impact their properties.

Initiatives for Economic Development: Staying current on community planning, infrastructure, and economic development projects provides valuable information about the potential for growth in certain locations.

Market Segmentation Techniques: Product Specializations

Since real estate markets are not uniform, being able to identify possibilities within certain sectors may be a tactical advantage. Among the techniques for market segmentation are:

- ★ ***Residential Segmentation:*** Investors may customize their tactics to target certain demographics by knowing the interests of different residential segments, such as first-time homebuyers, luxury house searchers, or retirees.
- ★ ***Commercial Sector Specialization:*** Investors may concentrate on market segments with distinct needs and trends by specializing in certain commercial sectors, such as retail, office spaces, or industrial assets. Investigating specialty housing markets, such as senior living communities, holiday rentals, or student housing, allows one to better understand certain demographic groups' requirements and preferences.

- ★ *Opportunities for Adaptive Reuse:* In certain markets, finding ways to repurpose old buildings for new use, or adaptive reuse, is a creative and sustainable strategy.

Tracking Regional and Global Trends from a Holistic Angle

There is global and regional connectivity among real estate markets. Among the methods for keeping an eye on regional and worldwide trends are:

- ★ *Global Economic Trends:* Recognizing patterns of commerce, geopolitical stability, and cross-border investment flows, as well as their possible effects on real estate.
- ★ *Regional Economic inequalities:* Investors may discover places with growth or recovery potential and regions suffering economic issues by recognizing regional economic inequalities.
- ★ *Technical Trends and Innovations:* Adopting technical trends and innovations, such as virtual reality, smart cities, and sustainable development, might influence how appealing real estate markets are.

★ ***Governance, Social, and Environmental (ESG) Aspects to Take Into Account:*** The growing emphasis on ESG issues influences decisions about real estate investments. Investors' analysis must consider social responsibility, sustainability, and governance procedures.

Final Thoughts: A Strategic Symphony of Understanding

Real estate market trends and projections need a symphony of approaches that balance macroeconomic data, data analytics, local knowledge, and international viewpoints. Proficient investors skillfully maneuver through the ever-changing dynamics of supply and demand, cutting-edge technology, and specialized possibilities across various market niches.

We will examine these tactics in more detail in next chapters including the real estate decision-making process. A strategic symphony of information is needed to create a successful investment portfolio in real estate, from macro trends that shape national economies to micro-level factors that define localities.

|3|

Essential Financial Fundamentals

This chapter goes over the most important financial aspects of investing in real estate. We will teach you about important real estate market measures like ROI, Cap Rates, and Cash Flow, as well as leveraging techniques and things to think about. This way, you can make smart financial choices in the real estate market. We also talk about how to handle financial risks, figure out your tax obligations, and make the most of your money to get the best results. Lastly, we talk about how important it is to diversify your wealth and include real estate purchases in your overall plan for your finances.

For the relevant case studies, articles , worksheets and free resources, you can visit: andonierealty.com

"I will tell you how to become rich. Close the doors. Be fearful when others are greedy. Be greedy when others are fearful."

— Warren Buffett

3.1 Real Estate Investment Math: ROI, Cap Rates, Cash Flow

Investors evaluate the performance and profitability of their real estate assets using a complicated range of formulas and measurements. When assessing the potential of a real estate investment, key financial metrics, including cash flow, capitalization rate, and return on investment (ROI), are essential. In this part, we will examine the mathematics behind these indicators and how they help with well-informed investing choices.

Return on Investment (ROI)

ROI is a basic statistic used to assess how profitable an investment is. It shows the profit or loss on an investment about its cost and is stated as a percentage. The ROI calculation formula is:

ROI = (Net Profit / Cost of Investment) X 100

A positive return on investment (ROI) denotes a successful venture, while a negative ROI implies a loss. ROI is a tool investors use to evaluate the entire performance of their real estate portfolio and compare the returns of various investment options.

Rate of Capitalization (Cap Rate):

The capitalization rate or cap rate is an additional important statistic in examining real estate investments. It offers a fast, standardized method of evaluating a property's possible return without considering finance or other investor factors. The Cap Rate formula is as follows:

Cap Rate = (Net Operating Income / Current Market Value or Purchase Price) x 100

The amount, which is shown as a percentage, gives an idea of how much money an owner might make from a real estate purchase. The entire property's revenue, less running costs (not including income taxes and mortgage payments), is known as net operating income, or NOI. The property's expected return, if bought with cash, is represented by the resultant Cap Rate, which is given as a percentage.

Cap rates are a useful tool for investors to evaluate the relative merits of various investment possibilities and pinpoint properties that meet their desired levels of risk and return. Though they may carry more risk, higher cap rates often suggest bigger potential gains.

Cash flow:

A crucial indicator called cash flow calculates how much money a real estate investment makes after all costs, including mortgage payments, are subtracted. It is a crucial sign of a property's sound financial standing and potential for profit. The following formula may be used to get cash flow:

Cash Flow= [Rental Income – Operating Expenses – Debt Service (Mortgage Payments)]

Rent income minus operating costs minus debt service (mortgage payments) equals cash flow.

A property with positive cash flow generates more revenue than it costs to maintain and finance, giving the investor a consistent flow of money. Conversely, negative cash flow indicates that the property isn't bringing in enough money to pay for its outlays, which might create difficulties for the investor.

To ensure that their real estate investments support their financial objectives—whether they create equity, generate passive income, or strike a balance between the two—investors examine cash flow.

Combining Metrics:

The combination of these three metrics—ROI, cap rate, and cash flow—offers a thorough insight into the financial success of a real estate investment. For example, a good ROI does not imply positive cash flow if the property has a high mortgage leverage. Similar to this, a high cap rate may suggest the possibility of substantial profits. Still, it only provides part of the story since it ignores financing costs and the property's unique qualities.

Savvy real estate investors combine these indicators into a comprehensive study that considers the local economy's status, the property's location, the possibility of appreciation, and their risk tolerance. It is important to understand that these indicators are not independent predictors of investment success but tools for making well-informed decisions.

To do real estate business computation, you have to carefully look at important factors like cash flow, cap rate, and ROI. Investors may learn much about a property's viability and financial performance from these measurements. Investors may make well-informed choices consistent with their risk tolerance and financial objectives by comprehending the mathematics behind these indicators and how they interact. Real estate investing is both an art and a science; to successfully traverse the ever-changing world of property ownership and management, one must possess a combination of financial acumen, market knowledge, and strategic planning.

3.2 Leveraging in Real Estate: Strategies and Considerations

In the context of real estate, leverage is the calculated use of borrowed funds, such as loans or mortgages, to raise the possible rate of return on investment. Leverage can potentially increase earnings, but it also comes with dangers and factors that investors must consider carefully. This section will examine the idea of leverage in real estate, the many approaches investors use, and the important factors that determine whether or not leverage is successful.

Recognizing Leverage

With less money, investors may manage a larger asset thanks to leverage. Investors may increase the possible profits on their investment by employing borrowed money. Leverage is often represented as the loan-to-value (LTV) ratio, which shows the proportion of a property's debt-financed worth.

LTV Ratio = (Loan Amount / Appraised Value or Purchase Price) X 100

For instance, the loan-to-value ratio (LTV) would be 80% if an investor obtained a $80,000 mortgage to buy a $100,000 property. This means that debt accounts for 80% of the property's worth.

Real Estate Leveraging Techniques:

- ❖ ***Conventional Mortgages:*** Getting conventional mortgages is a frequent way for investors to leverage their real estate holdings. The property is used as security for these loans, which usually demand a down payment.
- ❖ ***Owner-Occupied Financing:*** Using the advantageous conditions offered for owner-occupied homes, some investors finance investment properties using their houses as collateral.
- ❖ **Financed by the Seller:** Sometimes, sellers may provide bidders with finance. Investors who may not be eligible for conventional loans or would like more accommodating conditions arranged directly with the seller may find this useful.
- ❖ **Hard Currency Loans:** Hard money loans are high-interest, short-term loans from businesses or individual investors. They are more expensive but may provide funds quickly, making them appropriate for urgency.

❖ **Credit lines and loans:** With home equity loans and credit lines, homeowners can get money from the value of their main home. After that, the borrowed money might be used to invest in real estate. Investors may form joint ventures or partnerships with other people to combine their resources. Due to the possibility of pooled risk and cash, investors can take on bigger and potentially more lucrative ventures.

Questions to Ask and Dangers of Leveraging:

Leverage may increase profits, but it also carries hazards that investors need to be aware of:

Interest Expenses, Volatility of the Market and Ratio of Debt Service Coverage:

Interest payments are a cost of borrowing that may greatly influence an investment's overall profitability. A rise in interest rates may drive up these expenses, impacting returns and cash flow. The real estate market is not always stable. Leveraging their assets, investors may find themselves "underwater" if property prices fall and the existing loan balance exceeds the property's current worth. The Debt Service Coverage Ratio (DSCR) is a metric lenders use to determine if a property can provide enough revenue to pay off debt. A low DSCR may indicate financial strain and affect the conditions of qualifying for a loan.

$$\text{Current cash debt coverage ratio} = \frac{\text{Net cash provided by operating activities}}{\text{Average current liabilities}}$$

Risk Leverage, Limits on Loan-to-Value (LTV) and Erosion of Equity:

Leverage may increase profits, but it can also increase losses. Heavily leveraged investments might result in large financial losses if the market moves against you. The maximum LTV ratios that lenders may impose may restrict the amount investors borrow. Greater interest rates and stricter loan conditions often result from greater LTV ratios. A drop in real estate prices can reduce the equity in an investment, making it more difficult to refinance or sell the property.

Juggling Risk and Benefit:

To leverage real estate successfully, risk and return must be carefully balanced. Investors need to do a comprehensive financial analysis, including interest rate swings, market volatility, and the property's ability to generate revenue. Mitigating the risks related to leverage requires understanding the risk factors and implementing contingency strategies.

In summary:

In real estate investing, leverage is a potent instrument that allows investors to use borrowed cash to optimize profits. It is not without danger; however, it is crucial to carefully weigh your risk tolerance, market circumstances, and financial indicators. When it comes to leveraging, investors need to be aware of both the possible advantages and disadvantages and be ready to modify their plans in response to changing market conditions. In the end, leveraging has the potential to be a significant part of a profitable real estate investment strategy. Still, it also comes at a cost: careful planning, strict risk management, and a deep comprehension of the nuances of the real estate market.

3.3 Managing Financial Risks in Real Estate Investments

Considering the significant cash required and the many uncertainties present in the market, managing financial risks is essential to real estate investing. Various financial hazards may affect an investor's real estate portfolio's performance and profitability. The main financial risks associated with real estate investments will be examined in this part, along with practical methods for reducing and managing them.

Real estate financial risks include, Risk of Interest Rates and Risk to Liquidity:

Property Value Fluctuations: The status of the economy, local variables, and market dynamics all affect real estate prices. Market swings may impact property prices, affecting investors' equity and possible returns.

Effect on Financing Costs: Variations in interest rates greatly impact financing expenses. Increased mortgage payments due to rising interest rates might reduce cash flow and impact profitability.

Asset Marketability: Real estate is seen as an asset that is not very liquid. The current state of the market may not be ideal for an investor who has to sell a home soon, which might result in losses or cause delays in getting financing.

Credit Danger, Risk associated with operations and Currency Risks:

Tenant Default: Tenant default poses a credit risk in properties that generate revenue. Tenant nonpayment or unannounced eviction might negatively affect the cash flow of the property and the investor's capacity to fulfill debts.

Unexpected Expenses: Unexpected costs might arise from maintenance problems, unplanned repairs, or changes to local laws. These operational risks can negatively impact cash flow and the investment's financial performance.

Foreign Investments: If the value of the local currency changes relative to the investor's home currency, they may be exposed to currency risk while investing in international real estate. Changes in exchange rates may affect returns when repatriating money.

Techniques for Controlling Economic Risks:

1. **Increasing variety, Risk Evaluation and Due Care:** A real estate portfolio may be more resilient to certain risks by diversifying a range of property kinds, markets, and locations. A diverse portfolio is less vulnerable to the negative effects of underperformance in one particular property. It is important to carry out extensive due diligence before purchasing a

home. This entails evaluating the state of the market, the property's past performance, the possibility of appreciation, and the tenants' financial stability.

2. **Conservative Funding:** A financial cushion may be obtained by selecting conservative financing arrangements, such as lower loan-to-value (LTV) ratios. Higher leverage may enhance profits but also expose a person to interest rate risk and market changes.
3. **Fix-Rate Home Loans:** Reducing interest rate risk may be accomplished by selecting fixed-rate mortgages. The interest rate on a fixed-rate mortgage doesn't change over the loan term, giving debt service payments consistency.
4. **Management of Cash Flow:** It's critical to have a solid cash flow to handle unforeseen costs and market downturns. Putting aside enough money for maintenance, operating expenses, and vacant times is important.
5. **Insurance Protection:** Investors may be protected from unforeseen circumstances like natural catastrophes, accidents, or legal problems by purchasing comprehensive

insurance coverage, including property and liability insurance.

6. **Preemptive Asset Administration:** Resolving operational hazards requires the involvement of professional property management. Prompt identification and resolution of problems by competent management may reduce their effect on the property's performance.
7. **Analyzing scenarios:** Stress testing and other scenario analysis are useful tools for investors to evaluate the possible effects of unfavorable market circumstances. Proactive risk management is made possible by understanding how different events could impact the investment.
8. **Strategies for Exit:** Creating well-defined departure plans is crucial. Adjusting an investment plan or knowing when to sell a property depending on market circumstances might help reduce the risks associated with economic fluctuations.
9. **Compliance with Laws and Regulations:** Awareness of and abiding by local rules and regulations is essential. Changing rent control policies, zoning rules, or other legal

aspects may affect how financially viable an investment is.

10. **Monitoring and Adjusting for Risk:** Risk management in the real estate industry is a continual process that calls for constant observation and adjustment to changing market circumstances. Effective risk management requires regular evaluation of a real estate portfolio's financial standing, knowledge of market trends, and strategy modification in response.

Investors should be ready to adjust their investment plans in response to shifting market dynamics, interest rate fluctuations, and changes in the competitive environment. Adaptability and quick thinking are essential for managing financial risks in the ever-changing real estate market.

Successful risk management of finances is essential for real estate investing success. Investors must recognize, evaluate, and reduce the risks affecting their portfolios' performance. Investors may augment their capacity to endure market fluctuations and leverage prospects using prudent risk management techniques, such as diversification, cautious financing, and meticulous due diligence. Investors are well-positioned to handle the complicated real estate investing environment and achieve long-term financial success by constantly monitoring and adapting to shifting market conditions.

Technique	**Description**
Diversification	Enhance resilience through varied investments.
Conservative Funding	Use lower LTV ratios for stability.
Fixed-Rate Mortgages	Choose fixed rates for predictable payments.
Cash Flow Management	Budget for unexpected financial needs.

Insurance Protection	Obtain comprehensive coverage.
Preemptive Asset Management	Employ professional management for issue resolution.
Scenario Analysis	Conduct stress tests for risk readiness.
Exit Strategies	Develop adaptable exit plans.
Compliance with Laws	Ensure regulatory compliance.
Monitoring and Adjustment	Adjust to market shifts.
Adaptability	Modify plans swiftly as markets change.

Please note that this table is a simplified representation, and you may need to adjust the formatting based on your specific requirements or the platform you are using. Additionally, you can further customize or expand the table as needed.

3.4 Tax Implications and Financial Optimization

Investors looking to maximize their financial returns must comprehend the tax ramifications of real estate investments. A complicated web of tax concerns surrounds real estate ownership and transactions, which may greatly affect an investor's financial results. In this part, we will examine the main tax ramifications of real estate investments, along with tax code-compliant financial optimization techniques. This is a quick summary of what you can expect.

Tax Repercussions of Investing in Real Estate:

Rental Revenue: In general, income tax is applied to rental income. Nonetheless, investors can reduce their taxable income by deducting allowable expenditures, including depreciation, insurance, property taxes, mortgage interest, and upkeep. An example, if you need something to fix, like a light that went out, you can write that off in your taxes.

Tax on Capital Gains: Capital gains are the profits from selling real estate and are liable to capital gains tax. The holding term and the investor's income bracket are two variables that affect the tax rate. Capital gains taxes may be postponed using techniques such as tax-deferred exchanges (1031 exchanges), which reinvest sale profits into another identical property.

Appreciation of value: Throughout the property's useful life, investors may deduct a percentage of the asset's value via depreciation, a non-cash expenditure. By offsetting taxable rental income, this deduction may lower the total amount owed in taxes. Because nothing is eternal, buildings everyday crumble little by little, this is where you can have tax write off.

Deductions for Interest: Tax deductions are often available for mortgage interest on loans utilized for real estate ventures. Investors may maximize their financial position and lower their taxable income by taking advantage of this deduction. One thing to keep in mind, you can't tax debt.

Entities that Pass-Through: Investments made via pass-through companies, such as partnerships or Limited Liability Companies (LLCs), let individual investors receive income and deductions. Flexibility and possible tax benefits are two benefits of this arrangement.

1031 Exchange: When an investor sells one property and reinvests the profits in another similar property, capital gains taxes may be deferred under Section 1031 of the Internal Revenue Code. This tactic is often used to maximize tax consequences during real estate transactions. Trust me, you don't want Uncle Sam to take a huge cut for himself

Tax Credits: Tax credits for certain real estate investments, such as those connected with energy-efficient upgrades or historic preservation, may be available. These credits may directly decrease tax obligations.

Local and State Taxes: Jurisdiction-specific tax effects differ. State and local tax regulations may affect income tax rates, property taxes, and other financial factors, so investors must be aware of them.

Techniques for Financial Optimization:

Use of Deductions Strategically: Investors who maintain thorough records of their allowable costs should strategically optimize their deductions. This covers costs for upkeep, repairs, and enhancements to the property.

Financed with Tax Efficiency: The financial performance of an investment may be enhanced by choosing financing choices that minimize taxes. It may be beneficial, for instance, to use interest-only loans or arrange debt in a manner consistent with tax goals.

Expert Guidance: Consulting with real estate-focused accountants or tax experts is beneficial. These experts may provide customized guidance depending on the unique circumstances of an investment and the changing tax code.

Optimization of Entity Structure: Tax results for real estate investments may be maximized by selecting the appropriate corporate structure. Investors might assess the benefits of various organizational forms, such as partnerships, LLCs, and S companies, depending on their tax situation and financial objectives.

Making Use of Tax Credits Finding and using the available tax credits might help with financial efficiency. Credits that apply to investments should be known to investors, and they should try to take advantage of them.

Planning an Estate: A crucial component of financial optimization is estate planning. Investors may put plans in place to reduce inheritance taxes and ensure that real estate holdings are transferred to heirs in an orderly manner.

Ongoing Education: Tax laws are prone to change, so it's important to remain up-to-date on any revisions or new rules. Investors are guaranteed to be able to modify their strategy to comply with current tax rules via ongoing education on tax consequences.

Obstacles, Intricacy of Tax Laws and Specific Situations:

Tax minimization is a critical aspect of managing real estate finances, yet it comes with several challenges that investors should keep in mind. One key challenge lies in the dynamic and intricate nature of tax rules.

These regulations are subject to frequent changes, and staying abreast of these modifications can be quite challenging for investors. What was applicable and advantageous yesterday might not hold true today due to alterations in tax laws. Moreover, navigating through the complexities of these evolving tax rules can be a daunting task.

Investors often find it challenging to comprehend the intricacies and nuances of tax regulations, especially as they become more intricate over time. This complexity can create confusion and make it difficult for investors to make well-informed decisions about their real estate investments. Furthermore, strategies for optimizing taxes in real estate need to be tailor-made for each unique set of circumstances. There's no one-size-fits-all approach when it comes to tax optimization. What works perfectly for one investor might not be suitable or beneficial for another.

Variables such as investment goals, property types, holding periods, and individual financial situations greatly impact the effectiveness of tax strategies.

Hence, emphasizing the need for customized financial planning is crucial. It's imperative for investors to understand that a cookie-cutter approach won't suffice.

Each investor's situation is unique, requiring personalized strategies that align with their specific goals, risk tolerance, and financial capabilities. Seeking professional advice and tailored financial planning becomes essential in maximizing tax benefits and ensuring that the chosen strategies are optimal for an individual's circumstances.

Danger of Using Aggressive Methods:

When used improperly, several tax optimization techniques could result in legal problems. Investors should exercise caution when engaging in aggressive tax planning and consult a specialist to ensure compliance.

Financial optimization requires an understanding of and ability to manage the tax ramifications of real estate transactions. Through the strategic use of deductions, tax-efficient financing, and ongoing education on tax rules, investors may optimize returns, minimize tax obligations, and improve overall profitability. Notwithstanding the difficulties, cautious preparation, ongoing learning, and working with tax experts may enable investors to successfully negotiate the complicated real estate tax system and make choices that support their financial objectives.

3.5 Portfolio Diversification and Financial Planning

In real estate investing, financial planning and portfolio diversification are essential concepts. Diversification is distributing investing money across various assets to reduce risk. At the same time, financial planning is a comprehensive strategy for resource management and long-term financial objectives. This part will address the importance of portfolio diversification in real estate, go over the essential elements of financial planning, and show you how these ideas work together to maximize the returns on your investments.

1. Real estate portfolio diversification

Asset Class Diversity: Spreading risk may be achieved by diversifying among several real estate asset types, including retail, commercial, industrial, and residential buildings. Every asset class has a unique risk-return profile, and diversification reduces the negative effects of subpar results in a particular industry. Easiest way is through REITS.

REIT = Real Estate Investment Trust

Diversification by Region: Investing in many geographic regions might protect against unique market issues or regional economic downturns. By spreading out over many cities or regions, one may lessen their exposure to local hazards and take advantage of possibilities in expanding markets.

Diversity of Property Types: Diversifying by property type within each asset class provides an additional degree of risk reduction. For instance, an investor may have a combination of single-family houses, multi-family apartments, and holiday rentals in the residential sector.

Methods of Investing: Enhancing portfolio resilience may be achieved using various investment techniques, including long-term rentals, fix-and-flip investments, and real estate investment trusts (REITs). Various methods provide a well-rounded approach to risk management as they react to market circumstances in various ways.

Returns Adjusted for Risk: Enhancing risk-adjusted returns is the goal of diversification. Investors aim to maximize their returns for a given risk by balancing their portfolios with various assets at different risk levels.

Diversification of Asset Size: Investors may manage the possible returns and risks associated with various investment sizes by diversifying their real estate holdings according to their size, which can range from modest residential homes to enormous commercial enterprises.

2. Real Estate Financial Planning:

Establishing Objectives: The first step in financial planning is to identify your objectives. Investors state their goals to direct financial planning, whether producing passive income, increasing equity, or hitting certain financial benchmarks.

Assessment of Risk Tolerance: It's critical to comprehend one's risk tolerance. To match their investing plan with their risk tolerance, investors must assess how comfortable they are with market swings, possible losses, and general volatility.

Handling Cash Movement: Careful cash flow management is necessary for successful financial planning. Investors must account for unanticipated expenditures, mortgage payments, and property running expenses to maintain a positive cash flow and fulfill their financial commitments.

Financial Scheduling: It is essential to include tax planning in the financial plan. To maximize tax results, investors should investigate tax-efficient financing solutions, take advantage of deductions, and practice procedures like 1031 exchanges.

Reserves and Funds for Emergencies: Establishing reserves and emergency cash is a cornerstone of financial planning. Investors may manage unforeseen costs, empty times, and economic downturns with the support of a cushion without jeopardizing their overall financial stability.

Handling Debt: An essential part of financial planning is debt management. Investors should use leverage wisely, considering how interest rates affect cash flow and the portfolio's financial health.

Planning an Estate: Estate preparation minimizes tax repercussions and guarantees a seamless transfer of real estate holdings to heirs. This entails drafting trusts, wills, and other legal documents to protect and allocate assets by the investor's desires.

Periodic Review of Portfolios: The financial planning process is continuous and must be reviewed and adjusted frequently. Changes in the market, one's situation, and financial objectives may call for adjustments to the investment plan.

3. Financial Planning and Portfolio Diversification Work Together:

Risk Reduction: As a method of reducing risk, diversification fits very well with financial planning goals. Investors may increase the stability of their portfolios and lessen the influence of unfavorable market circumstances on their overall financial well-being by diversifying their holdings.

Aligning Goals: Financial planning and diversification work best when predetermined financial objectives are used to make investment decisions. As an example, an investor who is intent on making a consistent income stream would give priority to properties that provide income. Still, an investor looking for long-term growth could choose a more aggressive, growth-oriented approach.

Flexibility and Adaptability: Financial planning and diversification both place a strong emphasis on flexibility and adaptation. Investors must be ready to modify their financial strategies and portfolios in response to shifting market conditions, macroeconomic trends, and individual circumstances.

Comprehensive Risk Handling: Financial planning and portfolio diversification work together to provide comprehensive risk management. Through careful financial planning, investors manage risks associated with cash flow, Debt, taxes, and unforeseen occurrences, in addition to diversifying their asset holdings.

Building Long-Term Wealth: The combination of these ideas promotes long-term wealth accumulation. Diversification guarantees that the portfolio can withstand varying market conditions, and financial planning helps investors make wise choices that support their aspirations to accumulate wealth.

Portfolio diversification and financial planning are intertwined methods that enable investors to successfully manage the complexity of the real estate market and meet their financial goals. While financial planning offers a path for accomplishing long-term objectives, controlling cash flow, and maximizing tax results, diversification distributes risk over various assets. These ideas work well together, gradually making it easier for investors to build a strong and profitable real estate portfolio.

|4|

Property Selection and Evaluation

In chapter 4, we'll talk about the very important steps of choosing and evaluating properties for real estate business. It talks about how to choose places that will make you money, how important it is to do your research, and different ways to compare market value to potential growth. It also talks about the things that affect the value of a property going up or down and stresses how important it is to find special markets and unique business possibilities.

For the relevant case studies, worksheets and free resources you can visit: andonierealty.com

"Buyers decide in the first eight seconds of seeing a home if they're interested in buying it. Get out of your car, walk in their shoes and see what they see within the first eight seconds."

– Barbara Corcoran

4.1 Criteria for Selecting Profitable Properties

Choosing lucrative properties is one of the most important components of a successful real estate investment. To ensure that a possible property fits their risk tolerance and financial objectives, investors must thoroughly assess it using a set of criteria. In this part, we will explore the most important factors in choosing lucrative properties, offering investors a thorough manual for navigating the ever-changing real estate market.

1. Site:

When evaluating a property, conducting a neighborhood analysis is crucial as property costs and renter demand are influenced by factors such as local schools, public transportation availability, safety, and accessibility to services. Additionally, understanding local market trends is essential; investors should analyze current and historical data on sales trends, rental rates, and property prices to identify potentially appreciating areas.

Moreover, economic indicators like job growth, unemployment rates, and overall economic stability should be considered, as these can significantly impact property values. Investing in areas with strong economic growth prospects may enhance long-term profitability.

2. Features of the Property:

When selecting a property, an owner should choose a type that aligns with their investment strategy, be it residential, commercial, or industrial, each carrying unique risks and benefits. The property's age and condition are critical as they influence the potential repair and renovation costs; thorough inspections are necessary to assess any needed fixes or updates. Additionally, the size and layout of a property impact its functionality and attractiveness to potential buyers or renters. Understanding the preferences of the target audience is essential when determining a property's size and style. Features such as modern kitchens, energy-efficient additions, and attractive outdoor spaces can significantly enhance a property's value, making it more desirable at the time of sale or rent.

3. Metrics Related to Finance:

Cap Rate: As discussed earlier, the capitalization rate, or cap rate, is a measure of how much money a project might make. As an investor, you should always think about the whole danger and the state of the market, not just the cap rate.

Possible cash flow: For long-term real estate purchases, a good cash flow is important. You can figure out the property's cash flow by figuring out how much rent it will bring in and then taking out the taxes, mortgage payments, and other costs of running the business.

ROI: Return on investment, is a key metric that measures the profitability and cost-effectiveness of a project by evaluating the property's potential for appreciation and rental income generation. A positive ROI indicates a sound investment. Equally important are the financing terms, which encompass interest rates, loan duration, and down payment requirements. Favorable financing terms can significantly enhance the total return on investment, making them a critical aspect to review thoroughly before committing to a purchase.

4. Evaluation of the Market:

Understanding the dynamics of supply and demand in the local market is crucial for predicting future increases in property prices and rental rates. When demand for real estate is high and supply is limited, prices typically rise. Additionally, by examining recent sales and rental rates of similar properties in the area, investors can gauge market competitiveness and determine an appropriate price for their investment.

It is also vital to assess the prospects for market growth, considering factors such as population influx, improvements in infrastructure, and job opportunities. These elements help predict the market's potential expansion, making them essential considerations for informed real estate investment decisions.

5. Hazards and Counter- measures:

Understanding market risks is crucial for investors, especially in scenarios like economic downturns or oversaturated markets. It's essential to have contingency plans and mitigation strategies ready to address potential challenges. Additionally, assessing risks unique to a property, such as zoning changes, legal complications, or environmental issues, helps in evaluating the property's specific vulnerabilities. Having a clear exit strategy is also vital. Owners who have well-defined plans for divesting can swiftly adapt to changing market conditions, whether through selling, refinancing, or repurposing the property. These preparedness measures ensure more controlled and strategic handling of real estate investments.

6. Legal and Regulatory Considerations

Zoning rules are critical as they dictate permissible uses of land, so investors must understand local zoning laws to ensure their intended use is compliant. Additionally, tax considerations such as income taxes, property taxes, and potential tax benefits must be carefully analyzed to optimize financial outcomes.

Conducting thorough legal due diligence is also essential, as it helps uncover any liens, encumbrances, or legal issues associated with a property, ensuring legal safety and a clear title. When selecting profitable properties, investors should evaluate numerous factors including risk, location, property features, and economic indicators.

Making informed choices requires a deep understanding of the market, an assessment of risk tolerance, and alignment with financial objectives. Comprehensive research and knowledge of the local real estate environment are indispensable for making strategic decisions that foster long-term profitability and success in real estate investments.

4.2 Conducting Comprehensive Property Due Diligence

Performing thorough due diligence on a property is an essential stage in the real estate investing process. Before completing the acquisition, due diligence entails extensive investigation and evaluation of the numerous features of a property. This thorough inspection lets Investors discover any dangers, determine the property's worth, and make well-informed choices. In this part, we will examine each of the essential elements of thorough property due diligence and their significance in guaranteeing a lucrative and successful real estate investment.

1. Ownership and Title:

Conducting a title check is essential to ensure legal ownership of a property and to identify any existing liens, encumbrances, or legal issues. Investors must verify that the seller provides a clear title that is free of complications and saleable. Understanding the property's ownership history can also reveal its past uses and highlight any irregularities in ownership transitions, necessitating further investigation to avoid potential issues. Additionally, performing a property inspection is crucial for verifying that the property boundaries are accurate and that any structures are built in compliance with legal standards. This step helps prevent future disputes over borders and encroachments, securing a smoother transaction and ownership experience.

2. Visual Examination:

A thorough evaluation of a property's condition is carried out by trained professionals who inspect various aspects such as water, electricity, mechanical systems, roofs, and structural safety to determine its overall state. Additionally, investors should assess the property's surroundings for any environmental contamination issues, which is crucial for legal compliance and risk management. Ensuring compliance with land use and zoning regulations is also vital; any non-compliance could significantly impact the property's usability and value. Together, these evaluations help investors make informed decisions and mitigate potential risks associated with property investment.

3. Evaluation of Finances:

Reviewing the property's financial records, including rent rolls, spending reports, and income statements, provides a comprehensive understanding of its potential revenue and operational costs. This analysis is crucial for assessing the financial health and profitability of the property, enabling investors to make informed decisions based on its earnings capacity and expenditure patterns.

By evaluating market rent, investors ensure that the rental prices of the property are competitive by analyzing the rents of comparable properties in the vicinity. This study helps in setting optimal rent levels to maximize profits. Additionally, projecting future operating expenses, including maintenance, insurance, property management fees, and property taxes, aids in accurate financial forecasting. Together, these assessments allow investors to develop a comprehensive understanding of both potential income and expenditures, crucial for successful property management and profitability.

4. Adherence to Law and Regulation:

Ensuring that a property has all the necessary licenses and permits is crucial as unauthorized building projects or improvements can lead to legal and financial complications. Additionally, adherence to the latest building standards is important for both legal and safety reasons, with non-compliance potentially resulting in costly repairs or modifications. Investors should also investigate any easements, rights of way, or land use restrictions to better understand the land's limitations and potential issues. These checks help safeguard against unforeseen challenges and ensure the property's compliance with all regulatory requirements, enhancing its overall value and usability.

5. Analysis of Tenant and Lease:

Carefully evaluating all current leases is essential as it facilitates the understanding of the property's income stream through insights into lease terms, fee escalations, and tenants' responsibilities. Additionally, assessing potential renters by checking their credit scores and rental payment histories helps determine the risk associated with leasing to them. Knowing the dates when leases expire allows investors to prepare for potential vacancies and lease renewals, which could impact future cash flow. These steps are crucial for managing rental properties effectively and ensuring a steady and predictable income.

6. Evaluation of the Market:

To ensure that a purchase aligns with current market trends, investors should analyze similar homes on the market, comparing their prices and rental rates. Understanding the dynamics of supply and demand in the area is crucial for predicting future fluctuations in property prices and rents. Additionally, examining the market's growth prospects allows investors to make informed decisions about the long-term viability and potential value growth of a property.

7. A Look at Financing Issues:

To fully understand a property's financial situation, it is crucial to identify any existing debts such as loans, mortgages, or other financial obligations. Investors should also explore financing options and understand the terms of potential loans to make well-informed decisions regarding the financial aspects of an investment. Monitoring loan terms and interest rates ensures that financing arrangements are favorable and align with the investor's financial goals. These steps are essential for assessing the viability of property investments and ensuring that they fit within broader financial strategies.

8. Predicting financial outcomes:

Accurate financial estimates are possible for investors by thoroughly examining the financials and market dynamics. This guarantees that the investment aligns with the investor's financial objectives and helps with realistic financial planning.

Power in Negotiations: Investors possessing thorough due diligence gives them more negotiating leverage. Finding problems or inconsistencies lays the groundwork for negotiating advantageous conditions with sellers or modifying the purchase price as necessary.

Extended Durability: Evaluating the property's long-term sustainability involves considering its physical state, market potential, and regulatory requirements. Investors can make choices that support their long-term financial objectives.

Thorough property due diligence is crucial for real estate investors who want to succeed financially. Finding it entails carefully analyzing elements connected to the law, finances, physical environment, and markets to find possible hazards and possibilities. In addition to reducing risks, a thorough due diligence process lays the groundwork for wise choices, precise appraisal, and developing a profitable and long-lasting real estate investment portfolio.

4.3 Evaluating Market Value vs. Potential Value

A critical real estate investment research component is comparing prospective value to market value. Potential value considers the property's worth after modifications, renovations, or enhancements, while market value indicates the present value of a property based on variables such as recent sales of similar properties. This section will examine the importance of perspective and market value, the variables that affect both, and the tactics investors use to increase their returns.

1. Market Value:

Market value is the estimated price at which a property should exchange hands in an arms-length transaction between a willing buyer and a willing seller as of the valuation date.

Several factors influence market value:

- comparable sales use recent sales data of similar nearby properties
- location affects value through proximity to amenities
- schools, and transport

- the property’s dimensions, design, and features also play a role.

Additionally, the property’s condition, including necessary maintenance, and the local real estate market's trends, supply and demand dynamics, and economic conditions are all important determinants.

To estimate market value, several techniques are employed. Appraisers use diverse valuation methods and market data to determine a property's worth. Real estate brokers often perform Comparative Market Analysis (CMA) by analyzing past transactions and specific property features. Automated Valuation Models (AVMs) use technology to calculate property values based on data and algorithms.

For investors, understanding market value is crucial for making informed investment decisions. It serves as the starting point for assessing a property’s potential profitability, negotiating purchase prices, and aligning the investment with broader investment strategies.

2. Prospective Worth:

Potential value, or inherent value, refers to the estimated future value of a property after undergoing repairs, enhancements, or modifications. This value can be significantly influenced by several factors. Upgrades and renovations, such as adding new features or remodeling, can substantially increase a property's potential worth. Changes in local zoning laws that allow for higher densities or different uses can also elevate the property's value. Additionally, potential value considers the projected market trends and appreciation, as well as the development opportunities that could substantially enhance the value of undeveloped land or properties with development potential.

Several techniques are employed to determine this prospective value. The cost approach involves assessing the increase in property value relative to the investment in upgrades or enhancements. The income approach estimates future revenue streams to ascertain the value of income-generating assets. Development analysis involves evaluating the projected profits against the costs of developing properties with potential.

For investors, a thorough understanding of a property's potential value is critical. It allows them to identify opportunities for value-add strategies, such as strategic placement, thoughtful modifications, or leveraging potential development. By realizing a property's unrealized potential, investors aim to maximize profits, making potential value a key concept in investment decision-making.

3. Techniques for Increasing Profits:

Value-added approaches are a key focus for investors who target properties that have potential for improvement. Through repositioning, upgrading, or renovations, these investors aim to increase the value of a property significantly. Additionally, identifying development opportunities can lead to substantial increases in potential value, especially in areas that are experiencing growth or are subject to rezoning.

Accurate market timing also plays a crucial role; strategic timing enables investors to capitalize on their ability to predict market trends and make investments before property prices increase. Collectively, these strategies are central to maximizing the prospective value of real estate investments, allowing investors to enhance their returns effectively. Assessing the benefits and risks involved in prospective upgrades or modifications is critical for investors.

They carefully evaluate the potential value against the costs and risks associated with achieving that value to ensure a viable investment. Being adaptable is also crucial; investors must be ready to modify their strategies in response to shifting economic circumstances, competitive dynamics, and market conditions. This flexibility allows them to capitalize on opportunities and mitigate risks effectively, ensuring their investments remain aligned with the prevailing market environment.

4. Thoughts and Difficulties:

Fear of the Market: Unanticipated events, interest rate fluctuations, and economic concerns impact market and prospective values.

Inflating the Potential Value: Investors need to use caution when estimating future value. Financial problems and bad investments might result from unrealistic forecasts.

Dangers of Implementation: Value-add or development plans must be implemented well to be successful. Unexpected difficulties during the execution stage may affect the realization of the potential value.

Making real estate investing decisions revolves around the dynamic interaction between potential and market value. Investors should carefully evaluate a property's present market worth as a basis for their investment. They should then strategically investigate the property's prospective value by looking for value-added options, development opportunities, or market trends. Real estate investments may be profitable and effective if one can successfully negotiate these difficulties, adjust to changing situations, and appropriately assess potential and market values. Long-term real estate investors succeed with thorough due diligence, know market dynamics, and take a calculated approach to achieving potential value.

Here's the table:

Aspect	**Market Value**	**Potential Value**
Definition	Estimated worth based on current market data.	Future worth post-improvements.
Determinants	Sales, location, size, condition, market dynamics.	Upgrades, zoning, market trends, opportunities.
Methods	Appraisal, CMA, AVMs.	Cost, Income, Development Analysis.

Significance	Guides investment decisions, pricing, strategy alignment.	Targets enhancements, strategic growth opportunities.
Strategies	Value-add, market timing, adaptability.	Value-add, development focus, risk & timing assessment.
Challenges	Market uncertainty, value estimation risks.	Similar risks, emphasis on potential overestimation.

This table provides a structured overview of the key aspects, determinants, methods of assessment, significance for investors, strategies for maximizing returns, and considerations and challenges associated with evaluating market value vs. potential value in real estate investment.

4.4 Assessing Property Appreciation and Depreciation Factors

An essential part of real estate investment research is evaluating the elements contributing to property appreciation and depreciation. Property values are dynamic and affected by many variables related to and unrelated to the actual property. Investors may make well-informed choices, maximize profits, and manage the always-shifting real estate market by understanding the factors that contribute to appreciation and depreciation.

1. Appreciation Factors for Property:

The adage "location, location, location" continues to hold significant weight in real estate, with properties in desirable neighborhoods—characterized by easy access to amenities, top-notch schools, and secure environments—often appreciating more. Local trends are vital for investors to monitor to forecast future property values. Economic growth and development in a region, such as increased economic activity, infrastructural enhancements, and employment opportunities, typically elevate property values. The dynamics of supply and demand also play a crucial role; high demand coupled with limited housing supply often drives up prices, leading to appreciation.

Understanding overall market conditions and trends, such as interest rate shifts, demographic changes, and the general market sentiment, is essential for gauging the direction of property values. Property renovations and improvements, like modernizing interiors, enhancing curb appeal, or upgrading features, can significantly boost a property's valuation.

Furthermore, government investments in infrastructure—such as roads, parks, or transit systems—can enhance the value of adjacent properties. Historical performance of a neighborhood or market also provides insights into its resilience and potential for long-term appreciation. Lastly, shifts in demographics, like an influx of younger residents, can affect property values as they alter market demand, offering investors clues to anticipate future trends.

2. Depreciation Factors for Property:

Depreciation of property can result from several factors, including physical, functional, and economic influences. Physical impairment, such as wear and tear over time, contributes to depreciation, particularly when a property ages, is poorly maintained, or is exposed to harsh weather conditions.

Functional decline, also known as functional obsolescence, occurs when changes in consumer preferences or advancements in design and technology render a property outdated. Properties that fail to meet contemporary standards or lack desired features may experience depreciation. Additionally, economic downturns can lead to property depreciation; recessions or economic slumps often result in job losses, reduced consumer spending, and overall declines in economic activity, negatively impacting property values.

High vacancy rates in a building or neighborhood can signal a drop in demand, potentially leading to lower property values. Such vacancies can lead to neglect, deteriorating the community over time.

Property values may also be influenced by external factors, such as changes in municipal policies, zoning laws, or broader economic conditions, which investors must monitor as these can impact their portfolios. Moreover, a market saturated with properties that share similar characteristics can drive down prices due to increased competition and oversupply, contributing to property depreciation.

Technological advances can also affect real estate values; properties that lack modern amenities or are built with outdated infrastructure may depreciate as newer, more technologically equipped properties become more desirable. Lastly, properties in areas prone to natural disasters such as hurricanes, earthquakes, and floods are at risk of losing value due to the potential for significant damage, making them less appealing to buyers and investors.

3. Techniques to Reduce Depreciation and Increase Appreciation

Preventive upkeep is essential in avoiding physical degradation and maintaining a property's long-term value through proactive, routine maintenance. Transformative strategies, such as timely updates and renovations that align with current market trends, can significantly raise a property's value.

It's crucial to make upgrades that attract potential renters or buyers. Expanding into various markets and property types can help mitigate the effects of regional or localized depreciation and economic downturns. Staying knowledgeable and flexible allows investors to adapt their strategies in response to changing market dynamics, economic patterns, and regulatory modifications, thus minimizing risks and seizing opportunities.

Effective management of tenant relations is also critical; maintaining good rapport with renters can lead to lower vacancy rates as satisfied tenants are more likely to care for their living spaces. Additionally, thoroughly researching potential investment locations can identify communities with high appreciation potential and reduce exposure to depreciation risks.

Finally, employing expert counsel from specialists in property management, market analysis, and real estate can provide invaluable guidance in managing both depreciation and appreciation factors.

A continuous and essential component of successful real estate investing is evaluating the elements contributing to property appreciation and depreciation. Investors need to be on the lookout for changes in the market, keep up with regional developments, and put measures in place to increase appreciation and reduce depreciation risks.

Investors may support the long-term performance of their real estate portfolios and achieve their financial objectives by making well-informed choices based on their knowledge of the dynamic interactions between different elements.

4.5 Identifying Niche Markets and Unique Investment Opportunities

Real estate investors may establish a unique brand and increase profits using a strategic plan to identify specialized markets and special investment possibilities. Specialized areas of the real estate market, known as niche markets, may be defined by particular property types, target populations, or distinctive investment themes. This section will discuss the value of spotting niche markets, their advantages to investors, and methods for locating and seizing exclusive investment possibilities.

1. Being Aware of Niche Markets

In the real estate industry, niche markets refer to specific segments that deviate from more generalized categories, often focusing on particular types of properties, specific target audiences, or unconventional financing methods.

Examples of such specialized markets include student housing, which involves buying properties near educational institutions to rent to students. Another is senior living communities, which entails creating or acquiring properties equipped with facilities and services tailored for elderly citizens.

Additionally, there are vacation rentals, which concentrate on the market for short-term rentals in popular tourist destinations. Co-living spaces represent yet another niche, offering community living arrangements for young professionals or individuals interested in shared housing. These niches cater to unique demands, providing specialized investment opportunities in the real estate sector.

2. Advantages of Investing in Niche Markets:

Niche markets in the real estate industry often have fewer competitors compared to broader markets, resulting in less competition and allowing investors to capitalize on unique opportunities for potentially higher profits.

By focusing on a specific market segment, investors can develop specialized knowledge, which significantly aids in making informed investment decisions. Furthermore, investing in specialized markets provides a strategy for diversifying an investment portfolio, which can help mitigate risks associated with economic downturns or sector-specific issues.

This diversification can lead to increased profitability, as operating within a niche market may allow for pricing flexibility and the opportunity to achieve premium returns, especially when the demand within these markets is high and yet unmet. Additionally, niche markets are typically more responsive to new trends and shifting consumer preferences, enabling investors to quickly adapt and leverage changing market dynamics to their advantage.

3. Methods for Finding Specialty Markets:

Finding niche markets in real estate begins with comprehensive market analysis. This process involves scrutinizing customer behavior, demographic trends, and emerging needs to identify potential opportunities.

Additionally, paying close attention to local and regional dynamics is crucial as it helps uncover niche markets unique to specific areas. Each location has distinct needs or market gaps that present exploitable opportunities for savvy investors.

Moreover, cultivating industry connections and networking plays a pivotal role. Attending conferences, engaging with local real estate communities, and networking with experts in the field can provide valuable insights into new investment trends and specialized markets, enhancing the ability to make informed decisions and capitalize on niche opportunities.

Data analytics and technology: Finding trends and possibilities in the real estate market may be accomplished via technology and data analytics techniques. Potential niche markets may be identified by analyzing data on property kinds, rental patterns, and demographic changes.

Customer Feedback and Surveys: Understanding prospective renters' or purchasers' preferences and unmet requirements via surveys and feedback channels facilitates the discovery of niche possibilities.

4. Distinctive Investment Possibilities:

Exploring adaptive reuse and repurposing of assets offers unique financial opportunities, such as transforming historic buildings into mixed-use spaces or converting old warehouses into lofts. Additionally, the growing popularity of sustainable and environmentally friendly real estate caters to a niche market of renters or buyers focused on eco-conscious living, drawn to properties with green amenities or located in eco-friendly neighborhoods.

Technology-driven investments also cater to the evolving needs of the market, including properties equipped with smart home features or designed for remote work. Investing in real estate that supports arts and culture, such as spaces housing galleries, art studios, or cultural venues, targets a specific audience that values these elements.

Furthermore, the increasing focus on health and wellness has spurred investment in properties that promote a healthy lifestyle, featuring amenities like fitness centers, green spaces, or proximity to wellness services. Lastly, providing affordable housing solutions to underserved communities presents a specialized investment opportunity, potentially involving creative financing methods or unique yet cost-effective housing designs, meeting crucial societal needs while offering potential returns.

5. Reducing Risks in Specialty Markets:

Extensive due diligence is crucial, even in specialized sectors, as making well-informed decisions demands an evaluation of a niche's risks, prospective demand, and economic realities. Diversification within the targeted specialty can further reduce risks, such as an investor diversifying across multiple university cities within the student housing sector.

Investment strategies need to be adjustable, adapting to changes in niche markets to sustain success. Finding real estate niche markets and distinctive investment prospects requires a blend of strategic thinking, flexibility, and market knowledge. Successful investors utilize their understanding of upcoming trends, conduct careful research, and employ inventive ways to carve out a niche that meets market needs. Niche markets, whether targeting specific populations, adopting sustainable practices, or capitalizing on cultural trends, can lead to financial success and a distinctive, satisfying investment portfolio.

Aspect	**Description**
Understanding Niche Markets	Real estate niches like student housing, senior living, vacation rentals, and co-living spaces.
Examples of Niche Markets	Student Housing, Senior Living, Vacation Rentals, Co-Living

Benefits of Niche Market Investment	Reduced Competition, Specialized Expertise, Diversification, Higher Profit Margins, Adaptability
Strategies for Identifying Niche Markets	Market Research, Local Analysis, Networking, Data Analytics, Surveys
Unique Investment Opportunities	Repurposing, Sustainable Investments, Technology, Cultural Spaces, Health-Focused Properties, Affordable Housing
Mitigating Risks in Niche Markets	Due Diligence, Diversification, Adaptive Strategies

|5|

Financing Strategies

This chapter goes into detail about a number of important financial methods for real estate owners. We start by looking at mortgage choices and loan designs. Then we move on to more creative ways to get money, like partnerships and crowdfunding. Because we know how important it is to lower risks, we talk about financial tactics that can protect assets. Then, to make sure we make good decisions, we look at debt-to-income levels and financial health. Lastly, we look at ways to improve cash flow management, which is an important part of long-term success in real estate investing.

For the relevant case studies, worksheets and free resources you can visit: andonierealty.com

"Setting goals is the first step in turning the invisible into the visible."

- Tony Robbins

5.1 Exploring Mortgage Options and Loan Structures

Evaluating loan arrangements and mortgage options is pivotal in real estate investing, as the success and profitability of a venture hinge significantly on choosing the right financing strategies. Key considerations encompass interest rates and terms—analyzing fixed or adjustable rates, understanding duration, and potential fluctuations impacting overall loan cost and investment profitability.

Assessing the loan-to-value (LTV) ratio, understanding its correlation between the loan amount and property value, determines risk levels for lenders and potential favorable terms. Down payment requirements should be evaluated, as higher down payments may lead to better terms but necessitate more upfront capital. Exploring various loan programs, such as conventional loans, FHA, or VA loans, is critical, considering their distinct requirements and impacts on financing structures.

Understanding the influence of credit scores and financial histories on eligibility and interest rates is essential, emphasizing the importance of a strong credit profile for favorable terms. Also, it's important to think about how you'll repay the loan. This includes planning out regular payments over time (amortization schedules) and considering large, one-time payments at the end (balloon payments). Make sure these plans fit with your investment goals and expected cash flow.

The formula for calculating the monthly payment on a fixed-rate mortgage is:

$$M = \frac{P \times r \times (1+r)^n}{(1+r)^n - 1}$$

where:

- M is the monthly payment.
- P is the principal loan amount.
- r is the monthly interest rate (annual interest rate divided by 12).
- n is the number of payments (loan term in years multiplied by 12).

Assessing associated fees and closing costs is important, as these expenses significantly affect the overall cost of acquiring the property and should be factored into investment analyses.

Evaluating prepayment penalties is essential to understand potential limitations for future refinancing or selling strategies. Monitoring market conditions, interest rate trends, and economic forecasts informs decisions on optimal financing timings. Seeking advice from financial advisors, mortgage brokers, and real estate professionals provides valuable insights to navigate complex financing options and align decisions with specific financial goals and risk tolerance levels, ultimately maximizing potential profitability and success in real estate ventures.

1. The Value of Mortgage Choices

Capital efficiency and leverage, Mitigation of Risk and Handling Cash Movement

Leveraging the cash allows investors to manage a larger asset value with a comparatively lower initial investment, thanks to mortgages. This leverage increases potential profits on investment. Selecting the right mortgage helps lessen the dangers brought on by changes in the market. For instance, fixed-rate mortgages shield investors against interest rate volatility by offering consistency in interest payments. Effective cash flow management is possible for investors who choose their mortgage alternatives carefully. Adapting loan arrangements to the prospective revenue production of the property is one way to manage cash flow sustainably.

Options for financing have an impact on portfolio diversity. Investors may diversify their debt by selecting distinct mortgage terms and structures for the various properties in their portfolio.

2. Typical Mortgage Choices:

Fixed-rate mortgages have an interest rate that stays the same over the life of the loan, which helps owners plan their funds and budget more accurately. ARMs, on the other hand, have interest rates that can change based on changes in the market. ARMs may have lower rates at first, but the interest rates can change quickly, which can make total costs unpredictable.

Interest-only mortgages let users pay only the interest for a certain amount of time, which can be helpful for investors who want to get the most out of their short-term cash flow. Balloon mortgages have lower monthly payments during the loan term and a big "balloon" payment at the end. This type of mortgage is good for owners who plan to sell or refinance their properties before the term ends. Also, government-backed loans like those from the VA or FHA offer better terms and lower down payments for approved buyers, making it easier for people to get loans for real estate.

3. Considerations and Loan Structures:

The LTV (loan-to-value) ratio: The loan amount is shown as a proportion of the property's appraised value in the LTV ratio. Less risk for lenders is often implied by lower LTV ratios, which might lead to better conditions for borrowers.

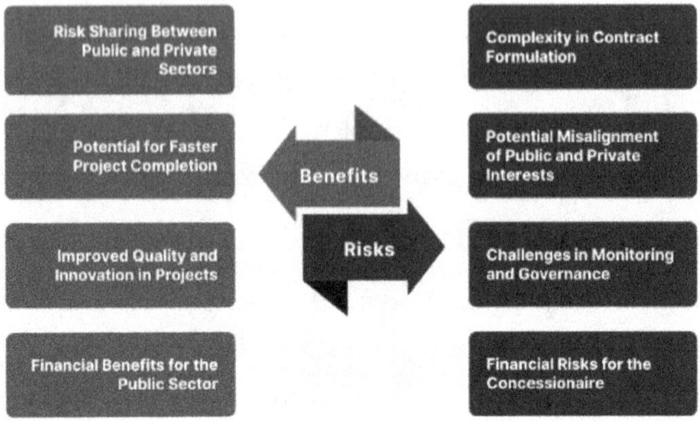

Loan terms are usually different, but 15, 20, or 30 years are popular. Most of the time, shorter loan terms mean lower total interest costs, but higher monthly payments. The repayment plan shows how payments are split between capital and interest over time. This lets investors pick designs that work with their investment strategies and financial goals. Some loans also have fees for paying them off early, which buyers need to know about and plan for in their long-term financial plans.

Also, it's important to know the difference between non-recourse and recourse loans. With non-recourse loans, the lender can only take back the property if the borrower doesn't pay, but with recourse loans, the borrower is directly responsible for the debt. Non-recourse loans are often chosen by investors who want to lower their personal financial risk.

4. Elements Affecting Mortgage Selection:

Investment Approach, State of the Market and Type of Property:

The investor's entire strategy should be in line with the mortgage that is selected. Fixed-rate mortgages may be advantageous for long-term, income-focused investments, while adjustable-rate or interest-only mortgages may be more appropriate for short-term, value-added initiatives.

The state of the market at the moment is quite important, particularly the movements in interest rates. Investors may choose fixed-rate mortgages in a rising interest rate environment to guarantee consistent payments. The kind of property being funded may impact the mortgage option. Multi-Family homes may need special considerations, and financing requirements for residential vs commercial buildings may vary.

Tolerance for Risk and Plan of Exit:

In selecting mortgage choices, investors want to evaluate their level of risk tolerance. If you're uncomfortable with interest rate risk, consider looking into adjustable rate mortgages (ARMs). It is advisable to consider the investor's exit plan, which may include selling the property, refinancing, or long-term holding. This affects the best mortgage arrangement for the financial venture.

5. The Mortgage Application Process:

Credit scores and credit histories are used by lenders to decide if a person is creditworthy. Having a good credit history can help you get a better loan deal. Interest rates can change based on credit score, which shows how important it is to have a good credit background. Lenders also look at the borrower's debt-to-income ratio by comparing how much money they make each month to how much debt they have.

A smaller number means that your finances are in better shape, which can lead to better loan terms. The loan-to-value (LTV) ratio and, by extension, the loan terms are also affected by the down payment amount. Usually, bigger down payments mean better terms and lower interest rates. To make the mortgage approval process easier, borrowers must provide a number of papers, such as tax records, proof of income, and information about the property. Having accurate and full paperwork can speed up this process by a lot. Lastly, investors should know how long it takes for loans to be approved. This is especially important in real estate markets where competition is high, so investors can plan their deals well and be ready for any delays.

6. Collaborating with Mortgage Experts:

Talking to experienced mortgage brokers or loan officers can be very helpful because they can give you useful information, walk you through the different mortgage choices, suggest the best arrangements, and make the application process easier. Also, it is very important to get help from both a financial and law professional when doing complicated deals.

Because they know a lot about mortgage agreements, taxes, and general financial planning, these professionals make sure that all parts of the deal are clear and legal. Investors should also think about getting offers from more than one loan and carefully comparing them. This method lets buyers look at contracts, interest rates, and fees all at once, which helps them make smart choices that will help them reach their financial goals.

One of the most important steps in the real estate investing process is researching mortgage choices and loan arrangements. It thoroughly assesses risk tolerance, market circumstances, financial objectives, and property details. A comprehensive investment plan, leverage, cash flow management, and other aspects must be considered when weighing the benefits and drawbacks of different mortgage choices. Working with mortgage experts and consultants may make securing finance for investors' investment goals easier. Selecting the appropriate mortgage is not only a financial but also a strategic move in the ever-changing real estate market that may determine the profitability and success of an investment portfolio.

5.2 Creative Financing Techniques: Partnerships, Crowdfunding

Creative financing methods like partnerships and crowdfunding have become cutting-edge in real estate investing. These strategies go beyond standard finance techniques and provide new ways for investors to share risks, fund projects, and take advantage of possibilities without traditional funding. This section will examine the ideas of crowdsourcing and partnerships, their advantages, and how real estate investors might use these innovative financing methods. This way it allows investors who don't have the full capital to still invest for the future.

1. Real Estate Partnerships:

In a real estate partnership, two or more people pool their money, expertise, and resources to invest in a project together. There are many types of partnerships, each with varying degrees of partner engagement and responsibility, including general, limited, and limited liability partnerships.

When it comes to real estate investing, each type of partnership has its own structure and perks. Because they are both responsible for the project's success, each partner in a general partnership is also responsible for all bills and responsibilities.

There are two types of partners in a limited partnership (LP):

- limited partners
- general partners

Limited partners give money and have limited risk, while general partners handle the investment and have more responsibility. Similar to limited liability companies (LLCs), a limited liability partnership (LLP) protects each partner from being sued.

Partnerships have a lot of benefits. They let buyers share their money, which makes more money available for bigger or more complicated projects. Risk is shared among partners, which makes it easier for individual buyers and may make the business more stable. Plus, each partner can bring their own special knowledge, skills, or networks, which can make the relationship stronger overall. Partnerships also give buyers access to more investment possibilities, some of which may be out of reach for individual investors. This creates new ways for the real estate market to grow and make money.

Even though real estate partnerships can be helpful, they also come with their own problems and things to think about that need to be carefully managed. It can get harder to make decisions, so partners need to be able to talk to each other clearly and agree on important issues to keep things running smoothly.

Profit sharing is also an important part that needs to be spelled out clearly in the partnership agreement so that there are no mistakes or disagreements between the partners. Because partnerships are complicated from a legal and financial point of view, it is important to have well-written partnership papers and other legal paperwork ready. These contracts spell out each partner's duties, duties, and financial contributions. They make sure that all legal areas are covered and that the partnership is set up for success.

2. Real Estate Crowdfunding:

Real estate crowdfunding generates money from many investors to finance a real estate project, each contributing a relatively small sum. Online crowdfunding services link real estate possibilities, and investors encourage this financing. This way, any investor can start with as little as $100 and have a fixed percentage ROI for a monthly or yearly revenue.

There are different kinds of real estate crowdfunding, such as: Equity crowdfunding lets investors get a piece of a project in proportion to the amount of money they put in. Investors get their money back when the project makes money or is sold. Debt crowdfunding is when users give money to project sponsors or creators in exchange for interest payments. The loan is then paid back over a certain amount of time. Crowdfunding that is hybrid combines loan and stock, giving investors a chance to earn interest and own a piece of the company.

Crowdfunding in real estate has a lot of benefits. It lowers the barriers to entry so that smaller investors can join real estate projects that were once only open to bigger investors. With this method, buyers can also spread their money out among several projects with different risk levels and yields. Crowdfunding sites also make project information clear and easy to find, which makes it easier for funders to get involved.

But there are problems and things to think about when it comes to real estate crowdfunding. Regulatory compliance is very important because the stocks industry is ruled by laws that both sellers and buyers must follow. There is also the risk that the project will fail, which means that investors could lose their money. This shows how important it is for both donors and investors to do a lot of research before investing. Also, funders usually don't have much say over project choices because the project backers still run the show. Lastly, market factors can affect the success of crowdfunding projects. For example, when the economy is bad or the market is volatile, the results may be different.

3. Making the Most of Real Estate Partnerships:

Finding partners whose resources and skills support each other is key to making real estate relationships work. One partner might be good at finances, and the other might be good at managing properties. This would make the team more equal. It's important to write up thorough partnership agreements that spell out each partner's duties, responsibilities, ways of splitting profits, and ways to settle disagreements.

Trust and good communication are very important for these partnerships to work. To have a good working connection, partners should keep the lines of communication open, agree on what the end goal is, and share regular reports. Additionally, partnership papers should clearly spell out how to end the partnership, including how to buy out partners, sell the property, or deal with other unplanned events. This way, everyone knows what to do when things change or problems arise.

4. Improving Real Estate Crowdfunding:

When crowdfunding for real estate, it's important to do a lot of research first. People who want to invest should do a lot of study on both the crowdfunding sites and the projects they are thinking about. This includes looking at the track record of the project sponsors and figuring out if the planned investment will work. Diversification can also help lower risks. Investors can make a well-balanced portfolio by spreading their money across a number of crowdfunding projects with different levels of risk.

It is very important for buyers to fully understand all the terms of their investment, such as the dangers, the projected length of the investment, and the possible profits. Attention must be paid to reading project papers and deals. Crowdfunding may be a more casual way to spend, but it's still important to keep an eye on things and take part. To make sure they make smart choices, investors should keep up with the market and check back on the projects they've put money into on a daily basis.

Real estate investing has changed due to creative financing strategies, including partnerships and crowdsourcing. These strategies provide special advantages, including risk sharing, increased access to capital, and the chance to work on various projects. However, they provide unique difficulties and concerns that need thorough preparation, investigation, and comprehension of the relevant financial and legal frameworks. Investors may access bigger capital pools, share risks, and combine capabilities via partnerships. Successful real estate partnerships need strategic alignment, well-written agreements, and open lines of communication between parties.

Similarly, real estate crowdfunding creates chances for a broader and more varied pool of investors. Reduced obstacles to entry, portfolio diversification, and open access to real estate developments are all advantageous to investors.

However, to successfully participate in crowdfunding projects, one must adhere to legal requirements, do due research, and understand the dangers involved. The decision between crowdsourcing and partnerships ultimately comes down to the investor's investing objectives, preferences, and risk tolerance. These innovative financing strategies allow investors to maximize their wealth and take advantage of various exciting real estate possibilities as the market develops.

5.3 Mitigating Risks through Financial Strategies

The real estate industry's inherent volatility may expose investors to risks from various sources, including economic and market volatility changes. Financial practices protects assets and puts them in a position to take advantage of possibilities. In this part, we will examine important financial techniques for reducing risk while investing in real estate.

1. **Identification and Assessment of Risk:**

Extensive Investigation, Scans of the Environment and Evaluation of the Market:

Investors must thoroughly investigate possible investments, looking at financial performance, property conditions, and market trends. Monitoring regulation changes, interest rate patterns, and overall economic circumstances are all part of routine environmental scans. Investors may foresee hazards and take appropriate action by solidly understanding the macroeconomic environment. A thorough market study is necessary to discover local trends, demand-supply dynamics, and possible changes in property prices. Analyzing the performances of similar properties offers insightful information for risk assessment.

2. Monetary Techniques to Reduce Risk:

Creating an ideal capital structure involves finding a balance between debt and equity that aligns with an investor's financial goals and risk tolerance. It's also prudent to set aside reserve funds for unexpected costs, vacancies, or market downturns, providing a financial safety net that allows investors to navigate challenges without compromising their portfolio's stability. Additionally, ensuring adequate insurance coverage for real estate assets is crucial to protect against risks such as natural disasters, liability claims, and property damage, with regular reviews and updates to insurance policies as risk profiles change.

Conducting stress tests on investment scenarios helps assess how portfolios might perform under adverse conditions, enabling investors to identify vulnerabilities and implement preventive measures. Diversifying real estate investments across different property types, geographic areas, and market niches reduces concentration risk and shields the portfolio from regional market slumps or sector-specific issues. Effective cash flow management is essential, involving careful monitoring of rental income and expenditures to maintain positive cash flow, adjusting for market rental rates and planning for potential vacancies.

Investors should also prepare for emergencies by developing contingency plans for various scenarios, such as economic downturns or unexpected property issues, enhancing their ability to respond swiftly and effectively. Lastly, performing consistent financial assessments allows investors to evaluate the performance of their investments, identify growth opportunities, and adapt strategies in response to changing market conditions, ensuring ongoing success and adaptability in their real estate ventures.

3. Instruments and Tools for Finance:

Hedging Interest Rates, Instruments Derivatives and Restructuring Debt:

Investors may be shielded from increasing interest rates by using interest rate hedging instruments like interest rate swaps or caps. By offering consistency in interest payments, these products lessen the risk associated with fluctuations in interest rates. One way to protect against changes in the market is to employ derivatives, such as futures contracts or options. Investors may use these tools to reduce the risk of fluctuations in real estate prices or interest rates. Investors may look into solutions for debt restructuring during difficult economic times. An investment's financial flexibility may be increased by negotiating advantageous terms with lenders or refinancing current debt.

4. Observation and Modifying Techniques:

Monitoring in Real Time, Modifiable Techniques and Creating Scenarios

Investors may remain ahead of such hazards by examining real-time economic statistics, tenant trends, and market situations. Proactive decision-making and risk minimization are facilitated by timely information. Because real estate markets are ever-changing, risk-reduction tactics must also be flexible. Investors must be ready to modify their strategy in response to evolving trends, shifting market circumstances, and economic changes. Creating many forecasts based on several economic situations is known as scenario planning. Investors may evaluate the effects of different variables on their portfolios and adjust their strategy by simulating possible outcomes.

Consulting with experts in finance and real estate is crucial. Experts in accounting, law, and finance may provide insightful guidance to help investors understand complicated financial situations and steer clear of trouble.

5. Making Use of Tax Techniques:

Planning for Tax Efficiency: Investing with tax efficiency in mind is a calculated move that will increase profits and reduce tax obligations. Investors should investigate the tax benefits, credits, and deductions relevant to real estate investments.

Exchanges (1031): Investors may postpone paying capital gains taxes by reinvesting the profits of selling one property into another using 1031 exchanges. This tax-deferral approach promotes portfolio expansion and improves liquidity.

Harvesting Tax Losses: Selling underperforming assets deliberately to offset gains and lower taxable income is known as "tax-loss harvesting." Adding tax-loss harvesting to a real estate portfolio may improve its tax efficiency.

Effective risk management via financial tactics is a continuous and essential component of real estate investing success. Proactive planning, flexible tactics, and financial instrument use are all necessary for effective risk management in today's changing market conditions.

Investors have to take a comprehensive strategy for risk reduction, considering variables including financial structures, tax consequences, and market circumstances.Investors should strengthen their portfolios against future difficulties by embracing diversity, creating reserve money, and putting appropriate capital structures into place. Regular financial assessments, stress testing, and contingency planning bolster a robust investment strategy that can withstand economic risks.

Moreover, using financial tools like debt restructuring, interest rate hedging, and derivatives offers more options for reducing risk. With these tools, investors may better control market and interest rate risks, increasing the overall stability of their real estate holdings.

Ultimately, real estate investing success in reducing risk requires sound financial judgment, market awareness, and flexibility. Adhering to these principles and using tactical financial tactics puts investors in a better position to protect their money and seize Expansion and profit-generating possibilities within the constantly changing real estate market.

Here's the table:

Aspect	Description
Risk Assessment & Identification	Conduct thorough due diligence on potential investments, monitor broader economic conditions, and analyze local market trends to identify risks and opportunities.
Financial Strategies for Risk Mitigation	Balance debt and equity, establish reserve funds, ensure adequate insurance coverage, perform stress tests, diversify investments, manage cash flows, plan contingencies, and regularly review financial performance to align with goals and mitigate risks.
Financial Tools and Instruments	Utilize interest rate hedging tools, derivative instruments for market fluctuation protection, and explore debt restructuring options during economic uncertainties.

Monitoring and Adaptive Strategies	Implement real-time monitoring of market and economic conditions, adjust investment strategies based on market changes, engage in scenario planning, and seek professional advice to inform decision-making.
Leveraging Tax Strategies	Optimize tax efficiency through strategic investment structuring, use 1031 exchanges to defer capital gains tax, and employ tax-loss harvesting to reduce taxable income and enhance tax efficiency.

This table provides a structured overview of the key aspects related to mitigating risks through financial strategies in real estate investment, covering risk assessment, financial tools, monitoring strategies, and tax considerations.

5.4 Understanding Debt-to-Income Ratios and Financial Health

Real estate investors need to understand debt-to-income ratios (DTI) and financial health since DTI is a key indicator of a person or entity's capacity for debt management and prompt payback. A financial metric known as the debt-to-income ratio (DTI) compares a person's total income to their debt payments. Understanding DTI ratios and keeping a clean credit record is critical for real estate investors to make well-informed choices and get advantageous financing arrangements.

$$\text{Debt-To-Income Ratio} = \frac{\text{Monthly Debt Payments}}{\text{Total Monthly Income}} \times 100$$

1. The DTI Explained:

The debt-to-income (DTI) ratio is one of the most important ways to figure out how financially healthy someone is. It is found by dividing the total monthly debt payments by the gross monthly income. It's written as:

DTI = (Total Monthly Debt Payments / Gross Monthly Income) x 100.

Most of the time, the answer is shown as a number. The different types of debt payments that make up this number are mortgage payments, credit card payments, auto loan payments, school loan payments, and any other normal debt responsibilities. A higher DTI rate means that a person spends more of their income paying off debt, which can affect their ability to borrow money and make financial choices.

2. The Value of DTI in Investing in Real Estate:

Lenders rely on the debt-to-income (DTI) ratio to assess a borrower's capacity to manage additional debt, making it a critical metric for determining loan eligibility and interest rates. A lower DTI ratio is generally viewed favorably as it indicates a smaller portion of the borrower's income is committed to debt repayments, suggesting a reduced risk of financial hardship.

For real estate investors, maintaining a favorable DTI ratio enhances their chances of loan approval since it demonstrates effective debt management. Additionally, investors utilize DTI ratios to gauge the affordability of undertaking further real estate investments. A lower DTI suggests greater financial flexibility, enabling investors to leverage more debt to capitalize on investment opportunities effectively.

3. DTI Category:

For example, the front-end debt-to-income (DTI) ratio looks at housing-related costs like taxes, mortgage payments, and property insurance. A lower front-end DTI means that housing costs take up less of a person's income, which means that housing costs don't put as much of a strain on their finances. A person's back-end DTI, on the other hand, includes all of their debts, not just their mortgage, but also their credit card bills and auto loans. This complete test gives a more complete picture of a person's general debt management, showing their overall financial obligations and debt-handling skills.

4. Understanding DTI Percentages:

A debt-to-income (DTI) ratio of less than 36% is usually seen as good. This means that less of a person's income is going toward paying off debt, leaving them with more money for savings or other spending. Most of the time, ratios between 36% and 43% are considered average, and ratios of 43% or more are considered high.

Higher DTI rates can be a problem because they show that a lot of income is going toward paying off debt, which could put a strain on the finances. Keeping your DTI ratio low is good for real estate buyers because it makes it easier for them to get loans with good terms. A good DTI percentage also lets owners take advantage of business chances and spread out their holdings, which improves their financial security and growth potential.

5. Enhancing DTI Percentages:

A debt-to-income (DTI) ratio of less than 36% is usually seen as good. This means that less of a person's income is going toward paying off debt, leaving them with more money for savings or other spending. Most of the time, ratios between 36% and 43% are considered average, and ratios of 43% or more are considered high.

Higher DTI rates can be a problem because they show that a lot of income is going toward paying off debt, which could put a strain on the finances. Keeping your DTI ratio low is good for real estate buyers because it makes it easier for them to get loans with good terms. A good DTI percentage also lets owners take advantage of business chances and spread out their holdings, which improves their financial security and growth potential.

6. DTI about Financing for Real Estate:

When lenders look at loan applications, DTI rates are one of the most important things they look at. Lenders are more likely to give money to investors with lower DTI numbers because they are seen as less dangerous. This good opinion can have a direct effect on the loan terms. For example, investors with lower DTI ratios may be able to get lower interest rates, which lowers the total cost of borrowing. Additionally, lenders may use DTI rates to figure out the largest loan amount an owner can get. Investors with lower ratios could get bigger loans because they were seen as less risky and more financially stable. Because of this, buyers who want to get good loan terms should make keeping the DTI ratio low a top concern.

7. Tracking and Handling DTI Throughout Time:

Regular financial checks should be made by real estate owners to see their debt-to-income (DTI) rates and general financial health. These regular checks make management more proactive and let financial plans be changed as needed. Also, changes in the market, interest rates, and the economy can all affect DTI ratios. Because of this, owners need to keep up with market trends and make changes to their plans as needed. Investors can make the most of their real estate investments and keep an eye on the market by planning their finances in a flexible way and keeping an eye on the market.

For Example: Think of an investor who has a 30% debt-to-income ratio. This suggests they pay off debt with thirty per cent of their gross monthly income. Lenders would look at this investor positively, and they could be eligible for attractive financing conditions, providing them with a strong platform to grow their real estate holdings.

Keeping good financial standing and comprehending debt-to-income ratios are essential for real estate investors. When deciding on an interest rate, approving a loan, and making other financial decisions, the DTI ratio is an important statistic. In addition to improving their financing prospects, real estate investors with favorable debt-to-income ratios are better positioned to take advantage of a wider variety of investment options. In the ever-changing world of real estate investing, persistent financial health and success are facilitated by proactive financial planning, intelligent debt management, and ongoing monitoring.

5.5 Strategies for Optimal Cash Flow Management

Effective cash flow management serves as the cornerstone of success in real estate investing, necessitating a meticulous balance between incoming revenues and outgoing expenses. It's a multifaceted approach that demands astute financial foresight and strategic decision-making.

Before diving into investments, conducting a comprehensive financial analysis becomes paramount—a thorough evaluation of potential income, expenses, vacancy rates, and risks allows for accurate cash flow projections.

Maintaining cash reserves serves as a buffer against unforeseen circumstances like sudden repairs, vacancies, or economic fluctuations, safeguarding against negative cash flow scenarios. Moreover, regular assessments of local market rents and adjustments to rental rates based on market trends can optimize income without alienating tenants.

Scrutinizing operational costs, negotiating vendor rates, and exploring cost-effective alternatives contribute significantly to expense management. Additionally, efficient rent collection systems and the enforcement of late fees can ensure consistent, timely payments from tenants.

Consideration of lease length and terms can provide stable income streams, reducing vacancy periods and turnover costs. Proactive property inspections and maintenance prevent larger, more costly repairs, thereby preserving property value and minimizing unexpected expenses.

Managing existing debts associated with the property, including refinancing at lower rates, is crucial in alleviating interest costs and enhancing cash flow. Staying updated on market trends, regulations, and investment strategies facilitates adaptation to changing market conditions, ensuring a resilient approach to cash flow management.

Diversifying the real estate portfolio across different property types and locations mitigates risk by spreading potential losses. Finally, professional property management services can streamline operations, tenant relations, and financial aspects, optimizing cash flow and bolstering long-term success in the dynamic real estate landscape.

1. Recognizing Real Estate Cash Flow:

A property has positive cash flow when the money it brings in is more than what it costs to run, like mortgage payments, property taxes, insurance, and repairs. This is a good situation because it means the house can pay for itself. On the other hand, a building has negative cash flow when its running costs are higher than its income. This mismatch in funds can put a strain on the owner's finances, and they often need to find extra money to make up the difference and keep the property running. Controlling these changes in cash flow is important for keeping the business's finances stable and making sure the project will make money in the long run.

2. Essential Elements of Management of Cash Flow:

In the real estate business, rental income is the main source of cash flow. Investors need to set property prices that are high enough to get people to move in, but low enough to cover all costs and still make a profit. To keep your cash flow healthy, you need to keep track of your operational costs like property management fees, care fees, real estate taxes, utilities, and insurance.

Additionally, a big chunk of cash flow is usually used to settle bills, like house payments. Investors need to carefully weigh the rental income they receive against their mortgage payments in order to avoid negative cash flow and the possible financial problems that can come after. This careful handling makes sure that real estate purchases are stable financially and make money.

3. Methods for Improving Cash Flow Management:

Investors need to do a lot of study on the market before they buy a property to fully understand market trends, vacancy rates, and local rental rates. This information helps you set the right rental prices so you can make the most money. Managing properties in a way that saves money is also important for lowering running costs. Investors can save money by getting managing fees that are competitive and hiring outside help for some tasks. Regular property checks are also important because they let owners find and fix repair problems quickly. Doing preventative maintenance not only keeps tenants happy, but it also keeps you from having to make expensive fixes. All of these tactics work together to help real estate investments be managed well and make money.

Choosing the right financial choices is a key part of handling cash flow well. To get the most cash flow from their investments, investors should look into borrowing terms, interest rates, and loan designs that work with their plan. It is very important to price rented homes correctly based on their features and the current market conditions. If you underprice them, you could lose money, and if you overprice them, you might have long gaps.

Tenant retention strategies, like letting tenants renew their leases, fixing problems with tenants quickly, and giving rewards for long-term leases, help lower openings and change costs, which stabilizes cash flow. Setting up an emergency fund is also important to cover costs that come up out of the blue, so that they don't hurt your cash flow.

Regular financial reviews are needed to see how investments are doing and find places where they can be improved. The best way to handle cash flow is to change tactics as the market changes. Cash flow can be improved even more by finding new ways to make money besides standard rental income, such as through business leases, short-term rentals, or adding features that make money. By maximizing after-tax gains, good tax planning that takes advantage of appropriate refunds, deductions, and rewards has a positive effect on cash flow.

It's also possible to save money and better control your cash flow by negotiating good terms with lenders, workers, and service providers. Using technology to keep an eye on finances, collect rent online, and handle properties can make things run more smoothly and save money on costs. Cash flow stays at its best when rental rates are changed based on quantity and demand in the market.

Let us imagine that an owner owns a house that brings in $500 every month in cash flow. This extra money lets the investor pay off debt and cover working costs while also setting aside money for future investments. This shows how important it is to plan carefully for both finances and operations when investing in real estate.

How Optimal Cash Flow Affects Investment Performance:

Cash flow that is just right gives owners the freedom to take advantage of new chances and help their portfolios grow. When owners have a good cash flow, they can think about making more investments, which helps them grow and spread.

This steady and positive cash flow also helps keep funds stable, so owners can handle unexpected costs, tough economic times, or short-term job openings without putting their general financial health at risk. A good cash flow also lets buyers put money toward paying down debt, which speeds up the process of building equity and makes long-term wealth creation easier. This approach not only makes money more stable, but it also sets people up for long-term success in their money-related activities.

Effective cash flow management techniques are essential to the success of real estate investments. If investors want to make sure that their portfolios are financially sound, they should concentrate on increasing income, reducing costs, and maintaining a positive cash flow. Effective cash flow management requires careful market research, economical property management, tenant retention, and smart financing.

Sustained cash flow optimization also benefits from the capacity to integrate technology, negotiate attractive terms, diversify revenue sources, and react to changes in the market. Prioritizing cash flow management helps real estate investors not only successfully negotiate property ownership difficulties but also set themselves up for long-term success and expansion in the ever-changing real estate market.

Here's a text representation of a table summarizing the key strategies for optimal cash flow management in real estate investment:

Strategy	**Description**
Market Analysis	Analyze local trends to set optimal rental rates and maximize income.
Cost Management	Negotiate fees, outsource tasks, and reduce operational costs for efficiency.
Property Inspections	Conduct regular inspections to maintain property condition and tenant satisfaction.
Strategic Financing	Choose financing that aligns with investment goals and optimizes cash flow.

Rental Pricing	Set rental prices based on current market conditions to maximize revenue.
Tenant Retention	Implement strategies to reduce turnover and stabilize cash flow.
Emergency Reserves	Establish funds for unforeseen expenses to protect cash flow.
Financial Reviews	Regularly assess financial performance and adapt strategies as needed.
Income Diversification	Explore alternative income sources like short-term rentals or commercial leases.
Tax Efficiency	Leverage tax incentives to enhance after-tax returns.

Negotiations	Secure favorable terms with service providers to reduce costs.
Technology Use	Use tech solutions for efficient property and financial management.
Rental Rate Adjustments	Adjust rental rates in response to market changes to ensure optimal cash flow.

This table provides a structured overview of the key strategies for optimal cash flow management in real estate investment, covering aspects such as market analysis, property management, financial reviews, and technology integration.

|6|

Real Estate Investment Strategies

This part gives you a wide range of methods for investing in real estate. We can help you whether you want to build wealth over the long term, make the most money in the short term, or take a sensible approach. We'll look at tried-and-true strategies like buy-and-hold and flipping, as well as mixed options and newer methods like REITs and syndications. Finally, we will help you make a financial plan that is unique to your needs and goals. So buckle up and get ready to see what real estate can do for you!

For the relevant case studies, worksheets and free resources you can visit: andonierealty.com

"The wise young man or wage earner of today invests his money in real estate."

- Andrew Carnegie.

6.1 Buy-and-Hold Strategies: Long-Term Wealth Accumulation

In the realm of real estate investing, buy-and-hold strategies represent a cornerstone methodology where investors procure properties with the intention of retaining ownership for extended periods—often spanning many years, if not decades.

The fundamental principle underpinning this strategy lies in the historical trend of property values witnessing an upward trajectory over time, thereby affording investors the opportunity to amass considerable equity and foster enduring wealth accumulation.

This enduring tactic is a linchpin of real estate investment, capitalizing on the dual benefits of consistent rental income augmentation and the appreciation of property value. Its essence encapsulates a nuanced interplay of several vital components, each contributing to its efficacy.

These encompass meticulous property selection based on growth potential, prudent financial analysis projecting long-term viability, and astute market assessment to discern trends influencing property appreciation. The buy-and-hold approach, while heralded for its potential to generate sustainable income streams through rental revenue, also hinges on the expectation of property values appreciating over time, thereby bolstering the overall return on investment.

However, despite its allure and potential, this strategy is not devoid of considerations: challenges such as property maintenance costs, potential market downturns impacting value appreciation, and the need for prolonged capital commitment underscore its inherent complexities.

Nevertheless, when executed judiciously, the buy-and-hold strategy emerges as a linchpin in the pursuit of long-term wealth generation, playing a pivotal role in fostering a diversified investment portfolio and offering a hedge against market volatility while steadily augmenting one's financial resources over time.

1. The Basis of Buy-and-Hold Techniques:

Buy-and-hold buying methods take advantage of the fact that real estate prices tend to rise over time. This means that buyers can build wealth as the property's market value rises. This method also offers a steady stream of renting income, as owners who rent out their homes can cover their debt and running costs, which increases the long-term value even more.

By keeping the property for a long time, buyers not only get annual payments on their debts, but they may also get capital gains if the value goes up. The property built up from these investments can then be used as a loan to reach other financial goals or make more investments in the future. This is called building wealth through long-term real estate investment.

2. Advantages of Buy-and-Hold Techniques:

There is a steady flow of cash coming in from rental income for buy-and-hold owners. This cash covers both the upkeep of the property and any debts that come with it. This way of investing also has some tax advantages, like being able to subtract running costs, property loss, and mortgage interest, which can greatly increase total profits. There is equity in a building that grows over time as buyers pay down the mortgage. As the loan amount goes down and is finally paid off, this process slowly changes from paying off debt to owning more assets. This raises the investor's net worth. This approach makes buy-and-hold buying even more powerful as a way to build long-term wealth in real estate.

In the past, real estate has been a good way to protect against inflation because property prices and rental income usually go up when inflation is taken into account. This means that saved capital keeps its spending power. People who use the "buy-and-hold" approach can also use the wealth they've built up in their current homes to pay for new purchases. This method lets investors grow their investment portfolios without having to bring in a lot of new money. This way, investors can take advantage of new chances while using the value they have already built up in their real estate assets.

3. Factors to Take Into Account for Effective Buy-and-Hold Strategies:

To make a good buy-and-hold business, you need to carefully choose the right property, taking into account things like location, property quality, potential for growth, and rental demand. Doing a detailed market study helps you find places that have a lot of growth potential and rental demand, which is important for making smart choices about where to buy real estate. Another important factor in the success of buy-and-hold plans is the structure of financing. To support their long-term investment goals, buyers should look for good mortgage terms, interest rates, and loan lengths.

For buy-and-hold owners, good property management is also very important. To make sure steady and regular rental income, it requires thorough renter screening, quick upkeep, and quick settlement of tenant issues. Another important factor is managing cash flow well, which means that rental income not only pays off debts and covers running costs, but also leaves some money in the bank for situations.

A buy-and-hold strategy also needs a long-term view. Investors need to be ready for long stretches of time when property prices, economic cycles, and market changes happen. This long-term view is very important for figuring out the tricky parts of real estate investing and making money over time.

4. Dangers and Obstacles:

There is a lot of market instability and economic factors that affect how stable property prices and the real estate market as a whole are. When investors use "buy-and-hold" tactics, they need to make strong plans to reduce risks and get ready for when the market goes down. Changes in the economy, like changes in interest rates and recessions, can also affect how well these tactics work. It is very important for owners to know what's going on in the economy as a whole and change their plans as needed to deal with problems.

Long-term property management also comes with its own problems, such as upkeep issues, renter change, and costs that were not expected. To keep the business going in the long run and avoid problems with cash flow, managers must be proactive. Investors can keep their income streams going and keep their investment accounts healthy by facing these problems head-on and adjusting to the constantly changing real estate market.

5. Strategies for Exit:

If an investor uses the "buy-and-hold" approach, they might want to look at their investments on a regular basis to make the most of the stocks they own. This process could include moving assets around to take advantage of new chances or selling buildings that aren't doing well to improve the general performance of the business.

Also, people who are getting close to retirement may want to sell their homes carefully to get their wealth and set up a steady income stream for their later years. Using 1031 swaps also lets buyers put off paying capital gains taxes by buying another property with the money from the sale of the first one. This way of deferring taxes gives real estate portfolio managers more freedom, so owners can keep and change their investment plans as needed over time.

In real estate, buy-and-hold tactics are an effective means of accumulating money over the long run. Over time, investors may significantly increase their net worth by using equity accumulation advantages, steady rental income, and property appreciation. Careful consideration of property selection, market dynamics, financing arrangements, and proactive property management are necessary for the successful execution of buy-and-hold plans.

Despite potential risks and hurdles, a well-executed buy-and-hold strategy is consistent with a prudent, long-term investing attitude. In the ever-changing real estate investing environment, investors who adopt this plan, remain aware of market circumstances, adjust their strategies, and use good property management techniques, set themselves up for long-term financial success and wealth creation.

6.2 Property Flipping: Short-Term Profit Maximization

Real estate flipping, sometimes called house flipping or property flipping, is a short-term investment strategy wherein properties are purchased to sell them fast and for a profit. The core of property flipping is finding distressed or undervalued properties, strategically improving them, and then reselling the upgraded property for a greater price. This approach necessitates a deep comprehension of the real estate market, the price of renovations, and the capacity to carry out timely and economical upgrades. In this part, we'll get into the essential elements of property flipping, reviewing the advantages, things to think about, and the steps required to maximize short-term profits.

1. Fundamental Ideas of Property Flipping:

Finding homes that have a lot of worth potential is the first step to successfully selling properties. This usually means looking for houses that have been foreclosed on, are in bad shape, or need repairs. Real estate flippers focus on carefully raising the value of a home by fixing it up and making improvements.

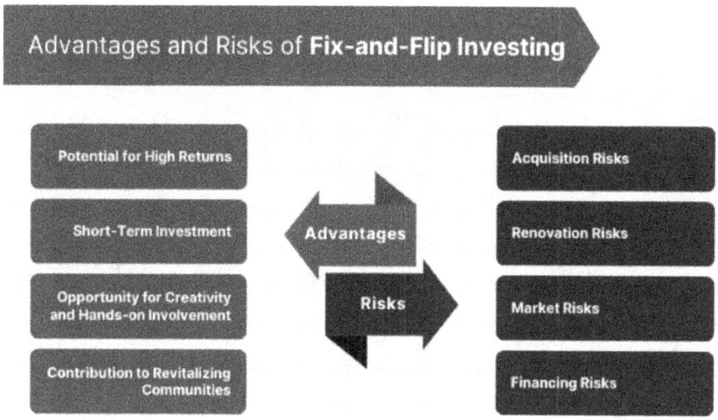

To make the house more appealing to potential buyers, these improvements could include making changes to the structure or the way it looks, as well as taking care of any upkeep issues that need to be fixed. When you're selling houses, time is very important. Flippers try to make the most money and cut down on keeping costs by buying, fixing up, and selling properties quickly. Their business plan will only work if they can turn things around quickly.

2. Advantages of Reselling Real Estate:

Flipping houses is a fast way to make money because owners can see a return on their investment very quickly because of how quickly they can buy, fix up, and sell homes. This approach gives flippers a steady way to make money right now; they can make money as soon as a property is sold and put the money back into new projects without having to wait for long-term growth or rental returns.

Property flippers also gain from market flexibility because they can quickly adapt to changes in the market. Because they are flexible, they can see and take advantage of short-term opportunities in markets that are always changing. Flipping properties also gives buyers the chance to get better at remodeling. This knowledge helps them correctly estimate repair costs and come up with cost-effective ways to improve properties, which makes it easier for them to flip houses for money.

3. A Look Into What Makes Property Flipping Successful:

In the world of selling properties, finding properties that can make you money requires a thorough analysis of the market. Knowing what customers want, what the local market is doing, and how much demand there is for restored homes helps you make decisions and spot profitable possibilities. It's also important to make a budget for repairs. Real estate buyers need to carefully predict remodeling costs to make sure that the improvements add enough worth without going over budget. It's important to flip properties on time; flippers try to make the most money and spend the least amount of money possible by managing the buying, fixing up, and selling processes well.

There are risks that come with selling houses, such as the unstable market and the difficulty of repairs. To deal with these problems and protect their assets, smart flippers use risk management methods. When it comes to money, flippers often use short-term options like hard money loans and lines of credit. These financial options are designed to support the quick turn-around that comes with selling, so you can get things done quickly in order to succeed with this fast-paced investment strategy.

3. The Methodology of Property Flipping:

People who sell houses usually find good deals on properties through a variety of sources, such as damaged property databases, sales, and real estate ads. Once a possible property is found, a lot of research is done to find out about its state, market value, and ability to be fixed up. The choice to go ahead with the purchase is based on this careful review. Flippers often strike good deals and try to make trades go quickly and smoothly so they can keep making money.

Following the purchase, the remodeling process starts, with changes that raise the property's value being the main focus. Flippers carefully oversee the rebuilding process to make sure that the changes meet the needs of buyers. The house goes on the market for sale after the repairs are done. Marketing tactics that work are used to get more people to see the products and buy them.

The final goal of flippers is to quickly sell the property at a good price that shows how much value the improvements have added. The difference between the purchase price and the sale price is the profit, less the costs of repairs and other costs. This means that the turning business was a financial success.

4. Dangers and Obstacles:

Flipping houses is a constantly changing business that is affected by changes in the market. When the economy goes down or buyer demand changes, it can have a big effect on how quickly and how much a property sells for. Unexpected problems, like delays or higher costs, often happen during renovation jobs. Flippers have to quickly deal with these problems as they come up. Also, if a property doesn't sell quickly, costs like property taxes, finance fees, and repairs can eat away at earnings. Time management is very important for keeping these costs as low as possible.

When it comes to closing strategies, property buyers who make money often put their profits back into a diverse strategy that includes both buy-and-hold and selling strategies. This helps find a mix between building wealth over time and making money right away. Some flippers choose to put their profits back into bigger projects, like business buildings or complexes with multiple units. This lets them take on bigger and more difficult projects. Instead, as flippers get richer, they may decide to cut back on flipping or stop doing it altogether, possibly switching to less time-consuming ways to spend or looking into other business opportunities. People may make this change because they want a different way of life or a different business goal.

Property flipping aims to maximize profits in the near term via dynamic and active investing. Property flippers may create wealth and produce active income by finding undervalued homes, carrying out well-thought-out improvements, and selling them swiftly. Renovating a home successfully requires skill with the market, risk management, and smart remodeling.

While flipping properties may provide rapid profits, investors must manage time-sensitive factors, complicated renovations, and market problems. When paired with thoughtful consideration and flexibility, a well-thought-out property flipping plan may be profitable for investors looking to make quick money in the real estate market.

6.3 Hybrid Strategies: Balancing Short-Term Gains with Long-Term Stability

Hybrid real estate investing methods include long-term wealth-building tactics like buy-and-hold and short-term profit-focused techniques like property flipping. The aim is to find a balance between building a steady, long-term portfolio and producing rapid returns. Acknowledging the advantages of immediate profits and long-term wealth building gives investors a flexible and adaptable real estate investing option. This part will examine the main elements, benefits, and factors to consider using a hybrid real estate strategy.

1. The Fundamentals of Hybrid Strategies:

Diversification: Hybrid strategies combine long-term and short-term investments to increase portfolio diversity. In various market circumstances, this diversity aids in risk management and return optimization. ***Handling Risk:*** Effective risk management is possible when short-term rewards and long-term stability are balanced. Although investors may be exposed to market volatility via short-term methods, the long-term component offers stability and resistance against transient swings.

Flexibility: Hybrid tactics may be adjusted to reflect shifting market dynamics. Investors might emphasize short-term and long-term investments based on variables, including market cycles, interest rates, and economic trends.

2. Elements of Hybrid Approaches:

In real estate, "property flipping," which means buying houses, fixing them up, and selling them quickly to make a profit, is a common way to make quick money. On the other hand, the buy-and-hold strategy is used to build long-term wealth. This means buying homes with the aim of keeping them for long amounts of time.

This long-term plan takes advantage of building wealth, rental income, and land value growth. Hybrid methods also help investors make the best decisions about when to focus on short-term gains versus long-term steadiness, which lets them make the best decisions for their investments. This adaptability can greatly improve the overall performance of an investment portfolio by letting buyers make changes based on their personal financial goals and the state of the market.

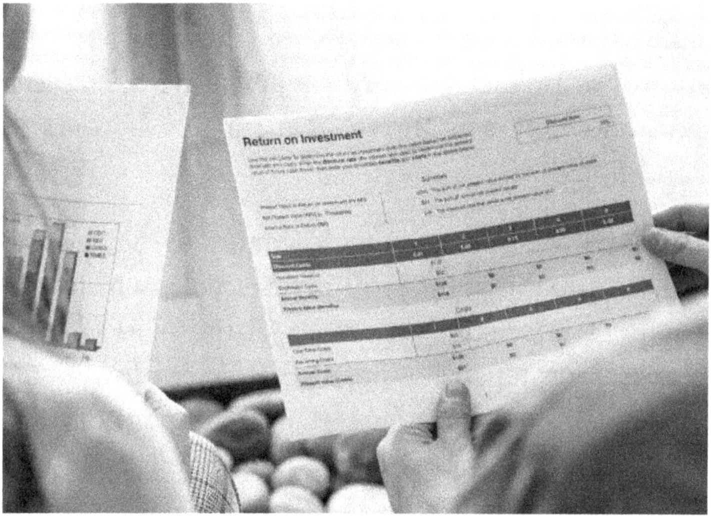

2. Hybrid Strategies' Benefits:

Real estate owners who use hybrid investment strategies can easily change their plans when market conditions change, which is very helpful in the fast-paced real estate market. This gives investors the freedom to switch their attention between short- and long-term goals based on how the market is moving and their own investing goals. Investors can make active income from quick sales and passive income from rented properties at the same time by combining short-term gains from activities like turning properties with long-term wealth accumulation through buy-and-hold strategies. This method of having two incomes not only spreads out sources of income but also improves financial security by creating a balanced portfolio that can thrive in a range of economic conditions.

Hybrid investment strategies naturally spread out risk by mixing short-term investments, which may be more affected by changes in the market, with stable long-term holdings that help lower the chance of losing money. This method not only protects against market instability, but it also opens the door to bigger projects.

When investors make money on short-term investments that do well, they can put the money back into long-term assets, which helps their portfolios grow over time. This kind of approach helps portfolios grow over time and people get rich. Hybrid methods also help buyers quickly adjust to changes in the market. When the market is busy, they might focus on taking advantage of short-term chances. When the market is slow, they might focus on tactics that will help them build wealth over the long run. This gives investors the freedom to change their strategies as the market changes, which ultimately increases their total financial success.

3. A Look Into Effective Hybrid Approaches:

To find the best mix between short- and long-term purchases, you need to carefully look at the market. Knowing how the market is doing right now is very important for buyers because it helps them make smart choices. When using mixed investment methods, it is important to do a full risk review. To make smart business decisions, people must carefully consider the risks and benefits of both short-term and long-term projects. Also, having a clear exit plan for both types of investments helps you make better strategic decisions, which is important whether you're buying houses or managing a long-term investment account.

To use mixed tactics effectively, you also need to carefully plan your finances. To reach their current and future goals, investors must wisely divide their resources, keep an eye on their cash flow, and make the best use of their financing options. Also, it's important to keep an eye on the portfolio's success on a regular basis. When investing, people should always think about the risks and benefits of each option and make changes as needed to keep up with the market. This constant watchfulness makes sure that the business portfolio stays strong and in line with strategic goals.

Practical Use:

As an illustration, to make rapid money, an investor could begin by flipping homes. For long-term wealth creation, they reinvest these earnings as they mount up in reliable, revenue-producing rental properties. The advantages of both active and passive revenue sources are combined in this strategy.

4. Difficulties and Strategies for Mitigation:

Market volatility can make it hard for hybrid investment strategies to work, but investors can lessen these problems by keeping up with market changes, using strong risk management techniques, and keeping a diverse portfolio. Financing these kinds of plans can also be tricky, since you might need different arrangements to properly pay short-term and long-term assets.

To make sure their mixed method is flexible and long-lasting, investors should look into financial choices that work with both parties' timelines and goals. Managing both long-term and short-term projects at the same time can also be hard from an operational point of view. Investors should reduce their processes and use technology to make their businesses run more smoothly and efficiently. Using technology together not only makes it easier to handle the complicated parts of mixed strategies, but it also helps investors adapt to a constantly changing market.

Real estate hybrid methods are a flexible and dynamic way to combine the advantages of long-term wealth building with short-term profit making. Investors may maximize returns while successfully controlling risks by diversifying their portfolios, balancing active and passive income, and responding to changing market circumstances.

Implementing hybrid solutions requires meticulously evaluating market dynamics, risk mitigation techniques, and financial planning. Investors adept at striking a balance between short-term profits and long-term security put themselves in a position to succeed in the dynamic world of real estate investing.

Component	Description

Short-Term Profit	Involves property flipping for quick returns.
Long-Term Wealth	Utilizes a buy-and-hold strategy for appreciation and income.
Portfolio Optimization	Balances short-term gains and long-term stability.
Flexibility	Adapts to changing market conditions and trends.
Risk Mitigation	Diversifies to mitigate market volatility.

This table provides a structured overview of the key components and considerations associated with hybrid real estate investment strategies, highlighting the flexibility, risk management, and advantages of balancing short-term gains with long-term stability.

6.4 Exploring REITs and Real Estate Syndication

Two unique yet well-liked real estate investment structures that provide investors with more ways to get into the real estate market are Real Estate Investment Trusts (REITs) and Real Estate

Syndication. Investors may take advantage of real estate possibilities via both processes, even if they do not own or manage buildings directly. We will examine the structures, advantages, and nuances of REITs and real estate syndication in this part and how they enhance diverse real estate investment portfolios.

1. REITs, or real estate investment trusts:

Reits, which stand for "Real Estate Investment Trusts," are ways to invest in and own property that makes money in a variety of places, such as retail, industrial, business, and residential. Since they are usually sold on big stock platforms, they give buyers a way to quickly get their money back when they lose it. Investors in real estate investment trusts (REITs) buy shares that give them ownership in the real estate assets that the REITs own.

The REITs handle and diversify these assets by sharing the money of many investors. Diversification is possible with REITs because they usually hold a wide range of income-producing properties. This lets buyers access a range of real estate assets and places without having to manage each property individually. Regular income payments and the chance for capital gain make

REITs a good investment for people who want to make money and grow their money as the value of the real estate they invest in rises. Unlike owning real estate directly, buying in REITs gives you cash because shares are easy to buy and sell on stock markets, which speeds up deals. Also, REITs are professionally run, so investors can trust that the management teams will make smart choices about buying properties, getting loans, and general management strategies.

2. Syndicated Real Estate:

A backer or syndicator finds the financial chance, negotiates terms, and handles operations in real estate syndication. A group of buyers pools their money to take part in a real estate project. When people invest in a syndication, they become limited partners. The host, who is usually a seasoned real estate professional, takes care of day-to-day tasks and makes decisions on their behalf.

Real estate syndications are different from REITs in that buyers own the land or project directly. This makes buying more participatory. It's possible that syndications have higher amounts of risk than REITs, but they also have the potential for big gains, which depend on how well the property or project does. Even though they don't have as much control over day-to-day business, syndication investors often have more access to and say over big choices than REIT investors. This depends on how the syndication is set up. When people invest in real estate through syndication, sponsors often put their own money into the project along with buyers to make sure that everyone's goals are met.

3. REIT Advantages:

REITs let buyers spread their money right away across a number of different real estate assets, which lowers their risk of losing money on a single property or market. Investors can easily get their money out of REIT shares, which gives them more options for buying and selling on the stock market. Investors who want to stay out of the details can choose REITs that are managed by experienced professionals.

This is because professionals are in charge of property management and deals. REITs are also required to pay dividends to owners from taxed gains. This makes them appealing to investors who want to make money. REITs make it easier for investors to get into a broad real estate portfolio than direct real estate ownership. This means that investors with small starting investments can do so.

4. Real Estate Syndication Advantages:

Real estate syndication lets investors own direct shares in certain buildings or projects. Compared to REITs, this gives buyers more power and information about their investment. Syndications, especially those that focus on value-added or risky strategies, could give higher returns than REIT investments that are more cautious. In real estate syndication, sponsors and buyers have interests that are similar.

This builds trust and confidence because sponsors have a personal stake in the project's success. Additionally, dealing in real estate syndication gives buyers the chance to learn about the business side of real estate investing, which can be helpful for those who want to learn more about the subject. Different investment strategies, like income-focused, growth, or value-add strategies, can also be used with syndications. This lets buyers choose projects that fit their needs and tastes.

5. Points to Remember:

Investors should think about how much risk they are willing to take before deciding between real estate syndication and REITs. Syndications may have higher risk than REITs, which are more stable. It is very important to think about how long the investment will last. Syndications usually require a more active commitment for a certain amount of time, while REITs are better for people who want a quiet, long-term plan.

Also, buyers should think about what they want to achieve with variety. REITs offer a lot of different options, while syndications may focus on certain methods or property types. Also, you should think about how much cash you need. Real estate investment trusts (REITs) make it easier for buyers who need to be able to buy or sell their investments quickly. Lastly, buyers should think about how much knowledge and involvement they want. Some may want to be more involved in making decisions, while others may prefer to stay out of it.

Real estate syndication and REITs have unique benefits and suit various investor tastes. Real estate investment trusts (REITs) provide immediate Diversification, liquidity, and expert management for passive, income-focused investors. Conversely, real estate syndication draws investors looking for a more involved position in certain real estate projects since it provides direct Ownership, the possibility of larger profits, and a more hands-on experience.

The decision between real estate syndication and REITs ultimately comes down to personal investing preferences, risk tolerance, and ambitions. Some investors could even include both in their portfolios to have a diverse and well-rounded exposure to the ever-evolving real estate investing landscape.

6.5 Crafting Personalized Investment Strategies for Specific Goals

Developing customized real estate investment plans for certain objectives is essential to asset management and financial planning. Investors explore real estate for several reasons, including portfolio diversification, tax advantages, capital appreciation, and passive income. Developing an investment plan that fits certain objectives requires thoroughly comprehending the investor's financial status, risk tolerance, and ambitions. This section will discuss creating customized real estate investment plans for certain objectives.

1. Determining Investment Objectives:

Capital gain is when an investor's real estate assets' value goes up over time. They can do this by using value-add methods, taking advantage of market trends, and focusing on buildings in places with a lot of growth. For some, the most important thing is to make a steady stream of idle income from real estate. Usually, this means buying things that bring in money, like rented homes, whose rent covers costs and leaves an excess.

There are big tax benefits to investing in real estate, like being able to subtract running costs, mortgage interest, and property depreciation. Investors can use these benefits to get the best tax situation for their financial goals. Many buyers also want to diversify their portfolios by buying real estate. This helps spread risk and could lead to better long-term results. Real estate can also be an important part of planning for retirement. Strategies for doing this focus on things like cash flow, property growth, and exit plans that help you reach your retirement goals.

2. Evaluation of Risk Tolerance

Investors must evaluate how much risk they are willing to take, considering variables like age, financial status, and volatility tolerance. While cautious investors may choose steady, income-focused strategies, others with a larger risk appetite may seek more aggressive ones.

It's critical to comprehend your susceptibility to changes in the industry. While some investors could feel at ease with real estate markets' cyclical character, others would choose less vulnerable techniques to economic downturns.

Considering Leverage: Financing solutions might be investigated by investors who are at ease with Leverage. Although it carries a higher risk, Leverage enables investors to manage larger assets with a smaller initial investment.

3. Adapting Techniques to Particular Objectives:

When investors want their money to grow, they usually look for assets that have the ability to add value. They look for growing markets or places that are set to grow. This approach could include building new homes, fixing up old ones, and planning when to enter and leave the market strategically. Passive income, on the other hand, means buying assets that bring in steady income, like business or residential rents. It's important to make sure that the buildings you buy are sound and have positive cash flow, and that they are managed well.

To get the most tax breaks from investing in real estate, you can use 1031 trades to delay paying taxes, structure your assets to get the most tax breaks, and stay up to date on changes to tax rules that affect real estate holdings. Another important approach is diversification, which means investing in different types of properties (residential, commercial, and industrial), places, and investment structures (like REITs and syndications). This spreads out the risks that come with having a concentrated portfolio.

Developing solutions for retirement planning may include combining income-producing and capital-appreciation properties. Investors may consider how rental income fits into their retirement cash flow demands and investigate exit plans that provide retirement liquidity.

4. Monitoring and Execution:

Putting a plan into action means carefully choosing properties. When doing your research, you should think about things like the property's quality, location, market trends, and its potential for future value growth. Another important step is to make sure that the financing models match the goals of the investors. This can be done with traditional mortgages, business loans, or partnerships.

Whether you choose professional property management or self-management, operational factors like renter relations, repair, and property management have a big effect on how well your plan works. Market factors must always be being watched, and buyers must keep up with changes in the real estate market, wider economic trends, and regulation changes. Strategies need to be able to change with the times, so they need to be able to check their portfolios, evaluate their success, and move resources around as required.

5. Obstacles and Their Reduction:

The real estate market is not always stable. Examples of mitigating techniques are diversifying, keeping up with market developments, and keeping an eye on the big picture to weather short-term swings.

Rental markets and real estate prices are susceptible to economic downturns. Techniques that combine strong risk management, enough liquidity, and conservative financing may lessen the effects of recessions.Changes to tax laws or real estate rules may impact investment plans. Keeping up to date and seeking advice from legal and financial experts may assist investors in adjusting to regulatory changes.

Developing customized real estate investment plans for particular objectives is a dynamic, iterative process. It requires a deep comprehension of an investor's goals, risk tolerance, and financial circumstances. Whether the target is tax optimization, diversification, capital appreciation, passive income, or retirement planning, a well-designed strategy fits these goals and adjusts to changing market circumstances.

Real estate investing success requires a well-thought-out initial plan, constant observation, tweaking, and proactive risk management. Long-term wealth creation and preservation are facilitated by a customized, goal-oriented approach that investors follow as they negotiate the intricacies of the real estate market.

|7|

Negotiation and Acquisition Skills

This part teaches you how to negotiate and buy things, which are important skills for getting good deals on real estate. There are many ways to negotiate well, and we'll talk about some of them. With their help, you can get homes at the best prices possible. It will also talk about how to build and keep good ties with agencies and sponsors. Lastly, we'll talk about the legal and moral issues that you need to think about to make sure your deals are honest.

For the relevant case studies, worksheets and free resources you can visit: andonierealty.com

"Let us never negotiate out of fear. But let us never fear to negotiate"

- John F. Kennedy

7.1 Effective Negotiation Techniques in Real Estate Deals

Negotiating effectively in the real estate industry is essential for obtaining business, fostering connections, and optimizing profits. Negotiating terms and conditions is a delicate art that calls for a mix of planning, communicating, and strategic thinking, whether buying or selling real estate. This part will look at several important and successful negotiating strategies in real estate transactions.

1. Careful Planning:

The foundation of every successful negotiation is a thorough grasp of the market. In detail, investigate the target area's property valuations, recent sales, and market trends. Understanding the state of the market lays the groundwork for wise bargaining. Examine the particular attribute that is of concern. Recognize its advantages, disadvantages, and special selling factors. Negotiators can successfully communicate the property's worth thanks to this understanding.

Establish specific goals before starting any talks. The negotiating process is facilitated by having well-defined objectives, which may include the desired purchase price, advantageous terms, or certain requirements.

2. Skillful Interaction:

It's important to listen to the other person actively. Negotiators may create offers that suit both sides' interests by thoroughly understanding their requirements, worries, and priorities.

Communicate briefly and plainly. Ambiguity may cause miscommunication and make negotiating more difficult. Give a clear explanation of your stance, your goals, and any requirements that are significant to you. A cooperative negotiation atmosphere may be produced by cultivating a good rapport with the opposing side. Finding common ground and building rapport via polite conversation provide the groundwork for fruitful negotiations.

3. Adaptability and Originality:

Discussions should be approached by negotiators with an open mind. Finding agreeable terms is more likely when one is open to other suggestions and solutions. In real estate discussions, complicated issues are often resolved. Results that please both sides may be achieved with imaginative thinking and a willingness to investigate new ideas.

It takes time to negotiate. Refrain from making hasty judgments or giving in to pressure. Negotiators that use patience often have more success in reaching their goals. Handle the negotiating schedule well. Purposefully applying time pressure or setting deadlines may create a feeling of urgency, which may influence the other party's choice.

4. Studies on Equivalent:

Examine the other party's motives. Negotiators may craft offers that appeal to the interests of their opponents by understanding what motivates their counterparts.During negotiations, leverage is obtained by learning the opposing party's goals and pressure points. It enables negotiators to concentrate on points of special significance for their opponent.

5. The Win-Win Strategy

Achieve a win-win situation in which both sides believe they have benefited from the agreement. Working together creates good connections and may open up future chances.Compromise is a common part of negotiation. Determine the areas where compromises may be made without sacrificing the main goals. An agreement is more likely to be reached when both parties are prepared to offer and take.

6. Making Good Use of Leverage:

Using knowledge as a weapon, Usually, the person with more knowledge is at a disadvantage. During discussions, use your understanding of the property, the state of the market, or other pertinent information as leverage. Leverage comes from having options, a Best Alternative to a Negotiated Agreement, or BATNA. Possessing workable options for when talks break down improves your negotiating stance.

Preserving Professionalism, During negotiations, professionalism is essential. Even under difficult circumstances, maintaining composure, etiquette, and composure helps to foster a productive negotiation environment. Written correspondence, including official letters and emails, must be written professionally and professionally. Written communication that is professional and clear promotes credibility.

7. Understanding When to Leave:

Recognizing deal-breakers is crucial. Avoiding undesirable agreements may be achieved by knowing when to end a discussion that doesn't serve your interests.Maintaining connections is essential, even if a contract is not completed. An important part of successful negotiating is to remain professional while keeping the lines of communication open for potential future business.

8. Following the Negotiation:

Once an agreement has been reached, ensure every detail is precisely and thoroughly recorded. Future misconceptions are less likely to occur when documentation is clear. It is advantageous to build a good connection after the transaction. Long-term success depends on having a good reputation in the field, which may lead to future partnerships or recommendations. Do a post-negotiation study to find areas for improvement and assess strengths and shortcomings. Over time, self-reflection and ongoing education improve negotiating abilities.

Regulations and real estate markets are ever-changing. Keeping up with market trends, legislative developments, and industry advancements guarantees that negotiators have current information.

9. Legal and Moral Aspects to Consider:

It is essential to comprehend and abide by legal requirements. The negotiators are responsible for ensuring that all agreements and proposals abide by local, state, and federal laws.Upholding moral principles fosters trust. Sincere and open discussions may result in long-term success and help build a good reputation in the business.

Real estate negotiating is an art that requires planning, communicating, and using strategic thought. Deals need negotiators to approach them with a thorough grasp of their objectives, the state of the market, and the opposing party's incentives. Real estate professionals may successfully negotiate difficult deals, establish strong connections, and accomplish desired results using negotiating tactics, including active listening, flexibility, and a win-win strategy. Professionalism, a never-ending learning process, and adherence to moral and legal requirements also influence long-term success in real estate negotiations.

7.2 Establishing Win-Win Situations for Buyers and Sellers

Creating win-win scenarios for sellers and buyers is essential to successful real estate transactions. Achieving mutually beneficial results makes transactions go more smoothly and builds strong connections that may lead to future possibilities in the fast-paced and very competitive real estate industry. Real estate professionals should consider the important tactics and factors covered in this section to create win-win circumstances for buyers and sellers.

1. Recognizing the Motives of Sellers and Buyers:

It is important to know why buyers are searching for a house. A family's necessity for a house may drive some purchasers, while speculators hoping to profit from property appreciation or rental revenue may drive still others. Agents may adjust their strategy by recognizing these reasons.Sellers may be motivated by several factors, including downsizing, moving, or taking advantage of gains in their property. By understanding the seller's objectives, agents may better create transactions that support their aims.

2. Adding Benefits for Purchasers:

Determining Requirements and Preferences

Agents can discern purchasers' unique requirements and inclinations through proficient conversation. This covers elements including budgetary restrictions, property attributes, and location. Buyers gain from agents who provide in-depth market knowledge. This contains data on market trends, property valuations, and prospective investment opportunities. ***Reaching Amicable Terms*** The goal of buyer-side negotiation is to secure advantageous conditions, such as a fair purchase price, appealing financing choices, or extra concessions from sellers.

Assistance During the Procedure, Purchasing real estate may be a difficult procedure. Agents who assist purchasers at every stage, from choosing a house to closing, add to a satisfying experience.

3. Adding Benefits to Sellers:

Sellers value agents highly who can correctly price homes based on thorough market research. This makes sure that prices are competitive to draw potential buyers. Using web ads, focused advertising, and professional photos, among other things, to reach potential buyers, good marketing strategies make the property more visible. It's important to negotiate strong deals that fit with the buyers' financial goals. This means talking about more than just price; it also means getting good terms and conditions. Giving sellers tips on how to improve their homes can also be helpful. For example, you could suggest small changes or arranging methods that will make the home more appealing to potential buyers.

4. Techniques to Create Win-Win Situations:

Active listening is the best way for agents to understand the wants and needs of both buyers and sellers, which lets them make plans that work for everyone. Making solutions that are specific to each party's needs, like coming up with new ways to finance the deal or fixing certain property problems, builds trust and honesty in the transaction. Finding answers that work for both sides is an important part of win-win negotiation tactics.

This usually means coming to an agreement on some things and being flexible on others. Long-term relationships are important to agents, so they try to set up situations where both parties can benefit. This can lead to referrals and return business. Teaching clients about possible problems, the trade process, and how the market works gives them the power to make smart choices and makes them happier with the result. To get through tough negotiations and come to an agreement that works for everyone, you need to be flexible and creative in how you solve problems.

5. Managing Obstacles and Resolving Disagreements:

When issues emerge, proactive conflict resolution is crucial. Promptly addressing problems and striving for solutions show that an agent is dedicated to making the process enjoyable for sellers and purchasers. ***Controlling Anticipations,*** Early management of expectations by both sides helps in the avoidance of conflict. Transactions go more smoothly when agents explain possible obstacles and establish reasonable expectations.

One strategy for settling disputes is to communicate clearly and consistently. Misunderstandings are reduced when open communication channels and problems are addressed transparently.

6. After-Transaction Monitoring:

Agents may get feedback and pinpoint areas for improvement by following up with customers and sellers with satisfaction questionnaires. Positive reinforcement reaffirms the importance of establishing win-win scenarios. A smooth transaction creates the foundation for networks of referrals. A never-ending loop of opportunity is created when happy buyers and sellers recommend the real estate agent to friends, family, or coworkers.

Creating win-win scenarios for buyers and sellers in real estate transactions calls for a calculated and compassionate approach. Real estate agents who prioritize learning about both sides' goals, desires, and preferences may develop solutions that benefit both parties. Agents create lasting connections and a solid reputation in the business by using skilful negotiating strategies, encouraging open communication, and taking proactive measures to resolve issues before they arise. Ultimately, creating win-win scenarios is a crucial skill for success in the fast-paced, cutthroat real estate industry.

7.3 Strategies for Securing Properties at Favorable Terms

Whether you are a developer, investor, or buyer in real estate, securing assets at advantageous terms is essential. The capacity to negotiate and arrange agreements that support your goals necessitates strategic thought, market awareness, and proficient communication. We will examine tactics that strengthen your negotiating position, improve deal structures, and support profitable real estate purchases in this part as we dive into ways for obtaining properties at advantageous terms.

1. Comprehensive Market Analysis:

First, do a lot of study on the market to find out about prices, trends, and how supply and demand work in the chosen area. Understanding these factors is the first step in having a well-informed conversation. Use Comparative Market Analysis (CMA) to look at the prices of similar homes in the area. This will help you negotiate from a position of knowledge and give you a way to judge whether the asking price is fair. Find buyers who are motivated, like those who are having trouble paying their bills, moving, or have been trying for a long time to sell their home. When buyers are motivated, they may be more open to negotiating and offer better terms.

2. Establishing Robust Financial Credentials:

Obtain Pre-Approval for Financing: Before beginning discussions, secure pre-approval for financing. Sellers are likely to see a pre-approved buyer as a serious and financially qualified purchase.

Cash Offer, if feasible, consider extending cash offers. Sellers find cash deals appealing because they may speed up the closing process and remove the uncertainty around mortgage approvals.

Showcasing Financial Stability: Exhibit dependability and stability in your finances. This might include proof of a stable income source, a clean credit history, and the capacity to pay for related charges like closing costs.

3. Techniques for Effective Negotiation:

Set clear, fair goals at the start of the talks. These should include clear top limits and the best terms. That makes it possible for focused bargaining to happen. Allowing a moment of silence after making an offer can be used as a strategy tool because it gives the other person time to think about their position and possibly change it. Focus on the things that make you more valuable, like being able to close quickly, having open terms, or being ready to meet specific selling needs. Pay close attention to and intelligently address the seller's concerns. This will show that you are effective in settling issues and improve your bargaining position.

4. Market conditions and timing:

Take advantage of the way the real estate market changes with the seasons. At different times of the year, buyers may be more willing to make deals, giving you better chances to negotiate. Look at the market's supply and demand balance. Keep in mind that buyers are usually more ready to negotiate and close deals in a buyer's market, where supply exceeds demand. Keep an eye on economic signs like interest rates and job growth, as they can have a big effect on the real estate market. If you time your talks so that the economy is doing well, you may be able to get better terms and outcomes.

Examine your alternatives for seller financing. In some situations, sellers could be open to financing a part of the transaction, giving you greater leeway to bargain for advantageous conditions.

Contingency Plans: Make thoughtful use of backup plans. Possessing realistic conditions in your offer, such as finance or inspection requirements, gives you flexibility and the chance to renegotiate if needed. Making a sizable, eager money deposit offer might demonstrate sincerity and commitment.

Proving your financial stability might also improve your negotiation position.

5. Networking and Developing Relationships:

Create bonds with brokers and agents in the real estate industry. Agents may provide vital information for negotiating methods since they often have insights into the conditions and intentions of sellers.Connect with wholesalers who could propane-market offers or homes in difficulty. Developing connections with wholesalers may open doors to possibilities not available to the general public.

6. Adaptability in Types of Properties:

Be willing to take into account various property kinds. Looking at various possibilities, such as houses in difficulty or ones with room for repair, may lead to better terms.Pay attention to the seller's preferences. A deal that benefits both parties is more likely if you know what matters most to the seller and adjust your offer accordingly.

7. Legal Due Diligence:

Perform extensive legal due diligence. Determine any title or legal concerns that could affect the property's value. Giving early attention to possible issues might provide you with a negotiating advantage. Consult with attorneys to review and advise on contracts. Legal counsel guarantees the conditions are reasonable and compliant with the law, strengthening your negotiation position.

8. Use Market Trends and Data:

Recent Sales and Market Data:

Use market trends and recent sales data during negotiations. Your viewpoint and the conditions you offer may be supported and justified by presenting proof of similar sales or market trends.

Knowledge of Seller's Purchase History:

Look into the seller's past purchases, if feasible. Understanding the seller's expectations and possible opportunities for bargaining may be gained by learning how much and when they paid for the property.

9. Exhibiting a Dedicated Nature:

If you want to stay in the property for a long time as a homeowner or investment, state so. If someone intends to preserve the property, sellers can be more willing to negotiate advantageous conditions.A good rapport with the seller can help the bargaining process. Forging a relationship and being genuine may foster a more pleasant environment that facilitates reaching an agreement.

Obtaining assets in the real estate industry at advantageous terms requires a comprehensive strategy that blends market expertise, skillful negotiating, and strategic thinking. Buyers and investors may strengthen their negotiating position by conducting extensive research, establishing solid financial credentials, and using innovative transaction structuring techniques. In addition, being strategic with time, establishing connections with business associates, and exhibiting dedication all play a part in acquiring properties at advantageous terms. These tactics enable people to negotiate successfully in a competitive and changing real estate market, eventually resulting in advantageous purchases and outcomes.

7.4 Building and Maintaining Relationships with Agents and Investors

Success in the real estate business mainly depends on establishing and maintaining connections with investors and real estate brokers. These connections may provide insightful information, entry to possibilities, and a professional network that all help to create a successful real estate company. This part will discuss the importance of establishing and maintaining relationships with investors and agents and the essential tactics.

1. The Value of Networks in the Real Estate Industry:

The real estate business depends on connections, which open up a lot of doors. Getting to know investors and real estate agents can help you find joint partnerships, business opportunities, and deals that aren't on the market yet. These connections give you important market data, like first-hand information about trends, the way things work in the area, and new possibilities.

This information is necessary to make smart business choices. It is normal for people in the real estate business to work together. Building relationships makes partnerships easier, which leads to joint ventures, co-investments, and resource sharing, all of which make real estate projects bigger and better. Strong relationships also help in talks, since people you can trust are more likely to share chances and work out terms that are good for everyone.

2. Relationship-Building Techniques:

By actively taking part in real estate workshops, seminars, and networking events, you can meet agents, investors, and other professionals in the field. Another good way to grow your network is to join a real estate company or association. These groups often put on events, lectures, and workshops where you can meet other pros in the same field.

Using social media sites like LinkedIn lets you connect with other professionals online and keep up with changes in your field. Participating in local community events can also help you make new friends in the area, which could lead to useful contacts with real estate agents and buyers. Giving buyers and brokers something of value, like joint projects, property insights, or market research, is a good way to get to know them and build strong, long-lasting relationships. Also, asking experienced owners or agents to be your guide can help you learn more about the real estate market and give you direction. This can help your career growth and network.

3. Maintaining Relationships and Communication:

Keep in touch with clients and agents on a regular basis to build ties that last. This means giving regular reports, sharing useful information, and keeping in touch. Show that you are trustworthy and skilled in all of your relationships to gain authority and trust, which are important for partnerships to work. Remembering important details about an investor's or agent's tastes will help you have more useful conversations and show that you value the connection. When you hit important goals in your portfolio or close a deal, celebrate with your team to improve your ties and create a sense of shared success. Finally, make sure that differences are treated in a productive way by communicating openly, actively listening, and focusing on finding solutions.

4. Joint Ventures and Collaborative Projects and Investments:

When resources and experience are pooled, collaborative ventures may provide win-win results.

Co-investing: Take into account the possibility of co-investing. Connecting with investors willing to co-invest enables pursuing more extensive or varied real estate projects and shared risk. Participate in seminars and networking events centered on teamwork. These forums provide chances to network with possible collaborators and discuss joint ventures.

5. Adaptability and Flexibility:

Flexibility is essential given the dynamic nature of real estate markets. Agents and investors value partners that exhibit resilience and strategic thinking in navigating and adapting to shifting market circumstances.When working with others, exercise flexibility. Establishing a collaborative and cooperative working relationship is facilitated by being aware of the objectives and preferences of investors or agents and modifying your approach appropriately.

6. Mutual Assistance and Reciprocity:

Encourage investors and agents in undertakings. Mutual support for one another, whether via recommendations, endorsements, or hands-on involvement in their startups, fortifies relationships and fosters community.Make sure your aims and mine are in line. The same goal and a shared vision increase the likelihood of long-term, fruitful cooperation.

Ongoing Education and Career Advancement:

Keep Up with sector Developments:

Remain current on developments and trends in the sector. Investors and agents value partners that are aware of the changing real estate market. b. Invest in Professional Development: Invest in your professional growth. Your dedication to ongoing education and development strengthens your reputation as a trustworthy and knowledgeable collaborator.

In the real estate business, cultivating and preserving relationships with brokers and investors is a continuous process that calls for commitment, communication, and shared success. These connections foster a cooperative and encouraging professional network and provide access to possibilities.

Through tactics like going to networking functions, providing value, and working on joint projects, people may create lasting relationships that contribute to their success in the ever-changing real estate industry. The durability and quality of these crucial professional connections are primarily dependent on the ability to continuously adjust to changing market circumstances, promote open communication, and keep a laser-like focus on common objectives.

7.5 Legal and Ethical Considerations in Real Estate Negotiations

In real estate discussions, legal and ethical issues are crucial since they form the basis of deals and connections in the sector. Adhering to established legal and ethical norms guarantees impartiality and transparency and safeguards the concerns of all stakeholders. In this part, we will examine the critical facets of legal and ethical issues in real estate negotiations, highlighting their importance, guiding principles, and function in upholding the industry's integrity.

1. The Importance of Legal and Ethical Aspects:

In real estate, upholding the law and moral principles is essential to establishing confidence and trust. Clients, coworkers, and other stakeholders depend on real estate professionals' integrity to keep their word and behave morally. A foundation for the protection of the parties to a real estate transaction is provided by legal considerations. Respecting the law and rules protects the interests of buyers and sellers by averting disagreements or legal issues.

Upholding moral principles is critical to an excellent professional reputation. Those in the real estate business with a reputation for moral behavior are more likely to draw in customers, recommendations, and joint venture prospects.Transaction-related legal problems or disputes are less likely to occur when legal requirements are met. Comprehending and abiding by legal and ethical protocols helps professionals manage obstacles and function reasonably.

2. Important Legal Factors to Take Into Account During Real Estate Negotiations:

Real estate transactions are based on contracts. Drafting precise, detailed, and legally enforceable contracts that specify the terms and circumstances of the agreement is necessary for legal considerations. It's common for sellers to be obliged to provide specific details on the state, past, or possible problems with the property. The legal ramifications of inaccurate disclosures underscore the need for openness.

Prohibit discrimination based on race, color, religion, sex, handicap, national origin, or family status. Adherence to these rules is crucial for real estate agents to guarantee fair treatment for all stakeholders. In real estate transactions, having a valid title is essential. Legal factors include exhaustive title searches to find any liens, encumbrances, or ownership issues that could affect the ownership transfer.Real estate agents must abide by all applicable local, state, and federal laws. This includes following zoning rules that may affect land use, environmental restrictions, and licensing requirements.Negotiation techniques must conform to legal limitations. During negotiations, lying, deception, or using force are all prohibited and may harm one's image in the business world.

3. Crucial Ethical Points to Keep in Mind During Real Estate Negotiations:

Being honest and open are important for doing the right thing in real estate. Agents must give correct information to clients, coworkers, and other people involved in the deal. Professionals must also keep client information private and not share it with other people without permission; this is a very important social task.

Ethically dealing with conflicts of interest means being open about any possible conflicts and taking steps to make sure they don't hurt anyone too much. As part of their moral duty, real estate agents must put their clients' needs first by giving them fair advice and not working in their own best interests. Another important part of ethics is fair business, which means that agents must make sure that everyone has an equal chance to negotiate, not discriminate, and treat everyone with respect and fairness. Maintaining professional competency is also very important, since real estate agents need to keep learning new things and getting better at what they do to give their customers the best service possible.

3. Juggling Legal and Ethical Issues:

When real estate agents make decisions based on facts and knowledge, they have to weigh their moral and legal duties and think about the effects of their choices. When dealing with complicated legal issues, talking to lawyers makes sure that choices are made in a way that is both legal and moral. Also, continuing education is important to keep up with changes in laws and morals. This helps real estate workers deal with changing legal situations and adjust their practices as needed.

4. Risk Management and Compliance:

To better handle legal and moral risks, real estate workers should set up clear internal rules and procedures for deals, statements, and communications to make sure they are followed. Regular reviews and checks of business activities help make sure that these standards are being followed, and they also help find and fix possible problems before they get worse.

Industry standards of ethics are often followed by real estate agents, according to the National

Association of Realtors (NAR). For example, the National Association of Realtors (NAR) offers its members a thorough Code of Ethics specifying behavior expectations.

State and Local groups: Professionals may be obliged to abide by specific codes of conduct established by state and local real estate groups. These rules serve as a guide for moral conduct and an addition to the law.

The foundation of real estate discussions comprises legal and ethical issues, guaranteeing the Honesty, openness, and equity of transactions. Building trust, defending clients' interests, and maintaining a favorable image within the industry require real estate professionals to negotiate a challenging terrain of legal requirements and ethical standards. Real estate professionals may support a healthy and moral real estate ecosystem by actively managing risks, upholding fundamental values, and appreciating the importance of legal and ethical issues. A successful and long-lasting real estate job requires a dedication to ethical behavior, ongoing education, and contact with legal experts.

|8|

Property Management and Maintenance

There is more to maximizing your return on investment (ROI) than just the first purchase. With the information in this chapter, you will be well-equipped to maximize your assets when we dive into the realm of property administration and upkeep. We'll discuss the advantages of effective property management, help you weigh the pros and cons of hiring a manager vs managing yourself, and provide tactics for maintaining your property as it increases in value. We'll also talk about sustainable and eco-friendly strategies you may use in today's ecologically concerned society. Ultimately, we will examine how improvements and renovations may raise the value of your home.

For the relevant case studies, worksheets and free resources you can visit: andonierealty.com

"Investing should be like watching paint dry or watching grass grow. If you want excitement... go to Las Vegas."

– Paul Samuelson, economist.

8.1 Importance of Efficient Property Management for ROI

Achieving a favorable return on investment (ROI) via real estate investing requires effective property management, which is crucial. It is impossible to overestimate the significance of effective property management as it directly impacts a real estate investment's profitability, level of tenant happiness, and overall success. This section will examine the many dimensions of effective property management for return on investment, emphasizing the components contributing to the bottom line and long-term performance.

1. Optimizing Rental Revenue

A key component of effective property management is determining the ideal rental rate. A well-managed property prices units strategically to maximize rental revenue without turning away prospective renters. It does this by using market data and demand patterns. Rent collection is guaranteed on time by a proactive approach to property management. Efficient processes for collecting rent and timely resolution of payment difficulties help maintain a consistent cash flow, which improves the property's overall financial performance.

2. Tenant Satisfaction and Retention:

Maintenance that is done on time is a top priority for good property management. This makes sure that problems are fixed quickly and the property is well-kept, which makes tenants happier. When renters are happy, they are more likely to repeat their leases, which cuts down on change costs and vacancies. It's also important to communicate clearly and effectively. Having open lines of communication with renters builds trust, helps solve problems quickly, and makes tenants happier, which lowers the risk of gaps. Creating a feeling of community is also important. Good managers focus on making the building friendly and taking part in neighborhood events, which helps keep tenants and makes living there a good experience.

3. Operational Efficiency:

Putting in place streamlined procedures is a necessary step for effective property management. Well-defined and well-organized processes minimize operational inefficiencies and save time and money, from lease procedures to maintenance routines. Using technology effectively increases productivity in property management. Rent collection, lease renewals, and maintenance requests may be handled automatically, simplifying operations, lowering administrative costs, and increasing Efficiency. Effective property management is characterized by anticipating problems and taking proactive measures to resolve them. Early detection of any difficulties, such as maintenance problems or tenant complaints, enables prompt treatment, preventing issues from worsening and affecting return on investment.

4. Budgeting and Cost Management:

Meticulous recording of expenses is a prerequisite for effective property management. When maintenance, repairs, utilities, and other operating expenditures are tracked, financial planning and budgeting may be done with knowledge. An essential function of property managers is budget optimization. Maintaining a solid bottom line and optimizing ROI are aided by cost analysis, service contract negotiations, and cost-saving measures.

A key component of effective property management is adherence to legal standards. Maintaining adherence to regional, national, and municipal laws reduces the possibility of legal problems affecting the property's credit rating. Property managers Property managers are in charge of overseeing insurance management. This includes choosing the right coverage, ensuring current policies, and effectively handling claims. In the case of unanticipated occurrences, the property's financial interests are safeguarded by effective insurance administration.

5. Reduction of Vacancies:

Property managers help lower the number of vacancies through these tactics. To minimize vacancy times, it is essential to understand target demographics, use internet platforms, and highlight the property's distinctive attributes to attract new renters. A crucial component of effective property management is thorough tenant screening. Carefully screening prospective renters lowers the possibility of renting to people with a bad credit history or a history of property damage, promoting long-term financial stability.

Skilled property managers prioritize preventive maintenance. Proactive maintenance and routine inspections help to protect the investment and provide a steady return on investment by preserving the property's value over time.Managers of properties evaluate the potential for strategic improvements. Finding upgrades that raise the property's worth and make it more appealing to renters helps to raise rental rates and boost the asset value of the property overall.

6. Partnerships and Investor Confidence:

Open and honest reporting to investors is a prerequisite for effective property management. Building investor trust via timely and accurate financial reporting, occupancy rates, and maintenance updates promotes long-term relationships and the possibility of further investments.

Property managers reduce risks for investors by effectively overseeing daily operations and handling hazards. Investor confidence is bolstered, and continuing investment in the property or portfolio is encouraged by the guarantee of professional management.

7. Adaptability and Market Dynamics:

Market dynamics adaptation is necessary for effective property management. By doing regular market research, property managers may maximize competitiveness and return on investment by modifying their strategy, pricing, and marketing initiatives to reflect changing market circumstances.Property managers may maximize property utilization by being aware of market needs. Finding ways to move or modify the property to accommodate shifting tenant needs improves its marketability and bottom line.

Achieving a favorable return on investment in real estate requires effective property management. The effects of good management are seen in many areas of real estate investing, from optimizing rental revenue and tenant happiness to operational effectiveness, cost control, and long-term asset preservation. By using a strategic strategy, property managers help the investment portfolio expand and succeed over time, in addition to providing short-term financial rewards. In the ever-changing and fiercely competitive real estate market, investors who understand the need for effective property management lay the groundwork for long-term success and resilience.

8.2 Hiring Property Managers vs. Self-Management Considerations

Choosing between self-managing a real estate investment and employing a professional property manager is essential for property owners. Every strategy has pros and cons, and the decision is based on several variables, such as the investor's background, time constraints, level of skill, and personal preferences. In this part, we will examine the pros and drawbacks of hiring property managers vs. managing yourself, highlighting the critical variables that property owners must consider before making this crucial choice.

1. Employing Property Supervisors:

There are many important reasons to hire a property manager, but the main one is that they know what they're doing. Property managers who are good at their job know the local real estate market, how tenants act, and the law, which helps them overcome problems quickly. Taking care of rental properties can take a lot of time, especially as the number of investments grows. By giving management tasks to professionals, property owners can focus on other things, like making more investments, working full-time, or having fun. Property managers are in charge of managing tenants, which includes screening applicants, renting out units, and meeting tenants' needs. This makes tenants happier, lowers turnover rates, and maximizes the economy's potential.

Property managers are also very good at making sure that industry laws and rules are followed. This lowers the risk of legal problems like renter fights or housing regulation violations. Organizing maintenance is another big job that property managers do. They use their networks of workers and service providers to make sure that maintenance is done on time and at a low cost, which keeps the property's value high and keeps tenants happy.

Property managers have the most up-to-date information on the market, which lets them look at rental rates, keep an eye on trends, and change their tactics to make the most money. This information about the market helps property owners make choices that are in line with the present situation. Property managers are also trained to deal with accidents and last-minute problems, making sure that the right steps are taken quickly to avoid long-term damage to the property or the owner's image.

Scalability is something that professional property managers give to people who own more than one property or want to grow their business. Their systems and procedures are made to handle a bigger number of properties, which speeds up operations and makes sure that all of their properties are managed the same way.

2. A Look Into Self-Management:

Cost reductions are a crucial factor to take into account when considering self-management. Self-managing property owners save money by not hiring a professional property management company. However, balancing this against the time and energy needed for efficient self-management is crucial.

Self-management gives property owners direct control over their finances, so they can make choices about everything from choosing tenants to choosing how to maintain the property that are in line with their own interests and goals. A lot of people who are busy buyers may like this amount of power. For some real estate buyers, taking care of their homes is a hobby they enjoy every day, which fits with their hands-on approach to investing. Self-management works best for property owners who live close to their homes because it lets them be more involved and deal with problems quickly and directly.

Self-management is also a great way to learn, especially for people who are new to investing in real estate. Owners can learn about the real estate market, how to deal with tenants, and how to keep their homes in good shape by having someone manage them. This method also lets owners make decisions that are flexible, so they can change their plans and solve problems based on their gut feelings and good sense, which can be helpful for people who are always changing and adapting.

Self-management is often more practical for property owners with a few properties, since handling more than a few properties gets harder as the number of them grows. If you want to grow your portfolio, it might be easier to hire a skilled property manager. Self-management fits well with the way of thinking of people who see real estate as an active investment and get pleasure from taking care of their homes.

3. Finding a Balance:

Some property owners choose a hybrid strategy that incorporates elements of both self-management and employing property managers. For instance, an owner could manage tenant relations while hiring experts to coordinate maintenance. This hybrid technique enables a tailored approach according to unique needs and preferences.Regular evaluations of the investment strategy are essential, regardless of the method used. Owners of rental properties should routinely assess the efficacy and efficiency of their management strategy, considering variables including return on investment (ROI), tenant happiness, and overall investment objectives.

Each property owner has different needs and considerations when deciding between hiring a property manager or managing themselves. Professional property managers provide knowledge, scalability, and time savings; self-management, on the other hand, gives financial savings, direct control, and firsthand investing experience. Achieving the ideal balance with a hybrid strategy guarantees that the management model of choice fits the owner's objectives, tastes, and requirements of their real estate holdings. Property owners must be flexible and conduct regular evaluations as they negotiate the ever-changing real estate management market to maximize return on investment and overall investment performance.

8.3 Maintenance Strategies for Property Value Preservation

Over time, maintenance techniques are essential to maintaining a property's value. Proactive and efficient upkeep guarantees the durability and operation of different parts, adds to the property's overall appearance, and increases tenant satisfaction. This section will examine the significance of maintenance techniques for preserving property value, including important factors, optimal methods, and the long-term effects on real estate investments.

1. Maintaining Asset Worth:

Preventive maintenance is one of the core tactics for protecting a property's value. Proactive actions and routine inspections reduce the likelihood of large-scale, expensive repairs later on by detecting problems early on and taking action to resolve them. Long-term asset value protection for the property is provided by this method.It's crucial to make repairs as soon as possible to prevent little problems from growing into bigger ones. When it comes to repairing a leaking roof, plumbing difficulties, or electrical issues, prompt and effective maintenance is essential to preserving the overall state and value of the property.

2. Contentment and Sustaining Tenants:

Resolving tenant maintenance issues immediately is essential to maintaining the property's value. Higher satisfaction levels result from responsive property managers or landlords who prioritize and promptly address tenant complaints. Lease renewals from happy tenants cut down on turnover expenses and vacancy times.

Preventive maintenance requirements can be found by conducting routine property inspections. Property managers can recognize signs of wear and tear, evaluate the state of appliances and systems, and resolve any problems before they affect tenant satisfaction or require more repairs. Teaching renters the fundamentals of upkeep on their properties may also help to preserve their worth. Giving renters instructions on how to do regular maintenance, like replacing the air filter or reporting problems right away, encourages them to participate in the general upkeep of the property.

3. Curb Appeal and Aesthetic Upkeep:

The property's landscape and exterior greatly enhance its curb appeal. Frequent upkeep of external areas, exterior cleaning, and gardening improve the property's aesthetic appeal. In addition to drawing in prospective renters, well-kept exteriors raise the property's perceived worth.Painting and small renovations are cosmetic enhancements that may revitalize the house's look. Updating paint and taking care of minor imperfections regularly improves the appearance and helps keep the property's market value.

4. Systematic Maintenance Planning:

Creating a maintenance schedule is smart. This calendar lists planned renovations, inspections, and routine maintenance. A methodical strategy guarantees that all aspects of property upkeep are covered and that duties are carried out reliably. Setting aside a specific maintenance budget is essential. Owners of real estate should budget for continuous maintenance expenses. Sufficient financing guarantees that updates and repairs may be made on time without jeopardizing the investment's overall financial stability.

5. Technology Integration:

Property management software makes Maintenance activities easier. These systems provide the ability to plan inspections, monitor repairs, and automate maintenance requests. Integrating technology improves productivity and guarantees that maintenance tasks are planned and recorded. Including smart home systems may help maintain the value of your house. In addition to improving the aesthetics of the house, intelligent gadgets like security systems, thermostats, and leak monitors also help to save energy and avert any damage.

6. Adjusting for Environmental Factors:

It's essential to modify maintenance plans by the local climate. While buildings in hot climates need protection from high sun exposure, those in areas with severe winters might need to take special precautions to prevent freezing temperatures. Maintaining the property by environmental conditions guarantees its resilience. Seasonal maintenance inspections are a proactive tactic. Property managers may evaluate the property's preparedness and take care of any problems from seasonal variations before the start of each season. This strategy protects the property's value and helps avoid weather-related problems.

7. Long-Term Planning:

Putting a life cycle analysis into practice entails estimating how long particular property components should last. Property owners may use this information to plan and prevent expensive last-minute shocks by promptly replacing and upgrading.

Making plans for strategic improvements helps maintain real estate's value. Essential amenities, like the kitchen or bathroom, may be upgraded to improve the property's appearance, stay competitive over time, and conform to current market trends.

8. Professional Property Management:

Hiring qualified property managers offers skilled supervision of upkeep tasks. Property managers contribute their industry expertise, vendor networks, and experience to make well-informed judgments about maintenance priorities and tactics.Skilled property managers are excellent at managing vendors. Because of their connections with reputable service providers and contractors, maintenance jobs are always allocated to qualified experts. The effectiveness and caliber of maintenance operations are enhanced by competent vendor management.

9. Documentation and Records:

It is essential to keep detailed records of every maintenance operation. In addition to helping to keep track of the property's maintenance history, documentation is a valuable tool for upcoming real estate transactions. Potentialstors or purchasers may want to see the property's maintenance records.

Participating in maintenance activities with the community promotes pride and a feeling of belonging. Community engagement is crucial in maintaining common areas and general property care, whether through collaborative efforts to clean up after shared events or organizing joint clean-up days.

A real estate investment's ability to retain its value and be successful depends on its maintenance plans. Proper maintenance extends beyond preventative measures and includes curb appeal, tenant satisfaction, systematic Planning, expert monitoring, and systematic Planning.

It also adds to the property's lifespan and financial success. In the competitive and dynamic real estate market, property owners who make maintenance a strategic component of their investment plan set themselves up for long-term success. In addition to attracting and keeping renters, a well-kept property maintains its worth over time by being a stable asset in the face of shifting market circumstances.

Category	Strategies	Details
1. Asset Value	Preventive Maintenance	Scheduled upkeep to prevent issues
	Timely Repairs	Quick response to repair needs
2. Tenant Satisfaction	Responsive Requests	Addressing tenant issues promptly

	Regular Inspections	Ensuring property is in good condition
	Tenant Education	Informing tenants about property care
3. Curb Appeal	Landscaping	Keeping exterior attractive
	Painting & Upgrades	Regular cosmetic updates
4. Planning	Maintenance Calendar	Scheduling regular maintenance tasks
	Budgeting	Allocating funds for upkeep and repairs
5. Technology	Management Software	Streamlining management tasks
	Smart Systems	Implementing efficient technology
Conclusion:	Importance	Crucial for property value and tenant retention
	Benefits	Attracts tenants and enhances appeal

This table provides a structured overview of the key maintenance strategies for property value preservation, organized into categories for easy reference.

8.4 Implementing Sustainable and Eco-Friendly Property Practices

Using environmentally responsible and sustainable property management techniques has become crucial. Property owners, managers, and investors are realizing the significance of implementing eco-friendly methods that save the environment, increase property value, and provide long-term cost savings as environmental consciousness on a worldwide scale continues to rise. We will examine the importance of adopting eco-friendly and sustainable real estate methods in this area and the main features, advantages, and factors to consider with this proactive strategy.

1. Conservation of Resources:

Conservation of resources is given priority in sustainable property practices. This covers the economical use of resources, water, and energy. Reducing resource consumption via technology and strategy implementation improves the environment and supports the global sustainability movement. One of the central tenets of environmentally friendly practices is reducing waste output. In addition to encouraging waste reduction among tenants and implementing recycling programs, property managers should emphasize using recyclable and sustainable materials in their building projects.

2. Energy Efficiency:

One practical step toward sustainable property management is upgrading energy-efficient appliances. Because these appliances use less energy, the total carbon footprint of the property is reduced, and utility bills are down for both property owners and renters.

Energy efficiency is increased by integrating smart home systems. These systems optimize energy consumption depending on occupancy and preferences by enabling intelligent control of heating, cooling, and lighting. Using innovative technology is compliant with current sustainability guidelines. A critical step toward sustainable energy practices is the integration of renewable energy sources, such as solar panels, into property design. Potential cost savings and a decreased need for conventional energy sources are among the long-term advantages, even if the initial expenditure can be more.

1. **Water Conservation:**

Low-Flow Fixtures: A simple way to save water is to install low-flow fixtures in kitchens and bathrooms. These fixtures contribute to reducing utility costs and sustainable water use by using less water without sacrificing functionality.

These techniques contribute to water conservation. This entails using xeriscaping techniques, building effective irrigation systems, and selecting native plants with lower water requirements.

3. Building Design and Construction:

A key component of sustainable building is using green building materials. Eco-friendly property practices benefit from using low-impact materials, such as recycled or recovered. Using materials that are supplied locally also lowers carbon emissions associated with transportation.Orientation, insulation, and ventilation are a few factors to consider while designing a structure. A well-thought-out design may optimize natural light, minimize the need for artificial lighting and heating, and provide a living or working environment that uses less energy overall.

4. Tenant Engagement and Education:

Including and educating renters about environmentally friendly behaviors is essential. Information on waste minimization, the value of sustainable living, and the saving of energy and water may be obtained from property managers. This encourages renters to engage in eco-friendly actions and cultivates a feeling of environmental responsibility.

Enacting incentive plans might encourage renters to embrace eco-friendly behaviors. This might include arranging eco-friendly activities, giving out rent reductions in exchange for energy-saving behaviors, or providing materials for sustainable living.

5. Standards and Certifications:

Obtaining a certification like the Leadership in Energy and Environmental Design (LEED) is a concrete approach to show your dedication to sustainability. Strict environmental standards, including indoor air quality, water conservation, and energy efficiency, are met by properties that have earned the LEED certification.These ratings serve as a standard for the energy economy. Property owners and managers may use ratings to assess the energy efficiency of individual assets, buildings, and whole portfolios.

6. Financial Advantages:

Over time, sustainable property practices often result in cost savings. Lower utility expenses result from energy-efficient equipment, renewable energy sources, and water conservation techniques. This improves the property's financial performance and attracts cost-conscious renters.Sustainable features increase a property's market attractiveness. Eco-friendly homes are often in higher demand as environmental awareness grows among renters and purchasers. This might result in better property prices and more chances for rental or sales.

7. Compliance with Regulations:

Adopting sustainable methods guarantees adherence to environmental rules. More and more governments and municipalities are implementing policies to support environmentally friendly building and property management. Keeping up with these rules helps promote responsible property ownership and helps avert any legal problems.

Materials and systems' lifespan and durability are considered by sustainable practices. Selecting long-lasting, high-quality materials helps the property last longer and requires fewer replacements and maintenance over time.Sustainable Properties are better equipped to adjust to shifting customer preferences and market trends. Eco-friendly features may draw in the broader spectrum of renters and purchasers as sustainability becomes an increasingly important consideration when making real estate purchases.

8. Continuous Improvement:

Data-driven decision-making is made possible for property owners and managers by regularly tracking the effectiveness of sustainable features.

Finding opportunities for improvement may include monitoring water and energy use and tenant participation in eco-friendly measures. Keeping up with developments in sustainable practices is critical. In environmental sustainability, new ideas and technologies are constantly being developed, allowing property owners to improve their green projects.

Implementing eco-friendly and sustainable property practices is a smart move for long-term real estate profitability and a responsible way to promote environmental stewardship. Sustainable techniques decrease environmental effects, provide financial advantages, and preserve property value.

These practices include energy and water saving, green construction materials, and tenant participation. By adopting these strategies, property managers and owners are leaders in an evolving real estate market, drawing in eco-aware renters and investors and fostering a more resilient and sustainable future.

8.5 Enhancing Property Value through Renovations and Upgrades

Enhancing a property's worth via improvements and renovations is a calculated strategy that may boost its market appeal and financial performance and improve its physical condition. Investing in well-thought-out renovations and enhancements may draw in better tenants, raise rental prices, and promote total property value for residential and commercial buildings. This section will discuss the importance of improving a property's worth via repairs and improvements, looking at important factors, well-liked tactics, and the long-term effects on real estate investments.

1. Reducing Obsolescence and Depreciation:

When addressing wear and tear on a home, renovations and improvements are essential. Structures and facilities might degrade with time, lowering the property's overall attractiveness. In a competitive market, well-planned improvements slow down depreciation and keep the home from becoming outdated.

Features and facilities must be kept current to maintain a competitive edge and draw in renters.

Modern designs and technology added to kitchens, baths, and common spaces improve the property's attractiveness and align it with current market trends.

2. Improving the Looks of the Property:

Attracting renters or purchasers mostly depends on curb appeal and first impressions count. Improving the aesthetics of entrances, painting exteriors, and upgrading landscaping have a favorable visual effect and set the tone for a well-kept home.

Renovating an interior's interior may change rooms and elevate a building's atmosphere. Updating paint colors, flooring, and lighting fixtures may all help create a modern, welcoming space that appeals to a broader spectrum of renters.

3. Adding Utility and Function:

Renovations provide chances to maximize available space. This might include rearranging layouts to improve functioning, providing storage options, or demolishing walls to create open floor designs. Effectively used properties attract renters who value practicality and ease of usage. Improving the property's fundamental plumbing, electrical, and HVAC systems enhances its general use. In addition to decreasing ongoing maintenance expenses and raising the property's long-term value, modern, effective systems also increase tenant comfort.

4. Energy Efficiency and Sustainability:

Cost savings and sustainability are enhanced when energy-efficient elements like windows, insulation, and appliances are included during renovations. Tenants who care about the environment are drawn to energy-efficient buildings, which may increase rental prices. Using eco-friendly materials and green building principles are examples of sustainable practices in renovations that go beyond energy efficiency. Sustainable elements help properties meet contemporary environmental regulations and attract renters who value eco-friendly living.

5. Adapting to Market Trends and Tenant Demand:

Property owners may adjust to changing market trends via renovations. This might include introducing facilities in demand right now, setting up co-working areas, or using smart home technologies. You can keep an eye on market developments to ensure the property stays appealing and competitive.

Renovations may be customized to satisfy changing tenant needs as they vary over time. Tenant satisfaction and retention are enhanced by features that meet the expectations of modern renters, such as modern finishes, updated appliances, and high-speed internet connection.

6. Competitive Positioning:

Renovations provide a chance to set the property apart from rivals. In a competitive market, unusual features, luxurious finishes, and avant-garde design may make the property stand out and draw in renters looking for exceptional living or working environments. A well-kept, remodeled home may fetch higher rental prices. When a property has excellent finishing, contemporary conveniences, and a well-designed living or working space, tenants are often prepared to pay extra. Increased cash flow and property value are closely correlated with premium rentals.

7. Budgeting and Strategic Planning:

A comprehensive needs assessment is the first step in strategic planning. Prioritizing repairs and allocating resources efficiently is made possible by identifying areas that need upgrading, considering tenant preferences, and assessing the property's general condition. A successful remodeling

depends on creating a reasonable budget. Real estate owners should carefully weigh the expenses and possible returns on investment before making changes that will have the most impact. Cost-control strategies guarantee improvements stay financially feasible and raise the property's value.

8. Risk Mitigation and Due Diligence:

It's essential to carry out expert examinations before improvements. Restorations are guaranteed to be founded on correct information when possible structural faults, code infractions, or concealed difficulties are found. Exercising due care reduces the likelihood of unanticipated difficulties throughout the remodeling process. Local building rules and regulations must be followed throughout renovations. Preventing legal complications and protecting the property owner's investment is achieved by ensuring all improvements comply with the legal standards.

9. Time-Related Issues:

When planning improvements, timing is crucial. Before starting any significant improvements, property owners should evaluate the state of the market, tenant demand, and economic variables. Timing improvements strategically will guarantee that they optimize profits and align with market demand. It's critical to reduce disturbance during renovations for buildings occupied by current renters. Effective communication with renters is essential for property owners. Phased renovation plans reduce tenant disturbance, and temporary relocation alternatives should be considered as required.

10. Investment Strategy for the Long Term:

One should consider renovations as a component of a long-term financial plan. Every rehabilitation project should be evaluated for projected return on investment by property owners, who should consider things like higher rental revenue, appreciation over time, and lower maintenance expenses. Renovations' flexibility to future market shifts is considered as part of long-term investment strategies. The property's ongoing worth is influenced by improvements and features that withstand the test of time and continue to draw in various tenants.

Upgrading and renovating a home to increase its value is a complex approach that calls for careful planning, wise choices, and an emphasis on long-term investment objectives. Renos improves a property's overall appeal, competitiveness, and financial performance by handling wear and tear, satisfying tenant expectations, and implementing sustainability. In the competitive and dynamic real estate market, property owners that strategically approach renovations, consider market dynamics and match improvements with tenant requests will be well-positioned for long-term success. A well-thought-out refurbishment plan raises the property's market value and ensures it will continue to be a profitable and sought-after investment for many years.

Category	Strategies	Details
1. Curbing Depreciation	Address Wear and Tear	Fix and maintain property
	Modernize Features	Update to current standards
2. Increasing Aesthetics	Curb Appeal Enhancements	Improve exterior look

	Interior Design	Upgrade interior
3. Adding Functionality	Space Utilization	Optimize space use
	Upgrade Systems	Modernize infrastructure
4. Energy Efficiency	Energy-Efficient Upgrades	Install energy-saving features
	Sustainable Practices	Implement eco-friendly practices
5. Strategic Planning	Needs Assessment	Identify renovation needs
	Budgeting and Cost Control	Manage renovation costs
Conclusion:	Enhance property value	Strategic, multifaceted approach
	Execute renovations well	Boost attractiveness and performance

This table provides a structured overview of the key considerations and strategies for enhancing property value through renovations and upgrades, organized into categories for easy reference.

|9|

Legal and Regulatory Considerations

You can handle the real estate industry's legal and regulatory environment using the information in this chapter. Making educated decisions requires knowledge of both local and federal legislation. In addition to guiding you through the legal procedures involved in purchasing real estate, we'll also look at risk mitigation and compliance tactics and dispute resolution techniques. To ensure that your assets are well-protected, the chapter also discusses legal measures for asset management and property protection.

For the relevant case studies, worksheets and free resources you can visit: andonierealty.com

"Creating a regulatory system that reflects the modern-day realities of financial markets is not as difficult as it may appear."

- Paul Singer

9.1 Understanding Local and Federal Real Estate Laws

Anyone working in the real estate business, whether they are developers, investors, agents, or property owners, must thoroughly understand state and federal real estate regulations. These laws form the legislative framework governing many facets of land development, property management, and real estate transactions. Handling the intricate legal terrain guarantees adherence, safeguards all stakeholders' interests, and reduces the likelihood of legal conflicts. We will examine the significance of comprehending municipal and federal real estate regulations in this part, as well as essential facets, legal issues, and stakeholder ramifications.

1. The Real Estate Laws' Legal Foundation:

Local and state governments are the central regulatory bodies for real estate legislation. Zoning laws, building codes, and land-use rules that specify how properties may be built and utilized are enacted by local governments. Although local laws are final, federal laws are also fundamental in the real estate industry. The federal government has adopted legislation about fair housing, anti-discrimination, environmental rules, and the financial elements of real estate transactions.

2. Transactional Compliance:

When completing property transactions, it is crucial to comprehend local and federal real estate rules. Compliance with legal standards is essential in property transfers, contracts, and disclosures to guarantee the legitimacy and enforceability of transactions. The transfer of property ownership is governed by real estate laws. To establish a clear and marketable title, Compliance with easement and encumbrance restrictions, deed recording processes, and title search requirements is essential.

Property Use and Zoning Regulations:

Zoning Ordinances specify the uses and developments permitted on property in a particular region. Property owners and developers must know these rules to ensure the site's intended use complies with local zoning laws. To depart from the norm regarding zoning, real estate laws often include procedures for securing deviations or special permits. Anyone planning to build or alter a property must know the requirements and procedures for getting these permissions.

3. Anti-Discrimination and Fair Housing Laws:

This law forbids discrimination in housing based on race, color, religion, sex, family status, national origin, or handicap. Real estate brokers, property managers, and landlords must abide by these anti-discrimination rules. A few states and localities have anti-discrimination laws and extra-protected classifications. Comprehending these distinctions guarantees thorough adherence to fair housing regulations across the board.

4. Environmental rules:

Property developers must consider and adhere to environmental rules, which include evaluations of possible environmental consequences. To prevent legal problems and possible liabilities, it is essential to comprehend the standards for environmental impact assessments and remedies. Protections for wetlands and endangered species are often included in real estate laws. Property development in locations with these characteristics may need specific permissions and adherence to environmental standards to avoid legal repercussions.

5. Regulations Concerning Financing and Mortgages:

This federal statute guarantees the openness of lending practices. Lenders and borrowers engaged in real estate finance transactions must comprehend TILA regulations.

The Real Estate Settlement Procedures Act (RESPA) mandates that lenders provide borrowers with certain information and control the closing process. Compliance with RESPA is crucial to avoid legal issues and guarantee honest and open real estate transactions.

6. Lease Agreements and Landlord-Tenant regulations:

When creating lease agreements, property managers and owners need to be aware of local and state regulations about landlord-tenant relations. Adherence to these legal statutes guarantees the enforceability of lease provisions and the mutual understanding of rights and obligations between the parties involved. Landlords must comprehend the eviction processes delineated in local legislation. Following the correct procedures for eviction avoids legal problems and guarantees a fair and legitimate settlement of tenant disputes.

7.

Professional Responsibilities in Real Estate:

State laws dictate the licensing standards that real estate agents must adhere to. Maintaining a legal and professional real estate practice requires understanding the licensing procedure, continuous education requirements, and ethical standards. Real estate agents have obligations to their customers, including loyalty, secrecy, and transparency. Maintaining professionalism and averting legal issues need understanding these responsibilities and adherence to ethical norms.

8. Consumer Protection Laws:

Federal and state consumer protection laws prohibit unfair and deceptive practices in real estate transactions. For fair and moral business practices to be ensured, Compliance with these regulations is necessary for all parties participating in real estate transactions.

To stop false information and dishonest tactics, rules govern real estate advertising. Advertising materials are guaranteed to meet legal requirements if one knows these restrictions. It is essential to comprehend the legal remedies accessible in real estate disputes. 10. Legal Recourse and Dispute Resolution: a. This entails being aware of the procedures involved in litigation, alternative conflict resolution techniques, and legal rights enforcement tools.

Real estate issues are often resolved outside of court via mediation and arbitration. A comprehensive comprehension of the benefits and constraints of these alternative dispute resolution procedures is crucial for effective conflict resolution.

Effective and legally compliant real estate transactions and operations depend critically on an awareness of both local and federal real estate regulations. A thorough understanding of the legal landscape is crucial for navigating the complexity of the real estate sector, as it affects everything from property transactions to environmental rules, fair housing legislation, and the obligations of real estate agents. Prioritizing legal Compliance helps stakeholders create a fair, honest, and moral real estate environment while reducing the possibility of legal problems. Real estate professionals are well-equipped to make educated judgments and maintain legal standards in the dynamic and ever-evolving real estate sector because they get ongoing education and keep up to date on legal advancements.

9.2 Navigating Legal Processes in Property Acquisition

An in-depth knowledge of the legal system is necessary to navigate the legal procedures involved in purchasing real estate, a crucial part of real estate transactions. To achieve a seamless and legally sound purchase, investors and buyers, whether buying residential or commercial properties, need to be well-versed in the legal processes and issues involved. This section examines the many facets of legal procedures involved in purchasing real estate, including essential details, preventive measures, and the role of legal knowledge in ensuring successful transactions.

1. Legal Considerations at First

Complete due diligence must be completed before starting the purchase process. This includes looking into the property's legal situation, including title searches, zoning compliance, environmental evaluations, and any liens or encumbrances that may be in place. Comprehending the property's legal framework is essential for a profitable purchase.

It's essential to comprehend how property ownership is structured legally. Purchasing property via a corporation, a partnership, or a person has different legal ramifications. The proper ownership structure must take time to consider investment objectives, liabilities, and tax consequences in accrual Agreements: a. Purchase Agreements: An essential contract in purchasing real estate is the purchase agreement. It describes the purchase price, deadlines, and contingencies, among other terms and conditions of the transaction. A purchase agreement's validity and clarity must be guaranteed to prevent disagreements throughout the acquisition process.

Legal procedures about the surreal estate purchases include counteroffers and negotiations. Comprehending these transactions' legal complexities is essential to arrive at mutually acceptable conditions and produce legally binding papers.

2. Financing and Legal Compliance:

It's essential to comprehend mortgage agreements and financing conditions if financing is a part of the transaction. A legally sound financing arrangement is ensured by disclosures that are transparent and in compliance with federal and state lending rules.

The buyer has legal safeguards when contingencies are included in the purchase agreement. Inspection, finance, and appraisal contingencies are examples of common contingencies. If specific requirements aren't satisfied, these provisions let the buyer back out of the agreement without facing legal repercussions.

3. Title Examination and Insurance:

An exhaustive title search is one of the most important legal procedures in purchasing a property. This entails looking through public records to confirm ownership, find any liens or encumbrances, and ensure the title is clear and marketable. Attorneys are often quite important in this procedure. Getting title insurance is standard when buying a property. To safeguard the buyer from financial damages brought on by unanticipated legal challenges with the property's title, title insurance offers protection against probable faults in the title.

Legal Adherence to Local Rules:

It is essential to adhere to local zoning and land use rules. Gaining knowledge of the property's potential uses and any local government limitations guarantees that the purchase complies with legal standards and prevents future issues.

Getting the required permits and permissions is a legal necessity, depending on the property's intended use. Permits for construction, the environment, and other regulatory approvals may fall under this category. Legal experts help with the permission procedure navigation.

4. Closing Procedures:

Money and legal papers must be transferred during the closing procedure to finalize the purchase. Escrow and closing agents are essential to guarantee that all legal criteria are satisfied, money is distributed correctly, and the title is effectively transferred. The deed, bill of sale, and closing statements are among the closing documents that legal experts draft and analyze. To complete the purchase and safely transfer ownership, it is essential to confirm the legitimacy and correctness of these papers.

5. Tax Implications and Legal Compliance:

Purchasing a property has tax ramifications, and attorneys may advise on tax-saving measures. This might include being aware of property tax assessments, capital gains tax, and possible tax breaks for certain purchases. In some circumstances, investors might want to look into a 1031 exchange, which enables them to reinvest sale profits into a property that is similar to their own, thus deferring capital gains taxes. For individuals looking to benefit from tax benefits, it is essential to comprehend the legal prerequisites and deadlines for a 1031 exchange.

6. Legal Challenges and Dispute Resolution:

Handling Legal Challenges: Even with meticulous preparation, legal issues might still arise while buying a property. These difficulties include border conflicts, title problems, or unanticipated legal roadblocks. Law professionals help resolve these conflicts via alternative dispute resolution, litigation, or negotiation.

Alternative Dispute Resolution: Mediation and arbitration are techniques that legal practitioners might use to settle disputes outside of the courtroom. Comprehending these procedures and their legal ramifications is essential to resolve conflicts effectively.

Completing any outstanding duties associated with the property, updating property records, and transferring utilities are all part of the post-acquisition legal procedures. According to the law, a smooth transition is guaranteed, and any legal problems are kept at bay during this stage. It's essential to ensure lease agreements and tenant rights are followed if the property has occupants already. Legal experts may advise on interpreting leases and handling legal disputes with renters.

7. Ongoing Legal Assistance:

To handle changing legal requirements, problems with property management, and possible legal challenges, property owners benefit from having continuing legal guidance. Building a rapport with legal experts guarantees you access to timely advice and assistance throughout your property ownership. Laws about real estate might change. Continuous legal assistance ensures ongoing adherence to the law and proactive risk management by assisting investors and property owners to adapt to regulatory changes.

In conclusion, a thorough grasp of the legal nuances of real estate transactions is necessary to navigate the legal procedures involved in property purchases. Legal experience is essential for obtaining a successful and legally sound property transaction, from contractual agreements and due diligence to title investigation, tax consequences, and continuing legal compliance.

Prioritizing legal concerns throughout the purchase process helps buyers and investors avoid legal entanglements and provides the groundwork for long-term success and compliance in real estate ownership. In the intricate process of acquiring property, legal experts are essential in offering advice, ensuring the law is followed, and defending the interests of all parties.

9.3 Ensuring Compliance and Mitigating Legal Risks

A complicated web of laws, contractual requirements, and possible legal challenges must be navigated to ensure compliance and mitigate legal risks in the real estate industry. Understanding and proactively managing legal risks is essential for the success and sustainability of real estate initiatives, regardless of whether you're a property owner, investor, developer, or real estate professional. In the dynamic and sometimes complex real estate field, this part examines the critical factors to consider while guaranteeing compliance and minimizing legal risks.

1. Compliance with Regulations: a. Local, State, and Federal Laws

Numerous municipal, state, and federal restrictions apply to real estate businesses. Respecting these rules is crucial, from fair housing legislation to zoning requirements. Regular audits and evaluations of regulatory modifications partly ensure ongoing compliance with legal obligations.

The usage and development of property are governed by environmental rules. To prevent legal ramifications and possible environmental liabilities, it is essential to comprehend and abide by rules about environmental impact assessments, hazardous materials, and conservation zones.

2. Contractual Compliance:

Real estate transactions are based on contracts. Ensuring contracts are carefully examined, prepared correctly, and adhered to the law. This covers all contracts related to real estate transactions, such as leases, purchase agreements, finance agreements, and others. Real estate deals often include precise deadlines and commitments stated in contracts. Following these deadlines and completing contractual duties is essential to avoid legal issues. Prompt documentation and communication aid in proving compliance and reducing hazards.

3. Risk Assessment and Due Diligence:

Due diligence is necessary for each real estate transaction. This includes financial studies, environmental investigations, title searches, and property inspections. Early risk identification enables well-informed decision-making and risk-reduction techniques. Creating and implementing risk mitigation techniques is essential to real estate operations. Regular risk assessments make Proactive risk management possible and may include insurance coverage, emergency preparation, and transaction structure to reduce legal liability.

4. Complying with Fair Housing and Anti-Discrimination Laws:

The laws against discrimination based on race, color, religion, sex, family status, national origin, or handicap must be followed. In addition to being required by law, ensuring adherence to these regulations encourages inclusion and ethical corporate practices. Real estate professionals engaged in leasing and sales must complete education and training to comprehend fair housing laws and anti-discrimination procedures. Professionals may stay up to speed on legal developments and are reminded of the significance of fair housing compliance via ongoing education.

5. Lease Agreement Compliance:

Property managers are responsible for ensuring lease agreements abide by applicable local landlord-tenant regulations. This entails being aware of the legal responsibilities of both parties as well as the eviction process and tenant rights. Leases with regular legal evaluations may assist in avoiding legal problems. Property managers and owners are responsible for keeping their properties livable. It's essential to comprehend and abide by legal requirements for property upkeep and repairs to prevent legal conflicts with renters and possible code infractions.

Financial reporting and adherence to accounting standards are aspects of real estate transactions. Not only does accurate financial reporting guarantee legal compliance, but it also gives stakeholders access to transparent and trustworthy financial data. Property owners and investors must abide by tax rules and regulations. This entails being aware of tax law changes that might affect real estate investments, depreciation schedules, and deductions. Getting expert tax guidance guarantees compliance and the best possible tax strategy.

6. Legal Advice and Professional Support:

It's critical to have access to legal specialists who specialize in real estate law. The involvement of legal counsel in transactions, disagreements, and decision-making procedures guarantees the timely identification and resolution of legal concerns. Regular legal audits of contracts, operational procedures, and real estate portfolios aid in the identification of possible risks. Legal experts may provide insights into new legal developments, industry best practices, and areas needing compliance attention.

7. Dispute Resolution:

Using methods like mediation or arbitration, which are forms of alternative dispute resolution, may be helpful in the case of disagreements. Alternative Dispute Resolution (ADR) techniques provide a way to settle disputes without drawn-out court cases since they are often quicker and less expensive than conventional litigation. A clearly defined litigation strategy is essential if litigation cannot be avoided. The lawsuit process may be steered by legal experts, who can guarantee strong arguments, persuasive evidence presentation, and protection of the parties' best interests.

8. Adjusting to Legal Changes:

Updates and modifications to real estate laws occur often. Monitoring local, state, and federal legislation changes regularly guarantees that real estate activities stay compliant and adjust to changing legal requirements.

Informing stakeholders—such as real estate agents, investors, and property owners—about legislative modifications is imperative. By taking a proactive stance, all parties are guaranteed to be aware of their legal obligations and to modify their actions appropriately.

9. Compliance with Technology and Data Security:

Adhering to data protection rules is essential in the digital era. It is legally required for property management systems, client databases, and communication platforms to comply with data security and privacy regulations. Confidential data is shielded from unwanted access by implementing robust cybersecurity procedures. Adopting industry-standard cybersecurity procedures and complying with data breach notification requirements are crucial elements of legal risk minimization.

In the real estate industry, ensuring compliance and reducing legal risks is a dynamic, continuous process that calls for attention to detail, knowledge, and a dedication to moral business conduct. Every aspect of real estate operations, including financial transparency, fair housing compliance, regulatory adherence, and legal assistance, adds to the total risk profile.

Prioritizing legal compliance helps stakeholders protect their assets and maintain the integrity and stability of the real estate sector. A robust legal framework that facilitates long-term and profitable real estate ventures must include regular legal evaluations, interaction with legal experts, and a proactive approach to risk management.

Category	Strategies	Details
1. Regulatory Compliance	- Local/Federal Laws - Environmental	- Adhere to regulations - Meet environmental laws
2. Contractual Compliance	- Review Contracts - Timelines	- Thorough checks - Meet deadlines

3. Risk Assessment	- Due Diligence	- Thorough evaluations
	- Mitigation	- Implement measures
4. Fair Housing	- Fair Housing Laws	- Follow regulations
	- Training	- Anti-discrimination
5. Property Management	- Lease Compliance	- Follow lease terms
	- Habitability	- Ensure habitability

This table provides a structured overview of the key considerations and strategies for ensuring compliance and mitigating legal risks in the real estate industry.

9.4 Dispute Resolution and Mediation in Real Estate

In the complicated world of real estate, mediation and dispute resolution are essential. Real estate is a dynamic and diverse sector, and as such, relationships and transactions may sometimes result in conflict, calling for efficient dispute resolution procedures. The importance of mediation and conflict resolution in the real estate industry will be discussed in this section, along with the advantages, disadvantages, and effects these methods have on different parties involved.

1. The Real Estate Dispute Landscape:

Conflicts over contracts, boundaries, property conditions, landlord-tenant concerns, finance, and disclosure requirements are potential causes of real estate disputes. Dispute resolution is often necessary since real estate transactions are complicated. Purchasers and sellers, landlords and renters, neighbors, developers, real estate experts, and even lenders can all be parties to a real estate dispute. Resolutions may be complex since each side may have distinct interests and viewpoints, yet commercial partnerships must continue.

2. Alternative Dispute Resolution (ADR) against Conventional Litigation:

In the past, traditional litigation—which included court cases, lawsuits, and perhaps protracted legal battles—was often used to settle real estate issues. Although a formal, regulated procedure, litigation may be costly, time-consuming, and aggressive. Because of its effectiveness and adaptability, ADR techniques like mediation, arbitration, and negotiation have become popular in the real estate industry. Compared to litigation, alternative dispute resolution (ADR) frequently produces speedier, more economical, and less cruel results by allowing parties to customize the settlement process to meet their unique circumstances.

3. Real Estate Mediation as a Crucial ADR Technique:

Through the voluntary and private mediation process, parties in conflict may work with a mediator—a neutral third party—to find a solution that works for all parties. In mediation, parties have more influence over the resolution than in arbitration, where the judge renders a legally enforceable ruling. In real estate disputes, mediation has several advantages. It promotes open communication, gives participants authority over the settlement process, and often keeps long-term relationships intact. In the real estate industry, where future partnerships may be potential, the informality of mediation might be very helpful.

4. Crucial Phases of Real Estate Arbitration:

The mediator usually gives an introduction before each side makes an opening statement. This prepares the ground for defining problems, setting objectives, and fostering a resolution-friendly environment. The mediator may hold separate sessions where the parties discuss their issues in secret and joint sessions when they are all present. This makes for deeper conversations and aids in the mediator's comprehension of the fundamental dynamics of the conflict.

The mediator assists parties in reaching a mutually agreeable resolution via guided negotiation. This might include discussing the underlying interests of each side and looking into innovative solutions and compromises. When an agreement is established, the parties usually record and sign it. After mediation, the parties reaffirm their commitment to the agreement at closure. Assistance after mediation or follow-up meetings may be offered to resolve any issues or guarantee the agreement is carried out as intended. Mediation is often faster and less expensive than litigation. Conflict resolution is enhanced by avoiding protracted court cases and related legal costs.

In the real estate industry, where continuing ties are typical, mediation promotes a more cooperative atmosphere, protecting connections crucial for future deals or joint ventures. Through mediation, parties may create solutions that address their needs and goals. This adaptability may lead to innovative and advantageous solutions that are not achievable legally.

Since mediation is private, candid dialogue is encouraged. Without worrying that comments they make throughout the process will be used against them in court, parties are free to voice whatever concerns they may have. Litigation can be emotionally taxing for all parties concerned. Because mediation is less aggressive, it often results in less stress and emotional strain and a more positive atmosphere for problem-solving.

6. Difficulties and Things to Take Into Account in Real Estate Mediation:

Since mediation is voluntary, all parties must agree to proceed. The efficacy of mediation may be improved if one side is willing. Disparities in power between the parties may affect the mediation procedure. Competent mediators know how to handle these situations and make sure that everyone has a chance to voice their concerns. Although mediation produces voluntary agreements, their enforcement may have issues. Before completing, the parties may decide to have legal counsel evaluate their agreement.

7. The Function of Legal Experts in Real Estate Mediation:

During mediation, parties to real estate disputes may elect to be represented by counsel. Legal experts may provide insightful counsel, guaranteeing that parties are entirely aware of their rights and the possible legal ramifications of any agreements. Choosing a skilled and knowledgeable mediator is essential. Legal experts may help choose a mediator with real estate experience and a proven track record of successfully resolving disputes.

8. Things to Think About After Mediation:

Parties must fulfill the agreement's provisions following mediation. Legal experts may oversee the agreement's implementation and handle potential post-mediation problems. A successful mediation might set the stage for further agreements and business dealings. When disagreements are resolved peacefully, parties may be more likely to cooperate on future real estate projects.

Mediation and conflict resolution are essential resources in the real estate industry. Because real estate transactions and relationships are complicated, creative and quick thinking is needed when resolving conflicts. In the real estate industry, mediation is a favored conflict resolution process because of its focus on relationship maintenance, tailored solutions, and voluntary involvement.

Legal experts are essential in helping parties navigate the mediation process, guaranteeing that decisions are made with knowledge, and enhancing the general prosperity and sustainability of real estate transactions. The mediation process will become even more critical as the real estate sector develops since it provides a resolution process that aligns with the industry's dynamic and interconnected character.

9.5 Legal Strategies for Property Protection and Asset Management

A complete real estate ownership and investing strategy must include legal tactics for asset management and property protection. Because real estate transactions include large sums of money, various hazards, and complex legal structures, putting into practice sensible tactics is essential to protecting assets, ensuring rules are followed, and maximizing the performance of a real estate portfolio as a whole. This section will examine important legal tactics that stakeholders, investors, and property owners may use to safeguard their assets and effectively manage real estate holdings.

1. Structures of Property Ownership: a. Choice of Legal Entity:

A fundamental tactic for property ownership is selecting the appropriate legal organization. Corporations, partnerships, limited liability companies (LLCs), and individual ownership are all options. Choosing the best structure may preserve assets, provide tax benefits, and reduce liabilities since each has legal and financial ramifications. Property owners often use several legal entities to separate their assets to lower the possibility that liabilities related to one property may impact others. This tactic reduces risk and protects specific assets from future lawsuits involving a particular property.

Risk Mitigation with Insurance:

A key tactic for safeguarding property is having enough insurance coverage. Policies may include liability insurance, property insurance, and specific coverage for risks like environmental problems or natural catastrophes. Sufficient insurance reduces monetary losses brought on by unanticipated circumstances and legal obligations. Reviewing insurance policies regularly guarantees that the coverage keeps up with the property portfolio's changing demands. To provide complete protection, policies must be updated to account for changes in property values, renovations, or the purchase of additional assets.

2. Protections Associated with Lease Agreements:

Creating well-structured lease agreements is a legal tactic that protects the rights of property owners. Clear agreements about rent, maintenance obligations, and dispute resolution procedures achieve smoother landlord-tenant interactions and a lower chance of legal disputes. Tenants may be assigned certain risks under lease agreements, such as property upkeep or adherence to rules and laws. Elucidating these responsibilities clarifies the proper allocation of risks and duties.

3. Regulatory Compliance and Due Diligence:

An essential legal tactic is performing extensive due diligence before purchasing real estate. This includes looking into land use limitations, zoning laws, environmental factors, and any liens or other legal constraints that may be present on the site. Comprehending these variables aids in averting future legal issues. Property owners must follow local rules and ordinances. In addition to being required by law, adherence to zoning laws, construction rules, and other legal requirements promotes the property's overall viability and success.

4. Financial and Tax Planning:

Employing a legal tactic to maximize financial results is tax planning. This might include using tax-efficient structures, maximizing any deductions that apply, and keeping up with any changes to the tax code that could affect real estate investments. By reinvesting the profits from selling one property into another "like-kind" property, property owners may use a 1031 exchange as a legal tactic to postpone paying capital gains taxes. This facilitates the growth of the portfolio without having an immediate tax impact.

5. Legal Due Diligence in Deals:

Including legal experts in real estate deals is an intelligent practice. Real estate attorneys are qualified to evaluate contracts, spot any legal issues, and provide advice that helps decision-making.

To guarantee a clear title, a comprehensive investigation is a legal tactic confirming ownership and finding liens. A clear title is essential to transfer property and avoid ownership-related legal problems.

6. Establishing Asset Protection Trusts:

Creating asset protection trusts is a legal tactic to safeguard assets from prospective creditors. These trusts may be set up to provide certain safeguards with continuing access to and enjoyment of the assets. When putting asset protection trusts into place, it is essential to have counsel from attorneys who specialize in estate planning and trusts. It takes legal knowledge to modify trusts to meet specific financial and legal objectives in this intricate area of the law.

7. Tenant Management and Screening:

Strict tenant screening procedures are a legal tactic that lessens the chance of renting to people with a track record of non-compliance or possible legal problems. Credit checks, background checks, and rental history verification are all part of proper screening.Good property management techniques are one legal tactic that helps safeguard assets. Preventing legal conflicts and preserving the property's value may be achieved by timely maintenance, attentive tenant communications, and strict adherence to lease terms.

Proactively creating legal response plans is a good idea. Whether a legal problem relates to a tenant conflict, a regulatory issue, or an unforeseen incident that affects the property's value, property owners should be ready to deal with it quickly and efficiently. Ensuring timely legal advice and help when required is ensured by maintaining access to legal experts. A thorough legal response strategy must include building connections with lawyers who understand the nuances of real estate law.

8. Dispute Resolution and Litigation Avoidance:

Using ADR mechanisms, such as arbitration and mediation, is a legal tactic to prevent drawn-out litigation. ADR offers a more adaptable and cooperative method of resolving disputes. Expert settlement and negotiating techniques are legal tactics that resolve conflicts out of court. It is possible to save expenses and time and maintain relationships by investigating settlement possibilities and negotiating in good faith.

Legal tactics for asset management and property protection are critical for negotiating the complex real estate market. Property owners and investors may maximize their real estate portfolios' financial and operational elements, maintain compliance with laws and regulations, and reduce risks using these tactics. Incorporating legal issues is essential to the long-term profitability and preservation of real estate assets. Legal experts are crucial in assisting stakeholders with these tactics because they provide invaluable knowledge and experience in the dynamic and intricate real estate field.

|10|

Market Trends and Adaptability

The real estate industry is dynamic and constantly evolving. You will get the expertise in this chapter to successfully manage these changes. We'll talk about the value of embracing innovation and technology, examine techniques for adjusting to shifting market trends, and reveal ways to remain ahead of the curve. We'll talk about analyzing and predicting market cycles so you can find the right times to invest. So fasten your seatbelts and get ready to command the market!

For the relevant case studies, worksheets and free resources you can visit: andonierealty.com

"Change is the law of life. And those who look only to the past or present are certain to miss the future."

– John F. Kennedy

10.1 Adapting to Shifting Market Trends and Dynamics

A key component of practical real estate investing and management is adjusting to changing market dynamics and trends. Because of its intrinsic dynamic nature, the real estate market is impacted by various variables, including demographic changes, economic situations, and technological breakthroughs. Investors and other stakeholders are better equipped to handle obstacles and seize new possibilities when they recognize how the market is changing and proactively modify their strategy appropriately. In this part, we will examine the significance of adjusting to evolving real estate market trends and look into tactics for being flexible in a constantly moving environment.

1. Recognizing Market Dynamics:

The status of the economy as a whole, inflation, interest rates, and real estate markets all have a significant influence. Demand for real estate may increase during economic expansion, while demand and property prices may decline during recessions. To predict changes in the market, investors need to keep an eye on economic data.

A significant factor in determining the direction of real estate markets is changes in the population, migration patterns, and age demographics. Investment possibilities may arise from increasing demand for housing and commercial space in locations where the population is growing.

Online transactions and virtual property tours are just two examples of how technology changes the real estate industry. It's critical to adopt new technologies to remain competitive and satisfy the changing needs of renters, sellers, and purchasers.

Modifications to government policies, zoning rules, and regulations may significantly impact real estate markets. Investors need to be current on legislative changes affecting property prices, development prospects, and investment approaches.

2. The Value of Adaptation

Modifying market conditions may bring up new hazards or intensify already-existing ones. Investors may proactively control risks by altering portfolios, shifting investing methods, or diversifying into other property kinds by adapting to these changes.

Market changes also provide possibilities for those ready to seize them. Flexible investors can recognize and take advantage of new trends, such as new investment models, shifting customer tastes, or the rise of specific areas. Preserving competitiveness requires keeping up with market developments. Regardless of the industry—property development, sales, or management—adjusting to changes in the market guarantees that companies stay current and continue to satisfy the demands of their target market.

3. Techniques for Changing with the Market:

The basis for adaptation is comprehensive and ongoing market research. This entails keeping an eye on economic metrics, researching demographic patterns, and keeping up with developments in technology and governmental regulations. To help them make wise judgments, investors should use analytics and data.

Attending conferences and networking events and interacting with colleagues in the field all provide insightful information about current market trends. Understanding regional peculiarities and prospective possibilities is facilitated by exchanging experiences and expertise with other experts. Using a deliberate method to reduce risk and adjust to market swings is the diversification of real estate portfolios. A diversified portfolio acts as a buffer against unfavorable market trends in specific industries by including a range of property kinds, locations, and investment techniques.

By using these techniques, investors may modify their strategy in response to changes in the market. A conservative investment strategy, for instance, may entail concentrating on stable, income-producing assets rather than high-risk investments during economic instability.

To remain competitive in the current real estate market, embracing technology is essential. This might include using data analytics for market insights, implementing property management software, and investigating digital marketing techniques to reach a wider audience. Real estate companies must have flexible business models that can react to shifting market conditions. These include investigating fresh sources of income, modifying their pricing strategies, or using cutting-edge methods of managing and developing real estate. Adapting to market trends requires an understanding of and ability to react to shifting customer preferences. Actively soliciting input, comprehending target audiences' requirements and preferences, and customizing services and products are all components of a customer-centric strategy.

4. Case Study: COVID-19's Effect on Real Estate:

A recent and significant example of how market dynamics may change suddenly is the COVID-19 epidemic. Trends in remote work, lockdowns, and customer behavior all greatly impacted real estate. As remote work grew more common, there was a decrease in demand for commercial premises and a rise in interest in suburban and rural residential properties. Quick-thinking investors swiftly changed course to satisfy the need for outdoor areas, home offices, and flexible lease periods.

It may be challenging to adjust to market changes, mainly if stakeholders are used to more conventional methods. A change in perspective and an openness to accepting change are necessary to overcome stagnation.

In volatile markets, finding the ideal balance between risk and reward may be difficult. Investors must make well-informed choices based on risk tolerance and investing objectives by carefully weighing possible possibilities against the associated hazards. Efficient resource allocation is essential when responding to market movements. This entails setting priorities for projects supporting strategic objectives and ensuring that financial commitments to marketing, technology, and real estate development provide measurable results.

Real estate investors and stakeholders may position themselves for long-term success by being proactive in their approach and flexible in response to changing market trends and dynamics. It takes constant learning, strategic planning, and dedication to remain ahead of the curve and adapt to changes in the economy, technology, or regulations. In a constantly changing market, real estate professionals who accept adaptation as a guiding concept are better able to manage uncertainty, take advantage of new possibilities, and create robust and profitable portfolios.

10.2 Embracing Technology and Innovation in Real Estate

In the real estate sector, embracing innovation and technology is a revolutionary force changing how properties are purchased, marketed, maintained, and experienced. Incorporating technological innovations has ushered in an age of efficiency, transparency, and improved user experiences. This section will examine the importance of adopting innovation and technology in the real estate sector and how these developments are changing the market.

1. The Modification of Real Estate Transactions:

The emergence of Internet listing platforms has significantly transformed the marketing and discovery of properties. A consolidated and readily accessible database of homes for sale or rent is made available by Realtor.com, Zillow, and others, enabling renters and purchasers to explore various possibilities quickly. Renters or prospective purchasers may virtually tour homes thanks to these technologies. Beyond still photos, this interactive experience gives an authentic feel of the property's configuration, style, and amenities. This is particularly important now because there may be fewer opportunities for in-person interactions, as there were during the COVID-19 epidemic.

The potential of blockchain technology to improve security and transparency in real estate transactions is being investigated. Blockchain-powered intelligent contracts may automate and simplify several transactional processes, eliminating the need for intermediaries and lowering the possibility of fraud.

2. Improvements in Property Management:

Property management software is now a must-have for landlords, property managers, and real estate professionals. It makes jobs like collecting rent, handling repair requests, and managing leases easier and more organized. With sensors and Internet of Things (IoT) devices, intelligent building technologies make it possible to centrally watch and handle systems like lights, HVAC, and security. This improves the renter experience, saves money, and uses less energy. By looking at past data and trends, predictive analytics for maintenance can predict problems that might happen. This lets property owners take care of maintenance needs before they happen, which means less downtime for tenants.

3. Reimagining Financing for Real Estate:

These platforms allow more prominent investors to participate in real estate projects. Due to the democratization of investing, more projects may be funded collectively by smaller contributions from individual investors. This invention opens up new funding and diversification options for real estate investing.

Fintech, or financial technology, has brought simplified and approachable real estate financing options. The financing process for residential and commercial buildings has been made simpler and faster by peer-to-peer lending platforms, digital underwriting procedures, and online mortgage applications. This process transforms physical real estate into blockchain-based digital tokens. This makes fractional ownership possible, opening up real estate investing to more people. Tokenization makes investments more liquid and lowers entry barriers for investors.

4. Improving Customer Experiences:

These technologies improve real estate customer experiences. Virtual staging, which involves digitally furnishing vacant areas, aids in helping prospective buyers see the possibilities of a given house. AR apps may overlay real-time property information when taking a physical property tour. Chatbots with AI capabilities are revolutionizing customer service in the real estate industry. These chatbots can arrange property viewings, help with property searches, and instantly respond to inquiries. This enhances response and interaction with possible renters or purchasers.

Machine learning algorithms suggest properties tailored to each individual based on user behavior and preferences. Users save time and increase the chance of discovering the ideal home by receiving personalized recommendations that fit their criteria, whether on listing platforms or via specialized real estate applications.

5. Ecological and Astute Development:

Eco-friendly and sustainable construction techniques are becoming more and more popular. As the need for sustainable living spaces rises, technologies like solar panels, energy-efficient HVAC systems, and smart thermostats help to produce environmentally friendly real estate.

The Internet of Things (IoT) is used for energy management in the real estate industry. Intelligent sensors and gadgets can maximize energy use, track resource use, and support the creation of ecologically friendly and energy-efficient buildings. The idea behind smart cities is using technology to improve inhabitants' quality of life. Intelligent urban planning combines connectivity, effective public services, and data-driven decision-making to build more livable and sustainable urban settings.

6. Overcoming Obstacles and Adoption Barriers:

Educating stakeholders about the advantages and possible hazards is necessary to overcome technological obstacles. Investors, customers, and real estate professionals need to know how these technologies may improve overall experiences, security, and efficiency. Data security and privacy are crucial as technology is increasingly incorporated into real estate operations. Gaining the confidence of stakeholders and consumers requires implementing strong cybersecurity measures and following privacy laws. Adopting state-of-the-art technology might have upfront expenses. However, the initial expenditure is often outweighed by the long-term gains in efficiency, cost savings, and enhanced experiences. Understanding the long-term benefits is essential for adoption to be effective.

In the quickly changing real estate market, embracing technology and innovation is not merely a reaction to shifting consumer preferences but a strategic need for maintaining relevance and competitiveness. Technology adoption increases productivity, enhances user experience, and creates new creative and sustainable real estate development opportunities. Real estate professionals, investors, and digital innovators will work together to build the future of real estate as the sector incorporates these developments, making it a more responsive, efficient, and connected environment for all parties involved.

10.3 Strategies for Staying Ahead in a Dynamic Market

Being ahead of the curve is a goal and essential in a dynamic real estate market. The industry is characterized by rapid changes brought about by economic changes, technological advances, and shifting customer tastes. Real estate professionals must take proactive approaches that foresee trends, welcome innovation, and guarantee resilience in the face of difficulties if they traverse this changing terrain effectively. This section will explore essential tactics for being ahead of the curve in a changing real estate market.

1. Ongoing Education and Industry Understanding:

Maintaining a competitive edge starts with a dedication to lifelong learning. Professional development and continuous education are essential investments for real estate agents. This entails keeping up with industry developments, attending conferences, and earning certifications to advance one's experience level. To predict changes in demand, price patterns, and new prospects, comprehensive and frequent market research is necessary. Experts may make wise selections using data analytics and trend analysis technologies based on current market information.

2. Welcome Technological Developments:

PropTech, or property technology, is changing the real estate market. Adopting PropTech solutions boosts productivity, enriches customer experiences, and simplifies operations. Examples of these technologies include blockchain apps, virtual reality tours, and property management software.

Making decisions based on data is essential to competitiveness in a changing market. Professionals may make well-informed strategic choices by analyzing operational indicators, customer behavior, and market data. These technologies may increase operational efficiency, improve customer service, and expedite repetitive activities. AI technologies such as chatbots, predictive analytics, and automated marketing campaigns help businesses remain competitive in the digital era.

3. Agile Business Models:

Real estate agents may quickly adjust to shifting market circumstances using agile business models. To adapt to changing customer expectations, this flexibility may include changing price methods, diversifying portfolios, or investigating new market sectors.

Marketing plans must adapt to changes in the tastes and behavior of their target audience. Digital marketing, social media campaigns, and targeted advertising may be constantly altered to reach target audiences.

4. Network and Collaboration:

Industry networking promotes cooperation and gives access to insightful information. Participating in professional groups, networking events, and industry organizations provides education, cooperation, and knowledge retention opportunities. Working with developers, technology suppliers, and other real estate experts may expand skills and generate new insights. Through partnerships and joint ventures, professionals may use complementary resources and abilities.

5. The fifth strategy is the customer-centric approach:

This strategy entails being aware of how customers' demands and preferences change over time.

Building long-term connections and being relevant in a customer-driven market requires asking for and receiving client input, conducting surveys, and paying close attention to their issues. A unique and unforgettable experience is produced when services are customized to each client's preferences. This can include tracking consumer preferences, anticipating requirements, and making personalized suggestions using customer relationship management (CRM) systems.

6. Risk Management and Resilience:

Experts may create proactive plans by foreseeing possible dangers using scenario planning. Identifying potential outcomes, such as market fluctuations or economic downturns, helps create backup plans to reduce risks. Using a diversified investment portfolio is a risk management tactic. Investing in various properties, places, and investment techniques might lessen the effects of industry downturns.

7. Keep Up to Date With Regulatory Developments:

Maintaining compliance and minimizing risk requires keeping current with legal and regulatory developments. Profession-specific legislation, tax codes, and zoning rules are updated regularly to guarantee that professionals follow the law. The real estate market can be significantly impacted by taxes, development, and land use laws. Remaining ahead of the curve in a constantly shifting regulatory landscape requires pushing for policies that promote business development and responding to policy changes.

Sustainable and Green Practices:

Changing consumer attitudes are reflected in the real estate industry's growing focus on sustainability and green practices. Remaining competitive in a socially aware market requires incorporating sustainable elements into projects, supporting energy-efficient technology, and following eco-friendly construction practices. Environmental, social, and governance (ESG) factors are increasingly important when making investment choices. Long-term profitability is improved, and more considerable public expectations are met when real estate processes acknowledge and include environmental, social, and governance (ESG) factors.

8. Talent Development and Staff Building:

Professional Development Investing in talent development is necessary to create a knowledgeable and flexible staff. A dynamic and resilient workforce results from offering training opportunities, encouraging innovation, and drawing on a varied talent pool. Fostering teamwork and creativity creates a climate conducive to developing creative ideas. Remaining ahead of the curve in a sector that is changing quickly requires cross-functional cooperation and a culture that embraces fresh ideas.

Surviving in a constantly changing real estate market requires a diverse strategy that values ongoing education, welcomes innovation, and adjusts to changing market circumstances. Professionals are better equipped to negotiate uncertainty and seize new possibilities when they embrace flexible business models, use technology, put the needs of their customers first, and proactively manage risks. Maintaining a competitive edge is not only a tactical benefit but an essential prerequisite for long-term prosperity and significance in the dynamic real estate sector.

Category	Strategies	Details
1. Learning	- Education	- Professional growth
2. Technology	- PropTech	- Adopt new tech
3. Agile Models	- Flexibility	- Adapt to changes

4. Networking	- Industry Networks	- Engage with peers
5. Customer Focus	- Understand Needs	- Know preferences
Conclusion:	- Comprehensive Approach	- Combine strategies

This table provides a structured overview of the key strategies discussed for staying ahead in a dynamic real estate market.

10.4 Analyzing and Forecasting Market Trends and Cycles

In the real estate sector, a key component of strategic decision-making is analyzing and forecasting market cycles and trends. Because of their intrinsic cyclical nature, real estate markets are impacted by various variables, including interest rates, demographic changes, and overall social trends. Successful real estate agents skilled at identifying and forecasting these patterns may reduce risks, make well-informed investment choices, and set themselves up to take advantage of new possibilities. This section will examine the significance of assessing and projecting real estate market cycles and trends and the associated approaches and factors.

1. Recognizing Cycles and Trends in the Market:

It's the economic factors, like inflation, unemployment rates, and GDP growth, that really shape real estate trends. When the economy is doing well, more people want to buy homes, which drives up prices. When the economy is bad, less people want to buy homes, which drives down prices. Interest rates also have a big effect on how much real estate costs.

When rates go down, demand usually goes up because it's cheaper to borrow money. When rates go up, demand goes down, which can affect property prices and business profits. Changes in population, movement trends, and age groups also affect real estate demand. For example, there is more interest in rented homes and cities in places where young workers want to live. It is also important to understand how supply and demand work in the market, since an undersupply can cause prices to rise and an oversupply can cause prices to fall. By looking at these factors, you can predict market trends and make smart financial choices.

2. The significance of market research

Real estate workers put reducing risk at the top of their list of priorities. They do this by closely studying market trends to spot possible downturns and figure out how vulnerable their stock is. Stakeholders can take steps to reduce risks and take advantage of chances by knowing the factors that affect the market. To make smart financial choices, you need to have a deep understanding of how the market works.

You can do this by looking at past data, present indicators, and predictions for the future. This could mean taking advantage of chances to buy properties that aren't worth as much or selling assets that are worth more than they're worth. Mastering the time of transactions is also very important. Market analysis is a useful tool for keeping track of sales, purchases, and other transactions. Professionals use information about the market to take advantage of good times or hold on to assets for when the market is expected to go up.

Market analysis has changed due to developments in data analytics and technology. Real estate experts use big data, machine learning techniques, and predictive analytics to glean valuable insights from large datasets. These resources may help with strategic decision-making by seeing patterns and predicting trends.

CMAs assess comparable properties in a particular market to ascertain their worth. CMAs are used by real estate agents to determine a property's current market worth, find comparable transactions, and evaluate the situation of the market as a whole. Evaluating the equilibrium between market demand and available attributes is critical to analyzing supply and demand dynamics. Professionals may use this study to determine if the market favors buyers or sellers, which impacts pricing policies and investment choices. Regression analysis looks at how variables relate to one another to find correlations and forecast future results. Regression analysis may be used in the real estate industry to simulate how several variables, like housing inventories, employment levels, and interest rates, affect property prices.

4. Factors to Take Into Account When Forecasting:

When trying to guess how markets will move, it's important to think about big picture economic problems, since they can have a direct effect on smaller market issues. As a result of knowing how changes in national and foreign economic data can affect property trends, real estate agents are always keeping an eye on these numbers. But changes in the local market, like job trends, zoning changes, and neighborhood growth, are just as important. These factors have a direct effect on property prices and the return on investments.

Also, it's important to keep up with changes to regulations, since changes to banking rules, tax laws, or zoning codes can have a big effect on real estate markets. For forecasts to work, it's important to think ahead about possible changes in regulations and how they might affect business plans and property prices. New technologies, especially PropTech innovations, can also change market trends and the way people buy, sell, and handle properties in the usual way. To effectively adapt to changing market conditions, real estate workers need to stay up to date on new technologies.

5. Difficulties in Projecting the Market:

Unforeseen occurrences may cause market projections to be disrupted. Examples of such events include natural catastrophes and worldwide pandemics. Real estate professionals' forecasting models must include risk scenarios and resilience strategies to accommodate unforeseen occurrences. A wide range of factors affect real estate markets, which makes forecasting challenging. The forecasting process becomes more complex due to market psychology, geopolitical developments, and consumer attitudes. Market sentiment may greatly influence real estate cycles. It might not be easy to gauge the mood correctly, but investor confidence, public perception, and psychological aspects can influence market dynamics.

Real professionals hoping to succeed in a fast-paced field must possess the critical skill set of assessing and predicting market cycles and trends. To make wise investment choices and reduce risks, one must be able to analyze economic data, use sophisticated analytics, and predict changes in supply and demand. Despite obstacles, maintaining a competitive edge requires a dedication to lifelong learning, using technology, and a sophisticated comprehension of regional and national market dynamics. Real estate professionals involved in market analysis and forecasting are in an excellent position to take advantage of the opportunities constantly changing in the real estate industry and navigate unpredictable times.

10.5 Identifying Opportune Moments for Investment in Market Shifts

Finding the correct times to invest in market changes is a strategic need for success in the ever-changing and cyclical real estate market. Numerous variables impact real estate markets, and timing the investment strategy's purchase, sale, or modification is essential to optimizing profits and minimizing risks. The importance of spotting when to invest in market changes will be discussed in this part, along with the factors and tactics real estate agents use to help them through these changes.

1. Comprehending Market Turnarounds:

It's important to understand that real estate markets go through cycles of upswings, downswings, expansions, and peaks. At each stage, owners face both chances and challenges, so they need to take a more complex approach to figuring out when to move. Things like GDP growth, job rates, and interest rates have a big impact on how the market changes. Real estate workers are very good at looking at these signs to predict changes and plan when to make investments.

Also, changes in the market are highly affected by how supply and demand work, with imbalances making markets buyer's or seller's. Investors can put themselves in a good situation by recognizing these imbalances. Also, keeping an eye on how people act and what they like is important for making smart business choices. Changing patterns of growth, demographics, and lifestyles have a direct effect on the market for certain properties. This shows how important it is to change tactics to meet changing customer needs.

2. Importance of Timing in Real Estate Investing:

Investors may profit from market opportunities by spotting favorable times. This might include buying properties at a discount when the market is down, seizing distressed sales, or carefully selling assets when the market is at its strongest.

One essential part of risk reduction is timing. Investors may manage their portfolios more resiliently, mitigate risks, and weather economic downturns by being able to recognize and react to market movements. Holding periods have an impact on real estate investments. Optimizing returns requires knowing when to join or leave a market segment, geographic area, or particular asset class. Real estate portfolios are more profitable overall when they are timed strategically.

3. Things to Take Into Account When Selecting the Right Times:

Finding the correct time to act requires in-depth market research and analysis. To guide their investment selections, real estate professionals use data on past performance, present market circumstances, and projected future growth. It is imperative to keep an eye on the state of the economy locally, regionally, and nationally. Gaining knowledge of employment rates, inflation, and GDP growth patterns may help one anticipate changes in the real estate market as well as the overall status of the economy.

The affordability and demand for real estate are significantly impacted by interest rates. Recognizing patterns in interest rates enables investors to prepare for shifts in borrowing expenses, which impacts demand for real estate and property prices. Local Market Understanding the subtleties of local market dynamics is critical. Certain areas become more desirable due to infrastructural development, employment opportunities, and population increase, which affects property prices.

4. Techniques for Spotting Perfect Moments:

A contrarian investment entails defying established market patterns. During periods of market pessimism, astute investors might spot favorable times to buy properties at reduced costs with the hope of future gain. This technique entails assessing various market conditions and how they can affect real estate ventures. Investors may create strategies tailored to unique market situations through industry-specific, geopolitical, and economic considerations.

By using an adaptive method, investors may modify their holdings in response to changes in the market. This may include diversification into several property kinds, geographical areas, or investing techniques to keep up with shifting market conditions. How well-performing assets might fare in unfavorable circumstances. Investors may find weaknesses in their portfolios and make changes to strengthen the durability of their real estate assets by stress testing them.

5. Difficulties in Recognizing the Right Times:

Finding favorable times may be very difficult when there is market uncertainty. Erroneous occurrences, abrupt economic changes, or geopolitical considerations may all contribute to uncertainty, making it challenging to forecast market movements precisely. Accurately timing the market is a notoriously tricky task. Investors need help following new trends and refraining from snap judgments. Incorrect timing changes in the market might lead to lost opportunities or unintentional risk exposure. -The amount of information available in the significant data age may be debilitating. Sifting through enormous amounts of information and picking out essential signals among the noise calls for sophisticated analytical techniques and a deep understanding of market fundamentals.

There are two aspects to real estate investing: the art and science of timing market change investments. Real estate agents must be well-versed in local market dynamics, new trends, and economic data. With careful planning and study behind them, investors may take advantage of market openings, position themselves favorably, and skillfully negotiate the intricacies of the real estate market. Even when there are obstacles, recognizing the correct times to invest in real estate is a crucial differentiator for success.

|11|

Scaling Your Real Estate Portfolio

You will like this chapter with the information and tactics needed to grow your real estate holdings and succeed in the long run. We'll go over how to increase and diversify your assets, talk about how to strike a balance between growth and risk, and show you how to leverage and scale your holdings. We'll also talk about how to manage several properties effectively. So grab a seat, and let's start creating your real estate empire!

For the relevant case studies, worksheets and free resources you can visit: andonierealty.com

"Progress always involves risk. You can't steal 2nd base and keep your foot on 1st."

– Fred Wilcox

11.1 Strategies for Expanding and Diversifying Investments

Expanding and diversifying investment strategies are essential for real estate professionals looking to improve their portfolios, reduce risks, and take advantage of more possibilities in the ever-changing real estate market. Successful investors understand that diversity is essential to maximize profits and safeguard their assets from market volatility as the sector develops. This section will examine the importance of increasing and diversifying real estate investments and astute experts' essential tactics to accomplish these goals.

1. The significance of diversification and expansion:

Real estate investors may maximize the risk-return profile of their portfolios by expanding and diversifying their holdings. Investors may increase the general resilience of their portfolios and lessen the effect of downturns in particular industries by distributing their investments over various properties, geographies, and asset classes.

The dynamics of real estate markets are dynamic and susceptible to continual change. Investors may respond to shifting economic, demographic, and industry-specific variables by carefully positioning themselves, capitalizing on new trends, and adapting to market developments with the flexibility that expansion and diversification provide. By using various income sources, diversifying an investment portfolio enables investors to optimize their profits. There may be differences in the revenue potential and appreciation rates of different property kinds, such as commercial, industrial, and residential. Capital appreciation and income production may coexist in a well-diversified portfolio.

2. Techniques for Growing and Changing:

One of the main strategies for diversification is geographic diversity, which involves investing in several geographic places. Local variables, population growth, and regional economic circumstances may significantly impact real estate markets. By lowering exposure to the risks connected to a particular market, geographic diversity acts as a buffer against regional downturns. Spreading risk and exposure by investing in a variety of property kinds. Every property—residential, commercial, retail, and industrial—has a different risk profile and market dynamics. Investors should carefully divide their assets across these categories to balance income stability and growth potential.

Using a variety of investment approaches increases diversification even more. Other strategies are buying and holding for long-term stability, flipping properties for quick profits, and participating in syndications or real estate investment trusts (REITs) for diversified exposure to more extensive portfolios. Diversifying across asset classes and real estate sectors is essential, in addition to property kinds. This might include investing in real estate, business buildings, industrial warehouses, or niche markets like hospitality or healthcare. Every industry reacts to economic cycles and market developments uniquely.

3. Things to Think About for Diversification and Expansion:

Conducting thorough market research and due diligence is essential before venturing into new markets or expanding one's real estate portfolio across multiple categories. This process involves analyzing legislative frameworks, assessing local market conditions, and evaluating potential risks and opportunities. Additionally, investors must align their diversification and growth strategies with their investment objectives and risk tolerance. While some may prioritize stable income, others might pursue more aggressive tactics to achieve higher returns, necessitating a balanced approach to risk and return. Furthermore, keeping abreast of economic and demographic trends is crucial for making informed decisions. A deep understanding of employment patterns, population growth, and emerging economic sectors helps investors in selecting optimal locations and property types for long-term development.

4. Methods for Growing Your Investments:

One way to expand investment opportunities is through joint ventures and partnerships, where investors can pool their resources and expertise to tackle more ambitious projects, venture into new markets, and share risks and rewards. Additionally, leveraging financing alternatives such as mortgages allows investors to grow their portfolios without committing large amounts of capital. However, optimizing leverage while managing risk necessitates a careful evaluation of financing terms, interest rates, and loan arrangements.

Exploring new development initiatives also presents growth opportunities, whether starting from scratch on construction projects, partnering with developers, or investing in undeveloped land. Such initiatives can provide access to emerging markets and help expand one's portfolio. Moreover, scaling property management procedures is vital for successfully managing an expanding portfolio. By streamlining processes and utilizing technology, investors can implement scalable property management systems that enable efficient management of an increasing number of properties.

5. Difficulties with Expansion and Diversification:

Increasing investment size and diversification brings with it complexity. Every market and kind of property has unique complexities and difficulties. Investors must manage these intricacies and know the many aspects that affect every investment. Good supervision is necessary when managing a diverse portfolio. The extra management cost that comes with managing a range of properties, locations, and investment strategies is something that investors need to consider. This includes upkeep of the property, interactions with tenants, and adherence to legal obligations.

Expansion and diversification depend heavily on timing. Inadequate timing in making choices may result in less-than-ideal outcomes. Examples include diversifying without fully comprehending market dynamics or joining a market at its peak. Investors need to implement plans precisely and evaluate the state of the market with great care.

Investors who want to prosper in the constantly changing real estate market should consider broadening and varying their real estate holdings. The combination of property type distribution, geographic diversity, and strategic investing techniques enables investors to maximize profits while minimizing risk and optimizing return. A well-constructed and diversified real estate portfolio may provide advantages such as improved resilience, better growth potential, and strategic positioning to take advantage of various market possibilities despite constraints. Strategic diversification and growth continue to be essential cornerstones of long-term success and portfolio optimization as real estate professionals negotiate the intricacies of the market.

11.2 Balancing Risk and Growth in an Expanding Portfolio

Balancing risk and growth is a fine art in real estate investing, especially when growing a portfolio. Numerous hazards are introduced by the real estate industry's dynamic character, including unanticipated market upheavals and economic downturns. Attaining maximum profits and growing one's investment portfolio both depend on pursuit. The pursuit section will examine the sophisticated tactics used by astute investors to manage an increasing real estate portfolio while finding the ideal balance between growth and risk.

1. Recognizing the Relationship Between Risk and Growth:

Real estate investments are subject to various risk factors, including fluctuations in interest rates, market volatility, and unforeseen events such as natural disasters or global crises. Understanding these risks is crucial for effective risk management. Investors typically set growth goals to diversify their portfolios, increase rental income, and capitalize on potential gains. Strategies to achieve these goals might include expanding into new regions, acquiring additional properties, or engaging in development projects. Furthermore, the trade-off between risk and reward is a fundamental aspect of investment strategy. Investments with higher growth potential often come with increased risk, prompting investors to carefully assess their risk tolerance and align it with their desired growth objectives. This balance is essential for achieving sustainable growth while managing potential risks effectively.

2. Techniques for Juggling Growth and Risk:

A key tactic for striking a balance between risk and growth is diversification. It is also known as a risk mitigation tool. Investing across a variety of property kinds, asset classes, and geographical areas increases the resilience of the whole portfolio by reducing the effect of a downturn in any area.

Figuring out the best mix of assets for a trader by looking at their goals, how much risk they are willing to take, and the current state of the market is called strategic asset allocation. By spreading their money out wisely among different types of real estate assets, this method helps buyers find the right mix between growth potential and risk exposure. It is also very important to do a full risk review and due diligence. Before putting money into an investment, investors can find and reduce risks by doing a lot of study on possible assets, market trends, and legal settings. Managing debt is another important part of a financial plan. Leverage can help you make more money, but it also raises your risk. So, getting the most out of borrowing money and staying away from too much debt are very important, especially during market downturns. This careful use of leverage helps keep the balance between risk and return in a good place.

3. Things to Think About When Balancing Risk and Growth:

Making educated investment decisions requires a keen assessment of economic and market conditions. Understanding whether the market is in an expansionary or contractionary phase helps investors determine the appropriate level of risk for their growth strategies. Additionally, considering the investment horizon is crucial for balancing risk and growth. Long-term investment strategies allow for a more measured approach that can withstand market volatility, whereas short-term initiatives might involve higher risks due to their rapid nature.

Moreover, it is essential to monitor market conditions and portfolio performance continuously. Investors must remain flexible, ready to reallocate resources, adjust their risk exposure, and modify their strategies in response to changing market dynamics. This ongoing monitoring and adaptation are key to maintaining a successful investment strategy.

4. Techniques for Controlling Risk in a Growing Portfolio:

Stress testing is a way to see how well a portfolio would do in bad situations by simulating bad things that could happen. Take a proactive approach: investors can find weak spots in their assets and put plans in place to lower risk. In this situation, it also makes sense to use tools for security and lowering risk. It is very important to have resources like liability insurance, property insurance, and financial goods that protect against certain risks, like changes in interest rates or exchange risks.

Planning for different market situations is also part of scenario planning. Investors can deal with uncertainty and lower their risks by thinking ahead about possible problems and chances. Another important risk management technique is to keep your cash on hand. Keeping enough cash on hand helps investors meet their financial responsibilities, take advantage of market downturns, and deal with unexpected problems, which makes their investment strategy more stable.

1. **Difficulties in Judging Risk and Growth:**

Real estate markets may be very volatile in uncertain times, making risk management difficult. Investors need to manage market volatility and create plans that consider unforeseen changes. Global economic issues such as financial crises or geopolitical events may impact real estate markets. Investors facing outside forces beyond their control may need help to strike a balance between risk and growth.

Regulatory Changes:

New risks may arise due to regulatory changes. Investors need to be updated on changes to local, regional, and federal rules that might impact their real estate investments and necessitate modifying their risk and growth strategy.

In summary, managing risk and growth in a growing real estate portfolio requires strategic thinking and flexibility, and it's a continuous process. Achieving the ideal balance between risk reduction and growth optimization requires a keen assessment of risk variables, diversification techniques, and constant market observation, all recognized by successful investors. Real estate investors should position themselves to negotiate obstacles and seize opportunities in the constantly changing real estate investment environment by implementing strict risk management procedures, using diversification techniques, and being flexible in reaction to market dynamics. Creating a stable and prosperous real estate portfolio requires striking a balanced balance between risk and growth.

11.3 Leveraging and Scaling Techniques for Sustainable Growth

Leveraging and scaling strategies are essential for a real estate portfolio to develop sustainably. In the real estate sector, investors often want to maximize their assets, improve profits, and increase their market share. While scaling refers to deliberately increasing the size and breadth of investments, leverage refers to employing borrowed funds to boost the possible return on investment. We'll look at the tactics used by astute investors in this part and the importance of scaling and leveraging methods for long-term real estate success.

Knowing How to Leverage in Real Estate:

When you borrow money to increase the possible rate of return on an investment in real estate, this is called leverage. When investors buy homes, they usually get a mortgage or some other kind of financing. This lets them handle assets with less of their own money. There are many benefits to leveraging. It lets buyers buy more homes and raise the value of the ones they're managing than they could with just their own money. Leverage can also greatly increase the returns on an investment, which could lead to bigger earnings. But using debt also comes with extra risks. When you borrow money, you have to pay interest on it. If the value of the property drops or the market gets worse, buyers may not be able to meet their loan responsibilities. So, in order to handle these problems carefully, good leverage management needs a thorough risk assessment.

When you borrow money to increase the possible rate of return on an investment in real estate, this is called leverage. When investors buy homes, they usually get a mortgage or some other kind of financing. This lets them handle assets with less of their own money. There are many benefits to leveraging. It lets buyers buy more homes and raise the value of the ones they're managing than they could with just their own money. Leverage can also greatly increase the returns on an investment, which could lead to bigger earnings. But using debt also comes with extra risks. When you borrow money, you have to pay interest on it. If the value of the property drops or the market gets worse, buyers may not be able to meet their loan responsibilities. So, in order to handle these problems carefully, good leverage management needs a thorough risk assessment.

Techniques for Efficient Leveraging

For real estate buying to use leverage effectively, loan plans must be optimized. Investors should look at a number of credit choices that fit their level of comfort with risk, their financial goals, and the state of the market at the moment. Some of these choices are interest-only loans, mortgages with changeable rates, and mortgages with set rates. Another important part of borrowing is keeping track of loan-to-value (LTV) rates. To keep the risks of too much debt to value to a minimum, investors must carefully consider the right debt-to-value ratio for each property. It is also important to find the Debt Service Coverage Ratio (DSCR). The DSCR checks to see if a property's working income is enough to cover its debts. By carefully looking at the DSCR, you can be sure that the property makes enough money to cover its debts. This protects your finances and lowers the risk of your investment portfolio.

Comprehending Real Estate Scaling:

In real estate, scaling means expanding business activities on purpose in order to build bigger companies or get into new markets. This growth could mean buying more real estate, spreading out into different types of assets, or looking for chances in new areas. Sizing up has many benefits, such as opening up new markets, making your business more diverse, and possibly making more money. When owners' assets get bigger, they can get economies of scale, more diverse income streams, and more power in negotiations. But growing also comes with some risks, such as more market exposure, problems with management, and more complicated operations. To make sure that real estate investments continue to grow and stay stable, the pros and cons of growing must be carefully weighed against the need for good management and strong risk-reduction plans.

Techniques for Successful Scaling:

One of the core techniques for successful scaling is portfolio diversification. This may be accomplished by investing in various asset classes, buying properties in various regions, or taking part in real estate investment vehicles such as REITs to get a broader exposure range. Property management techniques must scale adequately. Scalable methods and technologies are necessary for investors to manage an increasing number of properties efficiently. This entails using automation, outsourcing, and property management software as needed.

Working together via joint ventures and strategic partnerships enables expansion without exceeding budget. Together with other specialists in the sector, investors may combine their resources and experience to take on more significant projects and expand into new areas. Technology is essential to scaling. Investors may use data analytics, machine learning, and other technology tools to spot market patterns, optimize workflows, and make well-informed judgments. Digital platforms and automation improve scaling operations efficiency.

Combining Scaling and Leveraging:

In real estate, scaling means expanding business activities on purpose in order to build bigger companies or get into new markets. This growth could mean buying more real estate, spreading out into different types of assets, or looking for chances in new areas. Sizing up has many benefits, such as opening up new markets, making your business more diverse, and possibly making more money. When owners' assets get bigger, they can get economies of scale, more diverse income streams, and more power in negotiations. But growing also comes with some risks, such as more market exposure, problems with management, and more complicated operations. To make sure that real estate investments continue to grow and stay stable, the pros and cons of growing must be carefully weighed against the need for good management and strong risk-reduction plans.

Challenges with Scaling and Leveraging:

Uncertainty and instability in the economy can make it harder for owners to leverage and grow their assets effectively in the real estate market. People who want to get through times of market instability need to be very careful about how they handle risk. Also, operational complexity rises as investments get bigger. Investors have to deal with more problems related to legal compliance, handling properties, and managing tenants. To do this well, they need strong organizational structures and processes.

A big part is also played by money problems; not being able to get enough money can really stop growth and pressure. When the economy goes down or loan rules change, it can be hard for investors to get good financial deals. This means they need to be flexible and able to adapt to changing market conditions. Because of how many complicated factors are at play, smart planning and the ability to change are important parts of making money in real estate.

In summary, scaling and leveraging are essential elements of a real estate investment strategy for sustained development. To achieve more extensive and more diversified holdings, astute investors skillfully employ leverage to maximize returns and strategically grow their portfolios. Successful integration of these strategies requires sophisticated risk comprehension, efficient risk management procedures, and flexibility in response to changing market circumstances. Real estate professionals can successfully navigate the intricacies of the business, attain sustainable growth, and position themselves for long-term success in the constantly changing real estate landscape by utilizing prudent leveraging strategies, effectively managing risk, and implementing scalable operational approaches.

Leveraging in Real Estate	**Scaling in Real Estate**

- Involves using borrowed capital to amplify potential returns.	- Involves strategic expansion of investments for larger portfolios.
- Benefits: Increased ROI, control larger assets with less capital.	- Benefits: Diversification, economies of scale, access to new markets.
- Risk Considerations: Debt obligations, interest payments, market fluctuations.	- Risk Considerations: Operational complexities, management challenges.
Strategies for Effective Leveraging	Strategies for Effective Scaling
- Optimizing loan structures.	- Portfolio diversification across locations and asset classes.
- Managing Loan-to-Value (LTV) ratios.	- Implementing efficient property management practices.
- Evaluating Debt Service Coverage Ratio (DSCR).	- Strategic partnerships and joint ventures for larger projects.

Integration of Leveraging and Scaling	Challenges in Leveraging and Scaling
- Complementary strategies often used together.	- Market volatility and uncertainty impacting strategies.
- Synergy in risk management approaches.	- Operational complexity with portfolio expansion.
- Adaptability to changing market conditions.	- Financing constraints during economic shifts.

This summary table outlines the core aspects, strategies, integration, and challenges associated with leveraging and scaling techniques in real estate investment, offering a quick snapshot of the key considerations for sustainable growth.

11.4 Managing Multiple Properties Effectively

Real estate owners encounter various challenges as their portfolios grow, including efficiently managing many properties. Strategic planning, efficient procedures, and reliable systems are necessary to effectively administer various real estate assets to guarantee top performance, tenant happiness, and portfolio success as a whole. In this part, we will examine the critical factors and tactics for successfully managing many properties in the competitive and ever-changing real estate market.

Essential Things to Think About When Managing Many Properties:

A unified property management plan is essential for running a business well. Centralization brings together important tasks like upkeep, managing finances, and dealing with tenants. This makes all properties more productive and easier to coordinate. Also, handling a business that is growing requires technology and processes that can be expanded. When you combine automation tools, cloud-based platforms, and property management software, it makes it easier to handle data, communicate, and grow your business.

Professional property management services are also very helpful for people with large holdings. Investors can focus more on making smart decisions when they give tasks like dealing with tenants, planning repairs, and making sure the property meets all regulations to experienced property managers. Setting up strong ways for people to talk to each other is also important for managing properties well. Strong contact between property managers, renters, and other important parties helps problems get solved quickly, makes tenants happier, and keeps things running smoothly.

Techniques for Efficient Property Administration:

Standardizing processes and standards across properties is a good way to streamline operations in property management. This includes putting in place standard procedures for financial reports, maintenance, and leases, which encourage uniformity and make day-to-day activities run more smoothly. Also, strict processes for choosing tenants and checking them are necessary for handling homes well. By carefully checking out potential renters, property managers can lower the risk of lease violations, property damage, and late payments. This makes the business more stable and profitable. It's also important to plan upkeep ahead of time.

Preventive maintenance, fixing maintenance problems quickly, and frequent property checks all help assets last longer and keep tenants happy.

Managing multiple homes also requires good financial management and reporting. By using a unified accounting system to keep track of income and costs and making regular financial reports, owners can see how each property and the business as a whole is doing. This makes sure that everything is clear about money and helps people make smart decisions.

Using Technology to Manage Properties Effectively:

Property control software is very helpful for buyers who have a lot of homes to take care of. This technology makes it easier to handle a wide range of properties by combining data, managing regular tasks, and giving real-time information about how each property is doing. Additionally, adding smart home technology can make managing properties a lot easier. Devices like smart heaters, security systems, and keyless entry systems not only make renting a better experience for renters, but they also let property managers keep an eye on and run their properties from afar.

Cloud-based communication tools are necessary for sites that are spread out in different places. By letting teams handle tasks, share documents, and get real-time information, these tools make it easier for property management teams to talk to each other and work together. Predictive models and data analytics are also very important for making smart decisions. Investors can find trends, guess how properties will do, and make the best use of their resources across their holdings to ensure steady growth and stability by using data analytics.

Difficulties in Overseeing Several Properties:

Taking care of various sites makes operations much more difficult. Managing renter needs, organizing tasks, and keeping an eye on care in multiple sites requires putting in place the right organizational frameworks and efficient processes. It can also be hard to make sure that different types of traits and settings follow the rules. You need to know about zoning laws, renter rights, and other rules in order to stay out of trouble with the law and avoid fines. Keeping good relationships with tenants also takes extra work. To keep renters happy and satisfied, investors should put a high priority on good communication, respond quickly to problems tenants bring up, and build strong relationships with them. This all-around method helps to improve operations, keep up with regulations, and create a helpful space for renters, which all adds to the overall success of property management.

Techniques for Surmounting Obstacles:

Putting money into education and training for people who handle homes is important if they want to do a good job of managing various properties. Making sure that team members get enough training in industry rules, customer service, and how to use technology makes them much better at managing properties efficiently. Outsourcing non-core jobs like budgeting and property upkeep can also help businesses run more efficiently. With this approach, experts can take care of certain tasks, leaving owners free to make strategic decisions.

Performing regular performance reviews is also important for finding ways to improve each property and the business as a whole. Key performance indicators (KPIs) help owners look at operational, financial, and tenant-related factors. This lets them make smart choices that help the business grow and improve property management.

In summary, managing many properties successfully is a dynamic process that requires a blend of technology use, efficient procedures, and strategic planning. Centralized administration, expandable systems, and proactive approaches to upkeep and tenant interactions must be given top priority by investors. Regulatory compliance, consistent tenant interactions, and operational complexity may all be addressed via training, outsourcing, and ongoing performance reviews. Adopting these tactics helps real estate professionals succeed in a competitive real estate market by ensuring ongoing growth, tenant happiness, and overall success as they manage the challenges of managing various portfolios.

11.5 Creating Long-Term Value through Portfolio Expansion Strategies

To generate wealth and optimize profits over an extended period, one of the main goals of real estate investors is to create long-term value via portfolio expansion techniques. Portfolio expansion is the deliberate addition of additional properties, portfolio diversification, and growth-oriented strategies that support the long-term development and profitability of the real estate portfolio. This part will examine the critical factors and tactics astute investors use to build long-term wealth by growing their real estate holdings.

Essential Pointers for Expanding Your Portfolio:

For portfolio growth, investors need to do a lot of study and analysis on the market. This gives them a base from which to build their investments. They need to look at the current state of the market, spot new trends, and know how the demographics and economies of the places they're targeting affect the real estate markets there. Also, it's important to do thorough risk reviews before adding to the stock. For long-term success, investors need to be aware of the risks that come with new purchases, changes in the market, and new rules.

They then need to come up with ways to lower these risks. Portfolio growth strategies should also be in line with the investor's general financial goals. Growth activities should be tailored to the investor's risk tolerance and specific goals to make the most money or capital gains. Diversifying your assets across different types is also important for building long-term wealth. After giving variety a lot of thought, adding residential, business, retail, or industrial properties to the portfolio can help spread risk and open up new revenue streams. This planned method makes sure that the investments are well-balanced and will last.

Techniques for Growing Your Portfolio:

Many people use geographic growth as a strategy to grow their real estate business. Investors look for new areas with good demographics, economic growth, and the chance that real estate will go up in value. This kind of variety not only lowers risk, but it also lets you take advantage of different ways that markets change. The portfolio is also more stable when it is spread out across different types of assets. To adapt to changing market conditions and take advantage of a wider range of business possibilities, investors may include a range of property types, such as office buildings, industry areas, or mixed residential buildings. Partnerships and joint projects are also very important for growth.

By working together, owners can go into new areas and take on bigger projects without having to pay for everything themselves. This allows for planned growth and diversification by sharing resources and knowledge. In addition, taking part in expansion and rebuilding tasks is a responsible way to grow. When investors buy underused buildings or vacant land and expand or renovate them in answer to market demand, they can add value to their portfolios and make them more valuable.

Using Technology to Advance Strategy:

Finding chances for strategic growth requires data-driven decision-making. Investors may use data analytics to evaluate market trends, property performance, and demographic changes, helping them make well-informed choices about what and where to buy. These platforms provide resources for locating properties, analyzing the market, and finding deals. By making it easier to find possible purchases, these platforms help investors increase the size of their portfolios more quickly.

Financial modeling and forecasting enable strategic growth by assisting investors in evaluating the possible return on investment and risk involved with new acquisitions. This data-driven strategy facilitates the selection of assets that support long-term wealth development goals.

Difficulties in Expanding Your Portfolio:

Uncertainty and market instability can make it very hard to grow a real estate business. Unexpected events, changes in the market, or changes in the economy can hurt growth plans. This is why adaptation and good risk management are important parts of a good business strategy. Adding to a stock often comes with financial restrictions as well.

Investors may have trouble getting good financing deals, especially when the economy is bad or loan rules change. This makes strategic financial planning very important. One more thing is that as a business grows, it gets harder to run. To keep things running smoothly, managing a bigger and more varied set of assets needs strong organizational structures, effective systems, and advanced property management techniques. These things are very important for managing the difficulties and difficulties of expanding your business in a market that is always changing.

Techniques for Surmounting Obstacles:

It is important for real estate investors to have strong risk management systems in place. To do this, growth plans need to be put through stress tests, flexible assets need to be kept to protect against market changes, and any new problems need to be dealt with right away to lessen the effects of market instability. Along with good risk management, effective financial planning is a must for getting around money problems. To successfully respond to changes in the economy, investors should figure out how much cash they need, look into a variety of financial options, and build strong relationships with lenders.

Also, organizational speed is very important for handling the growing practical complexity of a larger business. It is important for investors to make sure that their teams have the skills, information, and tools they need to handle a bigger and more varied business effectively. A strong business plan in the fast-paced real estate market is built on careful risk management, smart financial planning, and the ability to change with the times.

In summary, generating long-term wealth via portfolio expansion techniques is a deliberate and dynamic undertaking that requires a thorough understanding of investor objectives, risk considerations, and market dynamics. Astute investors use diverse growth tactics to create robust and lucrative portfolios, adopt technology tools, and use data-driven insights. Investors should position themselves for long-term success in the dynamic real estate market by using organizational agility, financial planning, and strategic risk management to surmount potential hurdles, including market volatility and operational complexity. The potential to generate long-term value ultimately rests on an expansion plan performed skillfully and aligned with the investor's long-term wealth accumulation goals.

|12|

Long-Term Wealth Building and Legacy Planning

This chapter looks into the realm of using real estate to create a legacy and accumulate long-term wealth. We will discuss how to create wealth for future generations, how to ensure an orderly transfer of assets via estate planning, and even how you may use your real estate holdings to support charity and the community. The chapter also discusses how using moral and responsible real estate practices may have a long-lasting beneficial influence. So fasten your seatbelt and get ready to safeguard your legacy for future generations!

For the relevant case studies, worksheets and free resources you can visit: andonierealty.com

"Annual income twenty pounds, annual expenditure nineteen six, result happiness. Annual income twenty pounds, annual expenditure twenty pounds ought and six, result misery."

-Charles Dickens

12.1 Establishing Generational Wealth through Real Estate

Building generational wealth via real estate is a well-thought-out and proven strategy that entails purchasing, upkeep, and administrating real estate holdings to deliver enduring financial gains to many generations. Real estate has particular chances for generating money and leaving a lasting legacy since it is a tangible and appreciating asset. In this part, we will examine the main factors, tactics, and advantages of using real estate to build wealth for future generations.

Essential Factors in Developing Generational Wealth:

Long-term, strategic planning that puts asset preservation and steady growth ahead of short-term benefits is needed to build wealth that lasts generations. Diversification and picking the right assets are very important in this process. Investors should carefully pick properties that have the potential to go up in value over time.

They should also think about spreading their risk across a number of different types of real estate to increase their income streams. Also, it takes careful financial planning to make sure that real estate purchases are in line with long-term goals. This includes figuring out what generational wealth is for, what the specific goals are, and how to make sure that assets are passed on smoothly to future generations. For successful wealth protection, it is also important to teach family members about real estate buying and encourage open communication. These steps make sure that future generations understand the importance and duties of handling real estate assets, which keeps wealth going from one generation to the next.

Techniques for Creating Generational Wealth:

Buying land in a smart way is the key to passing on wealth from one family to the next. Investors should look for properties that have strong economic indicators and can handle changes in the market. These properties should also show signs of long-term growth. Using real estate as a way to make smart financial decisions can help you get rich much faster. Using debt, buyers can buy more expensive homes, which increases the chance of passing on wealth and maximizes returns on capital spent. Focusing on properties that bring in money, like business spaces or rental flats, ensures a steady flow of cash, which makes the real estate stock more stable and offers ongoing financial support for future generations.

Smart tax planning is also important for passing on wealth from one family to the next. Investors should look into tax benefits related to real estate, like 1031 swaps and depreciation discounts, to get the most out of their money and pay the least amount of taxes over time.

Advantages of Using Real Estate to Build Generational Wealth:

Real estate has a long history of going up in value over time. This makes it a great way to preserve wealth and leave a valuable memory for future generations. If you choose the right properties and take good care of them, you can protect your wealth and give your children and grandchildren a steady stream of passive income. This money can be invested, used for school, or used to help family members when the economy is bad. Investing in real estate also lets you spread your money out among different types of properties and places, which lowers your total risk. Diversifying the stock keeps it strong even when the economy is unsure.

Investing in real estate is a smart way to protect against inflation. Real estate tends to appreciate over time while money loses buying power, offering a dependable way to protect purchasing power for coming generations.

Obstacles in Developing Generational Wealth:

When the economy is bad, property prices can drop by a lot, so you need a plan that is both planned and flexible to deal with market instability. Succession planning is important for making sure that the transfer of assets goes smoothly. It includes legal issues, lowering estate taxes, and making sure that everyone knows their part in handling family real estate. Family relationships and conversation can also be hard, because fights or mistakes can happen that make it hard to pass on wealth. To solve these problems and make sure that wealth is passed on peacefully from one generation to the next, we need to have open conversations and teach people.

Techniques for Surmounting Obstacles:

Diversification and good risk management are important for real estate portfolios that want to lessen the effects of market changes. To do this, they have to carefully choose homes, keep an eye on market trends, and change their plans when money conditions change. Hiring professional experts and estate managers is important for succession planning problems because they help set up trusts, lower tax bills, and make sure that assets are transferred smoothly to future generations. Family schooling and government are also very important for getting past problems that come up because of how families work. Setting clear rules, roles, and ways to communicate helps everyone understand and commit to the long-term goal.

In conclusion, using real estate to build generational wealth is a robust, long-lasting method that calls for careful planning and consideration. Investors may leave a legacy that will last for many generations by embracing a long-term vision, carefully selecting income-producing assets, and implementing efficient financial and tax planning. Diversification, expert guidance, strong communication, and governance frameworks may help overcome obstacles, including market volatility, succession planning, and family dynamics. Ultimately, pursuing generational wealth via real estate investing is a commitment to creating a long-lasting financial legacy that will provide future family members opportunities, success, and financial stability.

12.2 Estate Planning and Succession Strategies

The smooth transfer of assets and wealth from generation to generation is greatly aided by estate and succession planning. Careful planning is necessary for real estate investments, where physical and valuable assets are involved, to guarantee that the intended beneficiaries can efficiently manage, protect, and increase their wealth. The main points, approaches, difficulties, and solutions related to succession planning and estate planning in the real estate industry will be covered in detail in this part.

Essential Things to Think About When Estate Planning:

Creating a comprehensive asset register is the first step in estate planning, involving a detailed inventory of all real estate holdings, such as land, commercial buildings, and residences, along with ownership information, appraisals, and existing mortgages. Evaluating the appropriate legal frameworks for real estate ownership, such as limited liability corporations (LLCs), trusts, or other entities, is crucial to support succession and estate planning goals. Understanding and minimizing tax implications, including estate taxes, is a key component of estate planning. Strategies like gifting, establishing trusts, and leveraging tax exemptions can reduce the tax burden on heirs. Clearly defining succession goals and objectives is essential, including identifying beneficiaries, asset allocation, and specifying any terms or conditions for transferring real estate holdings.

Techniques for Successful Estate Planning:

Setting up Family Limited Partnerships (FLPs) and trusts can help protect and handle real estate assets. They can also help with tax planning, protect assets from creditors, and give assets to family members in different ways. Giving gifts, like making yearly payments, using gift deductions, or using tools like Qualified Personal Residence Trusts (QPRTs), can help you pass on real estate to your children while minimizing the effects of estate tax. Life insurance can help with estate planning by giving you cash to pay estate taxes or settle bills. This way, your real estate assets will be safe for your heirs. As a family-owned business or partnership grows, buy-sell agreements can help with real estate assets. They make it easier to sell or move ownership interests when an owner dies by offering an organized framework.

Obstacles in the Planning of Estates:

Real estate costs change all the time, which makes it hard to correctly value assets for estate planning. This means that the estate plan needs to be reviewed on a regular basis to make sure it stays useful. Family relationships and possible disagreements among relatives can make the process even more difficult, as they may have different ideas about how to handle or divide up the real estate interests. This means that effective communication and conflict resolution skills are needed. It's also possible for changes in the rules and regulations, especially tax laws, to affect how well existing estate planning strategies work. So, it's important to do regular checks and changes to make sure cooperation and get the most out of planning methods.

Techniques for Surmounting Obstacles:

It is important to keep up with changes in the market and the law by reviewing the estate plan on a regular basis. Reassessments are done on a regular basis so that changes can be made to reflect changing asset prices and legal issues. Setting up family meetings and encouraging open conversation is a must for handling family relations and possible arguments. Heirs can work together and understand better if the reason for the estate plan is explained and they are involved in the conversation. It's also important to talk to professionals like lawyers who help people plan their estates, financial planners, and tax experts. These experts can help you through the complicated process of estate planning, give you useful advice, and make sure the plan follows all current laws and rules.

Advantages of Sophisticated Estate Planning

Good estate planning keeps money safe for future generations by carefully handling things like taxes, appraisals, and who owns what. This makes it easy to pass on real estate assets. Good estate planning also makes sure that homes or businesses that bring in money keep running, so that the next owners can take over management tasks without any problems. By using tax-efficient arrangements and deductions, smart estate planning also lowers tax bills, making sure that a bigger share of the estate is left to children. This method makes it easier for families to pass on wealth from one generation to the next. This gives future generations financial protection and chances based on real estate assets.

In summary, succession planning and estate planning are essential elements of prudent and strategic asset management, especially regarding real estate investments. People may guarantee the seamless transfer of real estate assets to successors by attending to important factors, implementing ideas, and actively handling obstacles. Beyond just keeping money safe, the advantages include keeping things running smoothly, lowering tax obligations, and leaving a lasting legacy. To ensure that estate plans are updated to reflect evolving laws and regulations and to ensure the long-term success of real estate assets and the family heritage, it is essential that expert advisers be included in the process and that frequent reviews be conducted.

12.3 Philanthropy and Community Contribution through Real Estate Success

A revolutionary approach to wealth management, philanthropy and community service via real estate success highlights the beneficial effects that real estate investments can have on local communities and society. In this part, we will look at the main factors, tactics, advantages, and difficulties of using real estate success to support charitable causes and community improvement.

Essential Factors to Take Into Account When Thinking About Philanthropy and Community Contribution:

Real estate charity starts with understanding the social responsibility that comes with being successful. With a strong commitment to promoting good social benefits, real estate owners can make cities better places to live and work. Getting involved with local groups and figuring out what they need are important steps. For investors to make the most of their charitable efforts, they need to know the unique possibilities and problems of a given place. Aligning charity work with business ideals makes sure that the donations are in line with the real estate company's goal and brand. When real estate is used for charity, long-term survival is very important. Building strong partnerships with community partners and completing projects that provide long-term benefits are two ways to help communities grow in a way that lasts.

Techniques for Philanthropy and Community Contribution:

By putting money into cheap housing programs, real estate success can improve the health of the neighborhood. This could mean building cheap housing units, working with groups that fight for affordable housing, or baking projects that make housing more affordable. Contributing to the building of community assets like parks, schools, and medical facilities is another way to improve the quality of life for people. Developers of real estate can put money and time into projects that meet important local needs. When real estate businesses work with groups and non-governmental organizations (NGOs), they can use the knowledge of their established partners to make sure their charitable efforts are carried out well and have a bigger impact.

By giving communities access to resources and information, education and skills development programs empower communities. Success in real estate may finance initiatives that foster the person's and the community's development, such as mentoring, vocational training, and scholarships.

Benefits of Community Service and Philanthropy:

Real estate groups' public image and standing are greatly improved when they do charity work. Doing good things in the community gets people to back you, which builds trust and goodwill among all parties. Contributing to community development builds stronger bonds with local government and people, which makes it easier for new projects to start up. Giving to others helps build a permanent reputation in real estate, having a good effect on communities that goes beyond making money and improves the entity's long-term image. Also, people who work for real estate companies that care about giving back to the community often take pride in their jobs. Staff happiness and engagement go up when they take part in community service projects, which give them a feeling of purpose and satisfaction.

Challenges in Community Contribution and Charity:

Real estate companies have a hard time finding the right balance between making money and helping others. They have to make sure that their charity work helps the business stay in business and fits with its goals. Also, doing detailed community needs surveys is hard because you need to involve local partners, spend time and money, and talk to them to really understand the community's many needs. For charity efforts to have a long-lasting effect, they need to be planned strategically and supported over time. Real estate groups need to come up with plans for staying effective over the long term, since keeping up these efforts over time can be hard.

Techniques for Surmounting Obstacles:

One way to ensure that community donations align with company aims is to integrate philanthropic planning into overall business plans. This integrated strategy addresses the problem of balancing altruism and profitability.

Partnerships and collaboration with local NGOs, governmental organizations, and other stakeholders can address the complexities of community needs assessments. These partnerships enable more efficient and targeted charitable efforts by leveraging local knowledge. Establishing measurable impact metrics is crucial for ensuring long-term influence. Real estate organizations should set specific objectives, monitor progress, and routinely evaluate the success of their philanthropic initiatives to enhance sustainability.

In conclusion, real estate prosperity combined with philanthropy and community service is a potent combination that may bring about good change and leave a long-lasting legacy. Real estate organizations may support the growth and well-being of the communities in which they operate by considering the particular requirements of such communities, coordinating activities with corporate principles, and putting sustainable plans into practice.

The advantages surpass the excellent press, including improved employee morale, legacy building, and community relations. While there are obstacles to overcome, such as striking a balance between charity and profitability, real estate success may be associated with good social effect and community enrichment via collaborations, strategic integration, and a dedication to demonstrable impact.

12.4 Creating Lasting Legacies with Real Estate Assets

Real estate assets need a deliberate and strategic approach to wealth management beyond short-term financial gain to leave enduring legacies. This section will examine the main factors, tactics, advantages, and difficulties related to creating long-lasting legacies via the prudent use and maintenance of real estate assets.

Essential Things to Think About When Leaving a Legacy:

When people buy real estate with the goal of leaving a long legacy, they need to think about how their holdings will help future generations financially and personally. Protecting and increasing the value of assets is very important. This means choosing properties that will hold their value over time, keeping them in good shape, and keeping an eye on market trends to find growth possibilities. Complete law and succession planning is necessary to set up ownership in a way that minimizes taxes, supports family goals, and makes sure that assets are transferred smoothly to the next generation. Building a memory also requires a dedication to social responsibility and making a difference in the community. People who own property can make a change that lasts by giving back to the areas where their homes are located.

Techniques for Leaving a Permanent Legacy:

Giving money to conservation and preservation projects helps leave a valuable legacy by making sure that ancient buildings, culturally important sites, and natural areas will be around for future generations. Setting up foundation funds or trusts to protect and improve real estate assets gives them ongoing support and resources, which helps the growth of the community and the long-term stability of the land. Putting money into cultural and educational programs has an even longer-lasting effect, as real estate owners contribute to projects that improve their communities' education, arts, and culture. Legacy-building efforts are also strengthened by making nonprofit relationships with community organizations and groups. This lets real estate owners support causes that are important to them by using their current networks and skills.

Advantages of Leaving a Legacy:

Leaving lasting gifts is a good way to pass on wealth from one family to the next. Real estate owners can make sure that future generations will have enough money by keeping and growing their property and leaving a lot of value for the next generation. memory-building projects that help people improve a real estate owner's lasting memory by creating public places, enhancing culture, and boosting the economy.

This dedication to leaving lasting memories also boosts image and recognition over time, connecting real estate owners with positive social benefits and encouraging people and stakeholders to be friendly with them. Supporting culture and natural protection with money also improves society as a whole. People who own land can leave behind scenery, ancient sites, and ethnic groups that will be cared for by future generations.

Obstacles to Leaving a Lasting Legacy:

The maintenance and appreciation of assets are confronted with obstacles due to market dynamics and economic developments. Adaptive solutions are necessary since real estate prices are subject to fluctuations, and economic downturns may influence the overall financial health of assets.

It might be challenging to ensure a seamless transfer of assets when dealing with complex succession planning. Careful preparation and execution are necessary to address legal issues, reduce tax obligations, and specify successors' tasks. Maintaining many work endeavors over the long haul might be challenging. Real estate owners may need to modify and improve their charitable initiatives in response to community needs, economic situations, or leadership changes.

Techniques for Surmounting Obstacles:

Managing risks in a strong way is important for dealing with problems that come up when the economy and markets change. Real estate owners should look over their plans from time to time and make changes as needed to keep up with changing conditions. For succession planning to work, professional planners and lawyers must be involved. These experts can help with making effective succession plans, tax strategies, and managing the complicated legal system. Charity work also needs to be evaluated and changed on a regular basis to make sure it has a long-lasting effect. Real estate owners should keep up with how the community's needs are changing, stay in touch with their partners, and make changes to their strategies as needed to stay effective and current.

In conclusion, using real estate assets to leave enduring legacies is a deliberate and forward-thinking project that calls for a blend of strategic planning, community involvement, and dedication to good effect. Real estate owners may leave lasting legacies beyond financial success by considering intergenerational aspirations, protecting and valuing assets, and participating in charitable projects. Robust risk management, consulting with experts, and ongoing strategy reviews may help tackle issues, including market fluctuations, complicated succession planning, and maintaining charity. Ultimately, the goal of leaving enduring legacies via real estate assets embodies a comprehensive approach to wealth management—one that considers the welfare of coming generations, the sound effects on local communities, and a dedication to preserving the environment and culture.

12.5 Embracing Ethical and Responsible Real Estate Practices for a Lasting Impact

Adopting morally and responsibly-driven real estate strategies is essential to making an influence that lasts longer than just financial gain. This commitment entails incorporating social, environmental, and governance factors into decision-making processes to ensure that real estate investments favorably impact communities, the environment, and stakeholders' overall well-being.

This part will examine the main factors, tactics, advantages, and difficulties of adopting moral and responsible real estate activities.

Essential Things to Think About When Practicing Ethical and Responsible Real Estate:

Ethical real estate businesses put community involvement and social impact at the top of their list of priorities. They want to make places that are welcoming and good for everyone, improving the quality of life for locals while also thinking about how their actions might affect other people. It is also important to be environmentally beneficial, so projects use eco-friendly designs, energy-efficient technologies, and long-lasting building materials to leave as little of an impact on the environment as possible. Transparency and good governance are very important. Honest real estate agents uphold high standards of governance, make sure that financial information is clear, and follow all laws and rules. Ethical real estate practices try to make places available to a wide range of people, supporting equality and stopping overcrowding and other changes that leave some people out.

Ways to Adopt Responsible and Ethical Behaviors:

A fundamental approach is to engage and consult with stakeholders, which includes people, local communities, and advocacy organizations. Real estate professionals may make well-informed judgments that meet the community's requirements by getting feedback and comprehending different points of view.

It is very important to follow green building and sustainability standards if you care about the environment. Certifications like LEED (Leadership in Energy and Environmental Design) help real estate projects move toward eco-friendly building and design methods. Ethical investment screening looks at possible projects using social and environmental factors to make sure that investments are in line with ethical and long-lasting ideals. Fair housing and anti-discrimination laws must also be put in place to promote equality and inclusion. In order to make sure that everyone can find a place to live, ethical real estate practices actively work to get rid of discriminatory practices.

Advantages of Adopting Responsibly and Ethically:

Ethical behavior makes a real estate company's image and business much better. These practices build trust and goodwill among partners by doing good things for communities, putting environmental sustainability first, and keeping the government open and honest. Developing things that are based on doing things in an ethical and environmentally sound way often show that they can adapt to changes in the market and weather economic downturns better. Being decent and responsible also creates long-term value, since properties that take into account their social and environmental effects tend to go up in value over time, which is good for both communities and businesses. Companies that follow ethical standards also attract socially responsible investors. These investors are giving more and more weight to ethical factors when making investment decisions, which makes it easier for companies to form partnerships and get money.

Difficulties in Adopting Responsibly and Ethically:

Costs Poison: One issue is that being decent and responsible often costs more at first. For example, it might cost a lot to start using green technology and goods that last a long time. On the other hand, the long-term benefits often outweigh the costs in the beginning. Finding the Right Balance: Businesses, neighborhoods, and environmental groups all have different needs, and it can be hard to find a situation where all of them are met. Ethics says that these different goals need to be taken into account when making a plan that works for everyone. Regulatory Complexity: Another issue is how to handle the complexity of regulations and the fact that different places have different needs. Companies in the real estate business have to follow many rules and laws. When new laws and rules come out, they have to change how they do business.

Techniques for Surmounting Obstacles:

Life Cycle Cost Analysis: This method helps with money worries by letting real estate pros figure out how much ethical and environmentally friendly practices will save them in the long run. Putting money into these practices early on can lower costs over time and raise the value of assets. Effective Communication and Engagement: To balance interests, you need to communicate and interact with people in a useful way. To deal with different points of view, real estate companies should actively ask for comments, encourage open communication, and share information in a clear way. Full Compliance Management: Full compliance management tools make it easier to understand the complicated rules that apply to your business. Companies in the real estate industry can spend money on strong systems that keep an eye on changing ethical and environmentally-friendly rules and make sure they are followed.

In summary, adopting moral and conscientious real estate practices is a revolutionary strategy that surpasses conventional profit-driven frameworks. Real estate professionals may have long-lasting effects that benefit communities, investors, and the environment by considering social impact, environmental sustainability, and governance principles. Strategies like life cycle cost analysis, effective communication, and complete compliance management may be used to solve challenges, including cost considerations, stakeholder balancing acts, and regulatory complications. In the end, including morality and responsibility in real estate operations leaves a good legacy, promotes the production of long-term value, and establishes real estate companies as pioneers in environmentally and socially responsible development.

|13|

International Real Estate Opportunities

The world is at your disposal! The fascinating world of foreign real estate markets is unlocked in this chapter. We'll dive into investigating international prospects, provide you with foreign investment techniques, and help you negotiate the subtle cultural and legal differences in other markets. This chapter will provide you with the tools you need to successfully handle risks and difficulties. It will also show you how you may use overseas investments to diversify your portfolio and spur development. So fasten your seatbelts and get ready to discover the wide world of global real estate!

For the relevant case studies, worksheets and free resources you can visit: andonierealty.com

"He is not a full man who does not own a piece of land."

-Hebrew Proverb

13.1 Exploring Global Real Estate Markets and Opportunities

Understanding real estate dynamics on a global scale is necessary for exploring global real estate markets and prospects. The main factors, tactics, advantages, and disadvantages of entering international real estate markets are examined in this section.

Important Things to Take Into Account When Researching International Real Estate Markets:

Stability in politics and the economy: Investors need stability in politics and the economy to lower the risks that come with market volatility and global problems. These risks can be lowered by looking at a country's political and economic situations. Culture and Legal Differences: It's important to understand culture and legal differences in order to do well in real estate deals. Cultural norms and country law systems can have a big effect on these deals, and buyers need to fully understand these issues in order to deal with them successfully.

Trends in the Industry and Opportunities for Growth: To get the best return on investment, it's important to look at industry trends and opportunities for growth. Investors should look for places where population growth, economic growth, and new real estate possibilities are all looking good. Currency Exchange and Financial Risks: When dealing in foreign real estate, there are big risks with currency exchange and money. Changes in the value of a currency can have an effect on results, so investors need to be good at managing these risks to keep their investments safe.

Methods for Researching International Real Estate Markets:

Local Partnerships and Expertise: Real estate owners should take advantage of local knowledge and form partnerships as a smart move. Working with experienced professionals who know the ins and outs of a certain market helps you make better decisions and lowers your risks. Regional Diversification: One good way to spread risk is to spread assets across different areas. With this approach, buyers can take advantage of growth opportunities around the world and different market situations. Due Diligence: It is important to do a lot of research before making a decision. Before investing in a new market, investors should do a lot of study on possible dangers and look at the governing environment. This will help them make smart investment choices. Flexibility in Response to Local Laws: It is very important to be flexible when following local laws. Real estate owners need to know and follow the rules in each country, making sure that their strategies are tailored to the country's laws.

Advantages of Researching International Real Estate Markets:

Diversifying your portfolio: One of the best things about investing in real estate in foreign markets is that it lets you spread your risk across different countries and take advantage of different market situations. Access to High-Development Markets: International markets offer chances for fast growth, especially in growing regions and economies that are just starting out. This is especially true for real estate investments that could yield big profits. Resilience of the Portfolio: A widely varied portfolio is more likely to be durable because it is less likely to be hurt by changes in regional markets or economic downturns. This makes the portfolio more stable overall. Making Money with Market Trends: Investors can make money with different market trends in different parts of the world by spotting and taking advantage of certain market traits, like trends in development or technology progress, which sets them up for success.

Difficulties in Researching International Real Estate Markets:

Foreign Exchange Risks: Changes in currency can affect how profitable foreign real estate purchases are, so it's important to use good risk management techniques like hedging. Language and cultural barriers: These can make it harder to negotiate and come to an understanding. Setting up good ways to communicate and using local knowledge can help you get past these problems. Regulatory Complexity: To get around the complicated rules of foreign real estate markets, you have to carefully change your plans to follow local laws. Hedging Against Currency Risks: To protect themselves against bad currency moves and keep profits stable, investors often use hedging techniques that involve financial tools and swaps.

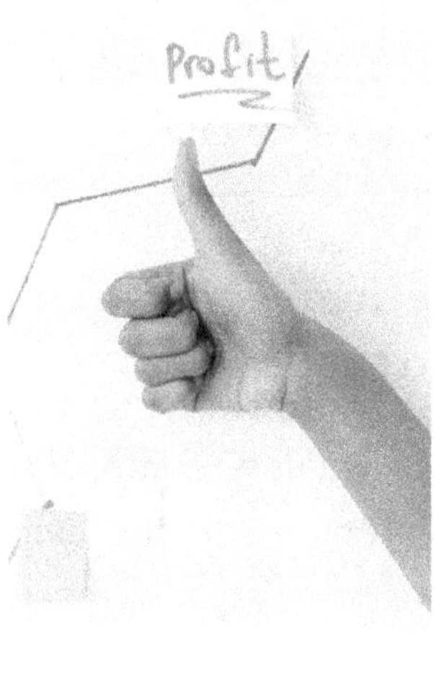

Effective communication is facilitated by engaging multilingual experts. Hiring individuals proficient in the native tongue and aware of customs and traditions improves the negotiating process and teamwork in general.

It's essential to monitor any regulation changes. To guarantee compliance and reduce legal risks, investors should set up strong procedures for monitoring and adjusting to changing rules in each market.

Investigating international real estate markets and prospects offers investors looking to diversify their holdings and profit from new trends a dynamic way to do so. Benefits include robustness, access to high-growth markets, portfolio diversity, and the chance to profit from emerging trends. However, drawbacks, such as regulatory complexity, cultural barriers, and foreign currency concerns, call for calculated strategies to be addressed.

Key tactics for navigating the complexities of international real estate transactions include:

- Forming local alliances.
- Carrying out extensive due diligence.
- Making adjustments to local rules.

Global real estate ventures ultimately come down to having a thorough awareness of the legal, cultural, and economic context of each market being pursued and a dedication to flexibility and calculated risk management.

13.2 Strategies for Investing in International Properties

Since cross-border real estate projects provide special potential and problems, investing in properties abroad demands careful consideration. In this part, we will go over important factors, tactics, advantages, and disadvantages of investing in foreign real estate.

Important Things to Think About When Investing in Foreign Real Estate:

Market Research and Due Diligence: Real estate owners need to do a lot of research on the market and do their homework. You need to know about the target country's laws, customs, and economy in order to make smart choices. This means looking at things like real estate laws, market trends, and possible risks. Currency Exchange and Financial Planning: It's important to think about currency exchange because changes can have an effect on profits. Investors should make thorough financial plans that include currency risks and possible ways to lower those risks. Local Laws and Rules: It's important to know the rules and laws in your area because each country has its own set of laws that govern real estate deals. Investors need to understand these details to make sure they follow the rules and reduce their potential risks. Tax Effects: You should carefully think about the tax effects in the target country. Capital gains, rental income, and property ownership taxes can have a big impact on the general profits of an investment.

Techniques for Purchasing Real Estate Abroad:

Local Expertise and relationships: Using local information and making relationships is a smart move. Working with experts in the law, property management, and real estate fields of the target country helps you understand new markets better and lowers the risks that come with them. Spreading risk and lowering the impact of economic downturns or global problems in any one area can be done by spreading investments across multiple countries.

This makes for a more stable investment strategy. Putting money into emerging markets: Putting money into emerging markets can be very rewarding. Even though these economies offer unique chances for growth, investors should carefully weigh the risks and unknowns that come with them against the possible benefits. Using Technology for Remote Management: It is necessary to use technology for managing properties from afar. Property management tools, video walks, and online platforms make it easier to keep an eye on things and talk to people, especially when people are far away.

Advantages of Purchasing Foreign Real Estate:

One of the main advantages is diversification, which also helps with risk mitigation. Purchasing real estate abroad diversifies an investor's portfolio overall, lowering reliance on the state of the economy in a particular nation and lowering the risk associated with certain regions.

When you invest abroad, you can take advantage of special chances that you might not be able to find in your own country. This includes interesting buildings, new markets, and real estate trends that are different from what the owner is used to in their home country. One more benefit is the chance of better earnings, since some foreign markets may have a lot of room to grow. Investors can get capital gains and higher renting income by finding new trends or markets that aren't being priced properly. Investing in other countries also subjects owners to changes in the world economy. They can take advantage of global economic growth through foreign real estate purchases by making sure their assets are in line with larger economic moves and trends.

The following are some difficulties when investing in foreign real estate:

Shifts in the value of the currency can be very difficult because they can affect the value of rental income and property prices, adding another level of risk and complexity. Legal and governmental threats change from country to country, so investors have to learn how to deal with different legal systems and could have problems with their contractual responsibilities, land ownership rights, and following local rules. Transactions can also be hard when there are language and cultural obstacles. To keep business methods clear and consistent, people must be able to communicate well and be sensitive to regional differences.

Techniques for Surmounting Obstacles:

One popular tactic to lessen the effects of currency swings is currency hedging. Financial instruments provide a degree of stability to profits by shielding investors from unfavorable fluctuations in exchange rates. It is essential to consult with and involve legal experts in the target nation. Investors may reduce legal risks and ensure compliance by using legal consulting and due diligence to assist them in managing the intricacies of local rules.

The enhancement of cooperation may be achieved via the use of cultural awareness and communication training. Cultural sensitivity training is necessary for property managers and investors to close communication barriers and build productive working relationships. Investing in foreign real estate means achieving diversity, exclusive prospects, and exposure to worldwide economic patterns. However, it provides difficulties because of exchange rate volatility, intricate legal and regulatory frameworks, and cultural disparities. Investors must first put due diligence, strategic alliances with local specialists, and in-depth market research to manage these obstacles effectively.

A well-rounded strategy includes diversification across national borders, using technology for remote management, and knowledge of possible hazards. In the end, foreign real estate investing necessitates risk management, strategic planning, and flexibility to the subtleties of other markets, guaranteeing that investors may profit while skillfully handling the related difficulties.

13.3 Understanding Cultural and Legal Differences in Foreign Markets

One essential component of international real estate investing is comprehending other real estate marketplaces' cultural and legal variations. Negotiating the complexities of various legal systems and cultural norms is essential to the success of cross-border real estate projects. In this part, we will go over the main points, tactics, advantages, and difficulties of understanding legal and cultural differences in international marketplaces.

Important Things to Keep in Mind When Interpreting Cultural and Legal Differences:

Social norms, speaking styles, and business practices vary a lot from country to country, and these differences play a big role in real estate talks. These differences can make it harder to negotiate, build relationships, and do business in foreign areas in general. Legal systems also vary a lot from one country to the next. To make sure they follow local rules, buyers need to know about property laws, contractual agreements, and conflict settlement processes. Different cultures have different rules about how to behave and do business. What is morally and socially okay in one culture might not be okay in another. To build trust and make business relationships that work, it's important to follow local business practices and show cultural knowledge. Also, different people can have very different ideas about who owns something and what their rights are when it comes to property. Because of this, investors need to know about local ownership structures, land tenure systems, and property rights in order to protect their assets and stay out of trouble with the law.

Techniques for Recognizing Legal and Cultural Disparities:

Relationships and local advisors: It's very important to talk to local advisors and make connections with people in the area. Working with experts who know the cultural and legal context can help you make smart decisions about how to do business in foreign markets. Cultural Training for Teams: It is very important to give business teams cultural training. Investors and their teams should get training to learn more about regional differences, speaking styles, and business etiquette so they can make more useful contacts in foreign markets.

Legal Advice and Research: It is very important to talk to lawyers in the country you want to buy from. Investors can understand and follow local laws better with the help of due research and legal advice. This makes sure that real estate deals follow the rules of the foreign market. Local influence: Having local influence is a good thing. By hiring local professionals like real estate agents, lawyers, and property managers, you can get useful advice and help from the ground up. This makes deals easier and helps you understand cultural and legal nuances better.

Advantages of Recognizing Legal and Cultural Differences

Understanding cultural differences helps people get along and trust each other, which lets businesses form good, long-lasting ties with local stakeholders. Being sensitive to other cultures can help you negotiate better by helping you understand how decisions are made, how to negotiate, and how to communicate, which can lead to win-win deals in foreign markets. Understanding the differences between laws is important for following the rules and lowering risks. This helps businesses get around the legal systems of other countries and stay out of trouble with the law. Investors are more likely to solve problems and be successful when their plans are in line with the legal and cultural rules of foreign markets. Being able to change to local business practices gives you a competitive edge.

Difficulties in Comprehending Legal and Cultural Differences:

Miscommunication and misunderstanding can happen because of cultural differences. For example, language hurdles, different ways of communicating, and different ways of reading business signs can all make it harder to complete a deal. Legal compliance risks are big problems because not knowing enough about local laws can cause people to break the rules without meaning to, which can cause legal problems and even financial losses. It's also possible to lose touch with other cultures. Not recognizing and respecting cultural norms can cause problems in relationships, slow down talks, and hurt investors' names in foreign markets.

Techniques for Surmounting Obstacles:

Continuous cultural education is important for owners and their teams. To stay up to date on cultural details, changes in the global market, and new trends, they should take part in programs that offer continuous learning. By knowing both cultures, cultural mediators and translators can help close communication gaps, making sure that messages get across correctly and encouraging good communication. It is important to hire lawyers who are experts in the real estate laws of the target country. This way, you can better understand the legal details and lower the risk of not following the rules. Training on cultural sensitivity is also a practical way to make sure that everyone on the team knows about business etiquette and cultural differences. This will help to avoid mistakes in cultural sensitivity and make conversations more effective overall.

A key component of a successful global real estate investment is knowing international real estate markets' cultural and legal variations. Establishing trust, cultivating healthy relationships, and guaranteeing legal compliance all depend on the capacity to negotiate a variety of cultural quirks and legal systems. A complete strategy for comprehending and adjusting to the distinctive features of international markets includes tactics like local alliances, cultural training, legal consulting, and ongoing education. Ultimately, investors are better positioned to negotiate obstacles, seize opportunities, and establish a long-lasting presence in international real estate when prioritizing cultural and legal knowledge.

13.4 Managing Risks and Challenges in International Investments

Managing risks and difficulties in foreign real estate investments is a difficult undertaking that calls for thoughtful deliberation, clever preparation, and flexibility. There are many unknowns when investing in overseas markets, such as cultural, legal, economic, and geopolitical aspects. This part will examine important factors, practical tactics, and the advantages of skillfully handling risks and difficulties in foreign real estate investments.

Important Things to Think About When Managing Risks and Challenges:

It is very important to think about geopolitical security because political unrest, policy changes, and geopolitical issues can all have a big effect on the real estate market. To predict and deal with these risks, investors need to keep an eye on and evaluate the global situation. Inflation, exchange rates, and economic downturns are all important economic factors that affect both property costs and rental income. To figure out how stable and likely to grow the target market is, investors need to do in-depth economic studies. Law and rule compliance is very important. Investors have to learn how to deal with different legal systems and make sure they follow local rules to avoid legal risks and problems that come from not following the rules. Cultural and social factors are both important. It's important to understand local tastes, habits, and cultural norms in order to communicate clearly, build relationships, and get people in the community to accept new housing projects. Lastly, market liquidity and exit plans are very important things to think about. Investors should look at how easy it is to buy or sell assets in the market and come up with good exit plans to lower the risks that come with changing market conditions.

Techniques for Handling Difficulties and Risks:

Diversification and Portfolio Allocation: One way to lower risk is to spread assets across different types of real estate and locations. A varied strategy helps lessen the effect of bad things happening in one market, which spreads risk more evenly. Extensive Due investigation: It is very important to do thorough due investigation. Spending time and money on thorough study that includes legal, financial, and market analysis helps with making smart decisions and finding possible risks.

Local Knowledge and Partnerships: It's important to use local knowledge and make deals with experts in your field. Local partners can help you deal with legal issues, make purchases easier, and give you useful information about how the market works. Tools for reducing risk: Using tools to lower risk, like insurance and financial swaps, can protect assets from things that might not go as planned.

These tools give you a way to protect your money from risks like global unrest, currency fluctuations, and more. Constant Monitoring and Flexibility: It is very important to keep an eye on the market conditions and the political situation at all times. Investors who are adaptable and aware of how things are changing can quickly change their plans to lower risks as they appear.

Advantages of Successful Risk and Challenge Management:

Improved Portfolio Resilience: Good risk management makes the portfolio more resilient, which means it can handle problems like economic downturns and unstable geopolitics better over the long run.

Legal Risk Mitigation: Taking care of risks ahead of time lowers legal risks. Investors can avoid legal problems by learning about local rules, making sure they are followed, and applying legal rights.

Best Returns on Investment: Best returns on investment come from managing risks well. By reducing the effects of bad things that might happen, buyers set themselves up to take advantage of good market conditions and make the most money possible.

Better Reputation and Trust: Investors' reputation and trust are improved when risk management is done well. Stakeholders and possible partners will trust you more if you have a reputation for handling problems well and lowering risks.

Obstacles in Risk Management and Solutions:

Uncertainties in the market provide difficulties. Diversification, careful due diligence, and ongoing monitoring to recognize and adjust to changing market circumstances are some strategies to overcome this. Complicated laws and regulations might be difficult to understand. To overcome this, one must use local knowledge, do extensive due diligence, and set up explicit compliance procedures to operate around regulatory systems. There are always geopolitical concerns when making foreign investments. Maintaining up-to-date knowledge of international geopolitical trends, having flexible investment strategies, and ongoing monitoring are all effective ways to mitigate geopolitical risks.

In conclusion, managing risks and difficulties in foreign real estate investments effectively is a complex task that requires a proactive and flexible strategy. Investors may create methods to reduce possible risks by considering important variables, including geopolitical stability, economic circumstances, legal and regulatory compliance, and cultural dynamics.

A strong risk management strategy must include diversification, extensive due diligence, local relationships, and the utilization of risk mitigation tools. Effective risk management may improve portfolio resilience, lessen legal risk, maximize profits, and improve the international real estate industry's standing. Although foreign investments always present certain difficulties, investors who successfully manage them set themselves up for long-term success in international real estate's exciting and lucrative world.

13.5 Leveraging International Investments for Diversification and Growth

A strategy method known as "leveraging international investments for growth and diversification" entails spreading real estate portfolios across worldwide markets to boost resilience, take advantage of various economic situations, and open up growth prospects. The main factors, tactics, advantages, and difficulties of using foreign investments for development and diversification will all be covered in this part.

Important Things to Think About When Using Foreign Investments:

Real estate buyers need to know about the world economic trends. By looking at economic factors like GDP growth, job rates, and inflation, you can find places where investing in real estate is a good idea. Diversifying your market is very important. Buying real estate in different countries and areas spreads your risk and makes you less dependent on the economic success of a single area, which makes your portfolio more stable.

It is also important to look at the risk-return ratio of each foreign market. When investors think about things like exchange rate instability, global stability, and the complexity of regulations, they need to carefully weigh the risks and possible benefits. Besides that, exchange rates are also very important. Investors should figure out how changes in the value of a currency affect their profits and use trading strategies to lower the risks that come with bad exchange rate changes.

Techniques for Making the Most of Foreign Investments:

Diversified Portfolio Allocation: Spreading assets across different asset classes and regional areas is a key way to lower total risk by making sure the portfolio isn't too focused on one type or market of real estate. Worldwide Market study: It is important to do in-depth study on the global market. To make smart financial choices, people who want to put their money in foreign markets should look at economic data, real estate market trends, and the rules and regulations that apply to those countries. ties and knowledge in the area: Using local knowledge and forming ties is a smart move.

Working together with real estate agents, lawyers, and property managers in each target market helps everyone understand and makes deals go more smoothly. Strategic Asset Allocation: It is very important to carefully allocate assets based on financial goals and market situations. To get the best yields and minimize risk, investors should look at how each asset class does in different parts of the world and change their holdings accordingly.

Advantages of International Investment Leverage:

One big benefit of having investments in many different countries is that it makes the stock more stable. Geographical diversification makes the stock less vulnerable to changes in regional markets or economic downturns, which promotes stability and long-term viability. Another benefit is access to markets with high growth. For example, foreign investments can go into new countries and rising economies, which can offer unique chances for real estate development and possibly higher profits. Currency diversity is also a good idea because buying in more than one currency lowers your exposure to the economy of a single country and lowers the risks that come with currency fluctuations, making your profits more stable. Overall, foreign variety can improve the risk-return profile, letting investors aim for higher yields while keeping portfolio risk under control.

Difficulties in Making the Most of Foreign Investments:

Investing internationally has some inherent geopolitical risks. Changes in government regulations, unanticipated geopolitical developments, or diplomatic disputes may affect real estate markets and provide difficulties for investors. This is a problem. Exchange rate fluctuations may influence returns and raise investor uncertainty. Therefore, it's important to have appropriate currency risk management techniques in place.

Investors face difficulties due to cultural and regulatory complications. One must possess flexibility and comprehensive knowledge to successfully negotiate the differences in corporate processes, legal frameworks, and cultural norms.

Techniques for Surmounting Obstacles:

To manage the risks that come with investing in other countries, you need to use a variety of trading strategies. Financial tools and swaps are ways for investors to protect themselves against threats like changes in the value of the dollar and problems in other countries. Investors can quickly change their plans and reduce new risks by keeping a close eye on the global social and economic scene and being able to adapt to new situations. It is a good idea to talk to local risk managers because they know a lot about the political, economic, and cultural parts of each market and can help buyers deal with problems and make smart choices.

In short, investors looking to create robust and dynamic real estate portfolios must strategically use foreign assets for development and diversity. International investments are a desirable alternative due to portfolio robustness, currency diversity, access to high-growth regions, and an optimized risk-return profile. However, for risk management to be successful, considerations including geopolitical hazards, volatile currency exchange rates, and cultural complexity must be considered. By implementing diverse hedging techniques, ongoing monitoring of worldwide circumstances, and consultation with local risk experts, investors may effectively manage obstacles and fully realize the potential of their international real estate assets. Ultimately, a well-rounded strategy that incorporates market analysis, risk reduction techniques, and strategic allocation leads to long-term success in the international real estate market.

|14|

Impact of Technology on Real Estate

This chapter delves into the fascinating realm of how technology is transforming the real estate sector. We'll look into the possible advantages and disruptions of blockchain technology, examine how smart home technologies might improve your properties, and discover how big data and analytics can enable well-informed decision-making. This chapter gives you the tools to take advantage of technology developments and provide your real estate ventures a competitive edge. So fasten your seatbelts and get ready to harness the power of technology!

For the relevant case studies, worksheets and free resources you can visit: andonierealty.com

"Certainly the advent of technology and electronic commerce has had an immense impact on the real estate industry."

— Michael Oxley

14.1 Tech Innovations Revolutionizing the Real Estate Industry

Technology advancements are bringing a new age of efficiency, transparency, and improved user experiences in the real estate sector. In this part, we will examine the major technologies that are transforming the real estate market and their profound effects on several facets of the sector.

AI and ML have become indispensable instruments in the real estate industry. These systems analyze enormous amounts of information to provide insights into market trends, property prices, and investment possibilities. AI-powered chatbots are used to communicate with customers, respond to their questions, and provide property details. Algorithms that use machine learning may forecast real estate growth or spot possible hAugmented reality (AR) and virtual reality (VR) are changing the way real estate is shown by letting potential buyers or renters take video walks from afar and by adding digital information to the real world to create realistic, engaging experiences.

This is especially helpful for picturing home improvements or building jobs before they happen. Blockchain technology is changing the business world by providing a clear and safe way to do deals, making it easier to buy and sell things with smart contracts, keeping an unchangeable record of who owns property, and allowing partial ownership through tokenization. The Internet of Things (IoT) improves property management and energy efficiency by letting you handle home features from afar and making sure that business building equipment works at its best to cut costs and support sustainability. Big data analytics is important for finding patterns, trends, and business possibilities. It also helps predict market trends, understand how customers act, and make property management methods better. 3D printing is changing construction by making it possible to make building parts quickly and cheaply. This cuts down on trash and construction time and makes it possible to build complex architecture designs.

Mobile apps and platforms are changing the way real estate deals are made by giving buyers, owners, and agents up-to-date information on prices, features of the area, and available listings, as well as by making it easier for everyone to talk to each other and offering features like geolocation and virtual reality. Property managers use predictive analytics to guess what repairs will need to be done, how renters will act, and what problems might come up. By looking at past data and trends, this saves money and makes operations run more smoothly.

Impact on the Real Estate Sector:

New technologies make things more efficient by cutting down on paperwork and actual work by streamlining processes. For example, AI can quickly look at big sets of data and come up with ideas that would take humans a lot longer to find. This helps with things like market research, deal processing, and property evaluation. Blockchain technology's decentralized and unchangeable ledgers make real estate transactions more open and safe. They keep an accurate and impossible to fake record of who owns property and what transactions have happened on it. Better accessibility is achieved through smartphone apps and online platforms, which let more people look at homes from afar and allow smaller buyers to take part in real estate projects through their partial ownership model.

AR and VR are changing the way creative real estate marketing is done by giving users engaging experiences and virtual tours. This lets developers show off projects before they are built and lets buyers see homes from anywhere. 3D printing and the Internet of Things (IoT) are two technologies that help save money and the environment. IoT devices help buildings use less energy, and 3D printing cuts down on wasteful materials in construction, both of which are in line with the industry's focus on environmentally friendly methods. Big data analytics makes it easier to make decisions based on data. It also gives real estate workers useful information about client tastes, market trends, and business possibilities. Predictive analytics makes it possible to handle properties in a proactive and planned way.

Obstacles & Things to Think About:

There are security problems with every technology. Even though blockchain is thought to be safe, hackers can still get into it. To keep private information safe, real estate agents need to use strong protection means. Adding new technologies to systems that are already in place can also cause integration problems. When real estate companies don't want to change, it takes careful planning and spending money on staff training to make the transition go smoothly.

Another problem is following the rules, since using tokenization and blockchain technology makes the law more complicated. Real estate agents have to keep up with changing laws to make sure they follow area rules. Also, technology can make things easier to access, but it can also make a digital gap. Differences in the real estate market can be caused by differences in how easy it is for different people or places to get technology.

In conclusion, technological advancements are transforming the real estate sector and paving the way for an accessible, transparent, and efficient future. These technologies, which range from blockchain-enabled transactions to AI-driven analytics, are improving current procedures and radically altering how real estate is purchased, sold, and maintained. By adopting these technologies, real estate professionals may obtain a competitive advantage by providing better services, more efficient procedures, and creative solutions to satisfy the changing needs of the contemporary real estate market.

14.2 Implementing Smart Home Technologies for Property Enhancement

In real estate, implementing smart home technology revolutionizes houses created, operated, and experienced. Including smart home technology raises the value of a house overall and improves comfort, security, and energy efficiency. This section will examine the essential elements of integrating smart home technology and their influence on improving properties.

Smart home technologies are based on home management systems, which let people control their security, entertainment, heating and cooling systems, lights, and other devices from a single location. Voice-activated helpers, such as Google Assistant and Amazon's Alexa, make life easier by letting you handle smart gadgets without using your hands. Intelligent lighting systems have customizable features that can change the mood, color, and brightness based on daily routines and resident preferences. Motion monitors and smart switches save energy by turning off lights in places that aren't being used.

They also make homes safer by letting a remote control make it look like someone is there. Smart security systems have high-tech features like motion alarms, doorbell cameras, smart locks, and smart cameras. These features let you watch your property in real time and get quick alerts on your smartphone. Networked heating and cooling systems, like smart thermostats and HVAC systems, save energy by learning what temperatures tenants like and changing them accordingly. Mobile apps that let you handle these systems from afar make them more comfortable and use less energy. Energy management systems keep an eye on and manage how much energy is used in real time. They do this by giving information about usage trends and finding places where energy can be saved, which lowers electricity bills and helps reach sustainability goals. Smart blinds and shades and other automated window covers change based on temperature, sunlight, and time of day.

This makes the best use of insulation and natural light to save energy. Smart cooking systems and intelligent equipment, like smart ovens, dryers, and freezers, can be watched and controlled from afar, and voice helpers make it easy to do things in the kitchen without using your hands. With voice control and built-in sound systems, smart TVs, and streaming devices, home entertainment systems make it easy to enjoy both music and video in a way that is completely engaging.

Effect on Enhancement of Property:

Adding smart home technology to a house makes it more modern, appealing, and useful, which raises its value. More and more buyers are looking for homes that have smart technologies built in.

They value the energy-efficient systems and extra features that make homes stand out in the market. Smart houses are more competitive in the real estate market because they appeal to tech-savvy buyers who like the ease and quality of life benefits of smart home features. Another benefit is that automatic systems like smart lighting settings and heaters make the best use of energy and lower power bills. This fits with the growing focus on living in a more environmentally friendly way. Intelligent security systems make homes safer by letting owners watch and control security measures from afar.

This gives extra protection and keeps people from breaking in. Voice-activated helpers, automatic lights, and temperature control are just a few of the smart home technologies that make daily life much easier and more comfortable. Smart home technology also makes homes flexible and ready for the future by making it easy to add new devices or update old ones as technology changes. These features are especially appealing to people who want to buy homes that can adapt to new technologies. Additionally, smart home technology allows for a lot of customizing, so people can make their homes more comfortable and unique for themselves, which makes living there better overall.

Obstacles & Things to Think About:

Adding smart home technology can be pricey at first, as you may have to pay a lot for high-tech gadgets and tools. But the possible return on investment in the form of higher property prices and lower energy costs may be enough to cover these costs. It can also be hard and take a lot of time to connect different smart gadgets and systems. Homeowners need to make sure that all of their devices can talk to each other without any problems. To fix compatibility issues, some devices may need to be installed and set up by a professional. The data that smart house gadgets gather makes people worry about their privacy and safety. Homeowners need to take extra steps to protect their smart systems from people who shouldn't be able to get to them. In response to these worries, makers are constantly working to improve security measures. Smart home technology may also have a learning curve for users, since it takes time to get good at using and managing all the different systems and gadgets. Clear instructions and easy-to-use tools can make this shift easier.

The integration of smart home technology signifies a paradigm change in the improvement of real estate, presenting a plethora of advantages ranging from heightened market competitiveness and property value to better security and energy efficiency. Smart home technologies are becoming a necessary component of contemporary life as technology advances, offering homeowners comfort, flexibility, and convenience. Despite some obstacles, smart home technologies have a significant overall influence on property improvement. They are reshaping residential real estate into linked and inventive living environments that will shape the future.

14.3 Blockchain and Real Estate: Potential Disruption and Benefits

Blockchain technology offers previously unheard-of levels of efficiency, security, and transparency and is set to transform the real estate sector completely. Blockchain technology can improve real estate transactions by streamlining procedures, lowering fraud, and boosting public confidence in the real estate sector. This part will examine the advantages and possible disruption of blockchain technology in real estate.

Real Estate Understanding of Blockchain:

Blockchain is a distributed, decentralized ledger technology that makes it possible to create a transparent, safe record of transactions. Within the real estate domain, blockchain functions as an unchangeable and impervious database, documenting every property-associated activity, from acquisitions and sales to rentals and property administration.

Possible Disruption in Real Estate:

There are several important sectors in the real estate sector that blockchain might potentially affect: In a traditional property transaction, several intermediaries are involved, such as banks, title firms, real estate brokers, and government agencies. Blockchain technology may expedite this procedure by allowing smart contracts—self-executing contracts with the terms explicitly put into code. This shortens transaction times, eliminates the need for intermediaries, and lowers the possibility of mistakes. Titles to real estate are essential legal documents that prove who owns what. Blockchain technology may provide a permanent and secure record of property titles, lowering the possibility of fraud and streamlining the title transfer procedure. Title management is made more effective by smart contracts, which can automatically transfer ownership rights when specific criteria are satisfied.

By converting property values into digital tokens, blockchain technology enables the tokenization of real estate assets. This makes fractional ownership possible, opening up real estate investing to a wider group of investors. Because tokens may be exchanged on blockchain-based platforms, tokenization can help increase market liquidity in the real estate sector.

Blockchain's decentralized structure protects it against fraud and hacking. Property records kept on a blockchain are safe and unchangeable without network consensus. This lessens the possibility of dishonest acts like title fraud, in which someone tries to transfer ownership without the proper authority.

- Blockchain's Advantages for Real Estate

Numerous advantages that might completely change the real estate sector come from using blockchain technology:

Blockchain technology is based on two main ideas: transparency and immutability. Authorized users can see all transactions on the blockchain right away, and transactions can't be changed after they've been recorded. This openness and inflexibility boosts trust among stakeholders, which makes disagreements and scams less likely. Blockchain technology can make real estate transactions much more efficient. Smart contracts automate the performance of contractual deals. This gets rid of middlemen and speeds up the transaction process, which speeds up the transfer of property and the close process. Another benefit is that blockchain cuts down on the need for middlemen and manual processes, which lowers the cost of transactions by cutting down on paperwork, administrative work, and human proof.

This makes it easier and cheaper to buy and sell real estate. Blockchain also makes global real estate purchases more flexible and easy to get into. Tokenization makes investing in real estate possible for people all over the world. This opens up the market and makes it easier to buy and sell partial ownership interests on blockchain platforms. Blockchain improves title management by keeping a clear and safe record of who owns a piece of property, lowering the chance of mistakes and scams, and making it easier to get title insurance and verify ownership. Blockchain-based smart contracts can also be used to handle lease agreements. These contracts automatically execute lease responsibilities like rent payments and renewal terms, so there is less need for human control and more compliance with agreed-upon conditions.

Obstacles & Things to Think About:

Uncertainty about the rules is a big problem for using blockchain in real estate, since the rules are still changing. Different law systems may have different ideas about whether or not blockchain-based activities are legal and acceptable. Because of this, the business needs to be able to deal with the confusion. It's also hard to combine blockchain technology with real estate systems and processes that are already in place. To get the most out of blockchain's benefits, old systems may need to be changed or replaced. This means that the sector needs to make sure that everything works together while also dealing with integration issues.

There are also educational hurdles. For example, some people in the real estate business are having a hard time understanding how blockchain technology works. So, programs that raise knowledge and teach people about the pros and cons of blockchain in real estate are very important for informing the public, buyers, and experts. Another worry is scalability, since blockchain technology is becoming more and more famous. A technical problem that needs to be solved is making sure that blockchain networks can handle more transactions without slowing down or losing their efficiency.

In conclusion, blockchain offers disruptive innovations and transformational advantages that have the potential to cause a major paradigm change in the real estate sector. An ecosystem for real estate that is more effective, accessible, and reliable may result from the inclusion of blockchain technology, which can streamline property transactions, improve transparency, and lower fraud. Despite obstacles, including unpredictability in regulations and educational hurdles, industry alliances and continuous advancements point to a bright future for blockchain in real estate. The real estate market may change significantly as players investigate and use blockchain technology, leading to a more open, interconnected world.

14.4 Big Data and Analytics in Real Estate Decision-Making

A disruptive age has begun in the real estate sector with the integration of big data and analytics, reshaping decision-making processes and giving experts in the field access to never-before-seen information. This section examines the significant influence of big data and analytics on real estate decision-making. It covers various topics: risk assessment, market trends analysis, property value, and consumer behavior comprehension.

Analytics and big data are essential for improving methods for property value. In the past, similar sales and professional opinions were major factors in property assessment. However, with the introduction of big data, a multitude of data is now accessible for examination. This includes past data on real estate transactions, trends in the area, economic indicators, and even opinions about a community on social media. Sophisticated algorithms may process this enormous amount of data to provide more precise and data-driven property appraisals. Real estate agents may use these insights to determine reasonable and competitive property pricing, which will help buyers and sellers make smarter decisions.

Knowledge of market trends is essential to making wise real estate selections. Large-scale datasets may be analyzed using big data and analytics, revealing patterns and trends that would otherwise go unnoticed. Market trends include shifting demographics, supply and demand dynamics, and real estate price variations. Real estate agents can forecast changes in the market, find new hotspots, and modify their tactics using predictive analytics. Thanks to this proactive approach, stakeholders are empowered to make strategic choices that align with the changing market environment.

Investing in real estate has hazards, and reducing these risks requires a thorough grasp of various variables. Big data makes risk assessment easier by giving real-time information on interest rates, economic indicators, and environmental elements. For example, information on hazards associated with climate change or natural catastrophes might affect real estate investment choices. Predictive modeling also helps investors and developers make risk-aware choices by estimating the probability of occurrences like economic downturns.

The decision-making process is improved overall, and real estate portfolios are made more resilient thanks to this data-driven risk assessment. Real estate agents may learn more about the preferences and behavior of their clients by using big data analytics. Through examining demographic information, social media interactions, and internet search trends, real estate brokers may better target niche markets with their marketing campaigns. Comprehending the preferences of customers facilitates the development of tailored solutions, therefore augmenting the entire customer experience. Analytics, for instance, may show which features and facilities are most important to prospective renters or purchasers, which helps real estate developers maximize their offers.

Big data analytics provides predictive capabilities that increase efficiency and simplify operations in property management. For example, predictive maintenance models may predict when building systems or equipment are likely to break, allowing property managers to plan repairs ahead of time. This strategy improves overall property performance, lowers maintenance costs, and minimizes downtime. Analytical techniques also improve rental prices by considering local market circumstances, economic data, and seasonal demand. A large amount of information for location intelligence may be obtained from big data, which is helpful when making real estate decisions. Advanced geospatial analytics can evaluate variables such as crime rates, environmental quality, local amenities, and accessibility to transit. The best places for new projects may be found using this data-driven method. It also helps determine how desirable communities are for renters or purchasers and how much a property may appreciate or decrease in value depending on its location.

Effect on the Making of Real Estate Decisions:

Business Strategies Based on Good Information: Big data can give real estate owners useful information that they can use to make smart business decisions. Investors can make choices that are in line with their financial goals and risk tolerance by evaluating dangers, looking at market trends, and knowing how people act. This leads to more value-driven and stable investment portfolios. Effective Property Management: Big data is used by property managers to make sure that property management is responsive and effective. By planning exactly when repair tasks are needed, predictive analytics helps keep property conditions up and running costs low. Additionally, data helps make choices about how satisfied and preferred tenants are, which increases the likelihood of keeping renters.

Accurate Property Valuation: Big data and analytics make property assessments a lot more accurate. Real estate agents can use more than just the usual methods to figure out what factors affect property prices. This lets them come up with more accurate pricing strategies and lowers the chance of overpricing or underpricing properties. Market Responsiveness and Adaptability: Real-time info lets people who make real estate decisions react quickly to changes in the market. To stay competitive, people in an industry can keep an eye on how the market is changing and what customers want. This lets them make changes to their plans before they happen. Better Experience for Customers: Big data analytics gives us information about how people act, which lets us connect with them in a more personalized way.

The marketing, communication, and properties that real estate agents and companies give can be changed to better meet the wants and tastes of their target market. This makes customers happier overall. Better Portfolio Management: Big data gives owners the tools they need to better handle their various real estate holdings. Investors can get the best returns and financial stability by constantly checking the success of their assets, keeping an eye on market trends, and analyzing risk factors.

Obstacles & Things to Think About:

Managing a lot of private data can be hard when it comes to security and privacy. To keep the data they collect and study safe and private, real estate agents need to put in place strong security measures. Legacy System Integration: It can be hard to add big data analytics to real estate systems that are already in place. There may be problems with compatibility with older systems, which means spending money on technology equipment and teaching staff. Compliance with regulations: Any use of "***big data***" in real estate must follow the privacy and data security rules that are in place. To stay out of trouble with the law, it's important to follow rules like the ***General Data Protection Regulation (GDPR)***.

Skill Set Needed: To use big data analytics, you need to have certain skills. Companies that deal with real estate might need to spend money to hire or train people who are good at data science, analytics, and machine learning.

In short, real estate professionals' approaches to property valuation, market analysis, risk assessment, and client interaction have changed paradigms due to integrating big data and analytics in real estate decision-making. Real estate decision-makers may boost efficiency, profitability, and customer happiness by using data to inform, strategize, and modify their decisions. Although some obstacles exist, such as data privacy concerns and integration difficulties, the advantages of using big data in real estate decision-making exceed these difficulties. The real estate market will increasingly depend on data-driven insights as technology develops, creating a more dynamic and adaptable environment.

14.5 Embracing Tech Trends for Competitive Advantage in Real Estate Ventures

A key tactic for obtaining a competitive edge in the dynamic and ever-changing real estate market is to embrace technological advances. In a time when technology is revolutionizing sectors, the real estate industry may take advantage of several tech trends to improve client experiences, streamline operations, and maintain a competitive edge. Property technology, or proptech, is expanding and includes cutting-edge solutions designed specifically for the real estate sector. Proptech tools and platform integration help real estate businesses increase productivity, improve client services, and simplify operations. Applications for proptech include anything from blockchain-based transactions and property management software to virtual property tours and smart home technology. Real estate projects may stand out, draw in tech-savvy clients, and keep up with emerging trends using proptech solutions.

These technologies have revolutionized the marketing and experience of real estate. Virtual property tours provide a genuine and immersive experience by allowing prospective renters or purchasers to view homes from a distance. By superimposing details about the surrounding area or prospective repairs, augmented reality may improve on-site property inspections. By providing unique and engaging experiences, real estate businesses that use VR and AR technology have a competitive advantage. This helps them draw in a wider audience and expedite the decision-making process.

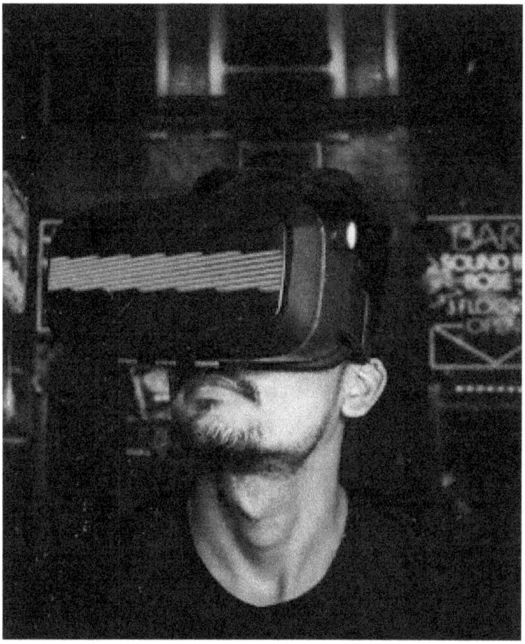

AI transforms how people look for properties. AI algorithms may analyze large-scale statistics to learn about user preferences, forecast changes in property values, and suggest customized real estate listings. Businesses in the real estate industry may greatly enhance customer satisfaction by providing customers with more relevant and accurate alternatives when they use AI-driven property search systems. AI may also automate repetitive chores, freeing up real estate agents to concentrate on developing relationships and making strategic decisions. In real estate, cloud computing has become a key component of effective corporate operations. Thanks to cloud-based collaboration tools and project management software, team members can communicate easily, even if they are spread out geographically. Centralized document storage, real-time updates, and improved collaboration are advantageous for real estate endeavors and may result in more efficient processes and expedited project schedules. Increased productivity and a competitive edge in project execution benefit from cloud solutions' flexibility and scalability.

Using chatbots and AI-powered customer support in real estate projects improves client engagement and response. By handling common questions, providing property details, and setting up appointments, chatbots free up human resources for more difficult jobs. AI-powered customer support may customize communications by making suggestions specific to the consumer's needs and preferences. Businesses in the real estate industry prioritizing prompt, knowledgeable customer service cultivate longer-lasting connections with their clientele, boosting client satisfaction and loyalty. Predictive analytics uses machine learning algorithms and historical data to predict future trends. Predictive analytics may help real estate investors by foreseeing market trends, prospective hazards, and property appreciation or depreciation. Real estate businesses may get a competitive edge in spotting profitable possibilities by using predictive analytics in their decision-making processes. This allows them to make data-driven investment choices, optimize portfolios, and stay ahead of market swings.

With their ability to provide customers with accessibility and convenience, mobile applications have become indispensable for real estate transactions. User-friendly mobile applications for real estate may make it easier to locate properties, take virtual tours, and even conduct safe transactions. Mobile applications make Instant updates and alerts possible by improving communication between customers and real estate agents. Businesses that use mobile technology meet the needs of today's customers, who are always on the move and get a competitive advantage in a market where responsiveness and accessibility are critical. Sustainability is starting to play a bigger role in real estate projects. Adopting green technology, such as solar power, eco-friendly construction materials, and energy-efficient building systems, not only supports environmental objectives but also draws in environmentally sensitive customers. Businesses in the real estate industry that prioritize sustainability stand out from the competition and help meet the rising demand for green buildings.

Adopting strong cybersecurity measures is crucial when real estate integrates technology. Securing private data, financial activities, and sensitive customer information is crucial. In an age when cyber risks are a major issue, ventures that emphasize data privacy and invest in cutting-edge cybersecurity solutions win customers' confidence and protect their brand. Social media platforms are essential for real estate marketing. Brand awareness may be increased, and a wider audience can be reached by partnering with influencers in the real estate and lifestyle industries and engaging in focused social media marketing. Using influencer marketing and social media trends, real estate businesses may develop a strong online presence, become trendsetters, and acquire a competitive edge in the digital market.

Effect on the Ability to Compete:

Better Engagement with Customers: Using tech trends in real estate makes customers more interested by giving them unique and personalized experiences. Businesses that put customer happiness first and use technology to adapt to changing needs are better able to build long-lasting relationships with their customers than their competitors. Cost Savings and Better Operational Efficiency: Real estate companies that are tech-savvy save a lot of money and run more efficiently. By automating chores that are done over and over, improving project management, and easing processes, you can lower costs, make more money, and gain a competitive edge. Differentiation in Marketing Strategies: Real estate companies can stand out from the rest by using cutting-edge technology in their marketing strategies. In a crowded market, these businesses stand out by offering unique services like AI-driven customer service, virtual property tours, and environmental programs that draw customers looking for new and valuable services.

Real estate projects that use new technologies show that they can adapt to changes in the market. Businesses that can quickly adopt new technologies and change with changing customer tastes are in a great situation to take advantage of new possibilities. These projects can also reach more people through internet tools, social media advertising, and mobile apps. Businesses can get more customers, connect more people, and get past traditional hurdles by following digital trends.

Obstacles & Things to Think About:

There can be big costs up front when you want to use cutting edge technology. Businesses in the real estate industry need to carefully choose tools that help them reach their goals and figure out how much money they will make back. It's also important to make sure that workers know how to use new technology properly, since pushback to change can slow down uptake. Putting money into training programs helps make sure the change goes smoothly. Protecting private info is more important as people depend more on technology. To protect customer info and follow data protection rules, real estate businesses need strong hacking steps. Real estate businesses also need to keep up with how technology is always changing. To stay on the cutting edge of new ideas, they need to keep spending money on research and development.

In short, adopting digital trends is not just a decision for real estate endeavors but a critical strategy for surviving and prospering in a cutthroat industry. Real estate endeavors that use technology acquire a multifarious competitive edge, from artificial intelligence-driven decision-making to virtual reality experiences and proptech integration. Tech-savvy businesses establish themselves as leaders in the always-changing real estate industry by prioritizing client involvement, operational efficiency, and flexibility in response to market shifts. Even if adopting digital trends comes with dangers, the transformational power of doing so far surpasses them, giving real estate endeavors the resources they need to prosper in a technologically advanced and dynamic future.

|15|

Alternative Real Estate Investment Avenues

This chapter deviates from the norm by looking at unconventional real estate investing strategies. We will explore the realm of real estate crowdfunding platforms, examine the advantages of Opportunity Zones as an investment opportunity, and examine their tax implications. We'll look at mortgage debt and real estate note investment for people looking for debt-based choices. Additionally, a full explanation of Real Estate Investment Trusts (REITs) and their benefits will be provided. In order to make sure you have a thorough knowledge of the wide range of real estate investment alternatives, we'll wrap up with analyzing specialized investments like holiday rentals and co-living spaces!

For the relevant case studies, worksheets and free resources you can visit: andonierealty.com

"Real estate investing, even on a very small scale, remains a tried and true means of building an individual's cash flow and wealth."

-Robert Kiyosaki

15.1 Investing in Real Estate Crowdfunding Platforms

The emergence of real estate crowdfunding as a disruptive and inventive investment strategy has allowed people to pool their resources and engage in real estate projects together. The appeal of investing via real estate crowdfunding platforms may be attributed to its accessibility, possibility for diversification, and capacity to enable participation in real estate enterprises with comparatively less cash. The mechanics of investing in real estate crowdfunding platforms are examined in this part, along with the benefits, factors to consider, and possible hazards of this cutting-edge investment option.

In real estate crowdfunding, many people contribute different amounts of money to help pay for a real estate project. Online sites make this process easier by putting buyers in touch with property owners or producers who need money. This way of dealing has opened up real estate to more people, giving them access to possibilities that were once only available to big institutional buyers. One of the best things about real estate crowdfunding is that buyers can easily get involved. Crowdfunding is different from traditional real estate investments because it lets people join projects with smaller amounts of money. This means that more buyers can join who might not have the money to buy property on their own.

Real estate crowdfunding lets donors spread their money around among different projects, areas, and types of property. By putting their money into more than one choice, investors can lower the risks that come with how well one property or market does. This makes for a more stable and varied investment strategy. Crowdfunding for real estate often offers the chance to make idle income. Depending on how the investment is set up, buyers may get money back through rental income or a share of the profits.

This is good for people who want to make money without having to manage homes.

In most cases, crowdfunding sites screen and handle projects, which means that donors can get professional knowledge. Due research is done by these platforms, which lowers risk and connects buyers with real estate experts who can give them useful information. Investing through crowdfunding sites makes it easier to manage your money than owning property directly. As long as these platforms take care of things like property upkeep, legal compliance, and financial reports, owners can focus on handling their assets instead of dealing with day-to-day practical problems.

1. Things to Think About for Investing:

Investors should thoroughly investigate the crowdfunding platform before investing. It is important to consider factors including the platform's reputation, track record, openness, and the kinds of projects it provides. Making an educated choice requires reading reviews, getting advice, and comprehending the platform's pricing schedule. Potential backers must carefully examine each project's specifics as listed on the crowdfunding website before investing. This entails assessing the project sponsor's or developer's expertise and the property type, location, and expected returns. Making wise investment choices requires having a thorough understanding of the risks and benefits related to each project. Although crowdfunding for real estate may provide diversity, investors must understand and control risks. Economic downturns, project-specific risks, and market changes may impact crowdfunding investments. Long-term success depends on putting a risk management plan into action and comprehending the risk-return characteristics of each investment.

Investors need to ensure that the crowdfunding site complies with all applicable laws and regulations and the projects it provides. A safe and legal investing experience depends on knowing the investment's legal structure, investors' rights, and the platform's compliance with securities laws. Before making any crowdsourcing investment, investors want to think about the exit options accessible. Understanding precisely how and when returns might be achieved is crucial, whether through selling real estate, refinancing, or other methods. The timing of the project and the kind of investment may affect exit alternatives.

2. Possible Hazards:

Local, state, and federal issues, as well as interest rates, may all impact real estate market volatility. Investors need to be ready for any changes in the market that might affect the performance and worth of their crowdsourcing investments.

There are a variety of hazards associated with real estate projects, such as unanticipated costs, construction delays, and shifts in consumer demand. Determining the risks involved in any project in detail is essential to making wise investment choices. Compared to publicly listed assets, real estate crowdfunding investments often need more liquidity. Particularly if the investment horizon is long-term, investors should be ready for the risk that their wealth may remain locked up for a considerable time.

The crowdfunding platform's effectiveness directly impacts the profitability and dependability of an investment. Risks unique to a platform might include fraud, insolvency, or poor management. Investors are advised to select trustworthy platforms with a solid track record and open business practices. Regulatory changes in the real estate or crowdfunding sectors may impact the operating environment for crowdfunding platforms and investors. It's critical to keep up with regulatory changes and modify investing plans as necessary.

Investing in real estate crowdfunding platforms offers people a strong chance to participate in real estate projects with comparatively less money and less administrative work. Many different types of investors find it an attractive alternative because of its benefits, which include accessibility, diversity, potential for passive income, and access to professional experience. However, a successful real estate crowdfunding investment plan requires considerable thought, research, and risk management. Investors may take advantage of the advantages of real estate crowdfunding while navigating the intricacies of the always-changing real estate investing environment by comprehending the platform's dynamics, evaluating particular projects, and being aware of possible hazards.

15.2 Exploring Opportunity Zones for Tax Benefits and Investments

As a smart strategy for real estate investment and economic growth, investigating Opportunity Zones for investments and tax advantages has drawn much attention. Opportunity Zones are areas set aside by the U.S. government to attract private investment in regions experiencing economic hardship. They also provide investors with special tax breaks and work to boost employment and economic expansion. The main features of Opportunity Zones, their tax advantages, and factors to take into account for investors wishing to profit from this investment option are covered in this section.

The Tax Cuts and Jobs Act, enacted in 2017, created Opportunity Zones. The U.S. Department of the Treasury has recognized these zones, which are localities that are economically challenged and have been designated by state governors. The main goal of offering tax breaks to investors who place money in approved Opportunity Zones is to entice private investment to help these struggling communities recover.

Principal Tax Benefits:

The ability to postpone capital gains taxes is a primary advantage of investing in Opportunity Zones. If an investor reinvests their capital gains from the sale of an asset within 180 days of the sale, they may postpone paying taxes on those profits. The deferred tax is due by December 31, 2026, or when the investment is sold, whichever comes first. Long-term investments made in Opportunity Zones may be eligible for a capital gains tax reduction and deferral. A 10% discount on the deferred capital gains tax is available to investors holding their QOF investment for at least five years. The decrease rises to 15% if the asset is retained for at least seven years.

The biggest inducement is the possibility of tax-free earnings on investments held for at least 10 years. Any increase in the Opportunity Zone investment's value that an investor keeps for ten years or longer is tax-free upon sale.

Using Qualified Opportunity Funds (QOFs) to make investments:

Investors must fund a Qualified Opportunity Fund (QOF), an investment entity created to invest in Opportunity Zone assets, to benefit from the tax advantages. These funds must invest at least 90% of their assets in eligible Opportunity Zone properties to be self-certified, which may be done by filing a document to the IRS.

Within Opportunity Zones, Qualified Opportunity Funds may invest in various assets, such as operating companies, infrastructure projects, and real estate developments. Due to this flexibility, investors can choose projects that complement their experience and investment objectives. Before investing in a qualified opportunity fund, investors should thoroughly investigate it. This entails assessing the investment strategy, track record, and projects in which the fund has invested. It is crucial to comprehend the fund's management team and their background in Opportunity Zone investing.

Investor considerations:

Investments in Opportunity Zones are intended to be made over an extended period. Investors should carefully assess their investment horizon because the greatest tax advantages are obtained when an investment is kept for a minimum of 10 years. Shorter investment horizon holders may not be able to realize the tax-free profits fully, but they could still benefit from deferral and reduction. Investments in economically troubled regions may entail risks, even when Opportunity Zones provide tax benefits. Investors should evaluate the risks connected to the enterprises or projects located in the Opportunity Zone, considering the potential for community growth, regulatory issues, and market dynamics.

It's critical to comprehend the Opportunity Zone's local dynamics. Investors need to conduct comprehensive market research, appraise the likelihood of economic expansion, and gauge the level of demand for the projects they are contemplating. Making wise investing selections requires having a thorough understanding of the local market. Investments made in Opportunity Zones are intended to benefit the targeted communities and provide financial rewards. The possible social and economic advantages that investing in these regions may have should be considered by investors. Comprehending neighborhood needs and interacting with local stakeholders may augment the overall effect of investments made in Opportunity Zones.

Compliance with Opportunity Zone laws is crucial to guarantee that investors may fully benefit from the tax advantages. Investors should collaborate closely with tax specialists and legal consultants to maintain compliance with regulatory obligations and negotiate the complicated regulatory environment.

Community Development Impact:

Promoting economic growth and employment creation in underprivileged areas is one of Opportunity Zones' main objectives. The effort seeks to develop infrastructure, establish sustainable enterprises, and stimulate local economies by drawing private investments to these places. In addition to looking for financial gains, investors may be influenced by matching their investments with the more general community development objectives.

In conclusion, Opportunity Zone investments provide a unique chance for people to take advantage of tax breaks while assisting in recovering economically struggling areas. Opportunity Zones are a desirable choice for strategic investors due to the possibility of lower and postponed capital gains taxes and tax-free returns on long-term investments. However, it's essential that investors evaluate the risks, carry out extensive due diligence, and match their investment plans with the more general objectives of community development. Through this approach, investors can effectively manage the intricacies of investing in Opportunity Zones and attain financial gains and constructive social influence.

15.3 Investing in Real Estate Notes and Mortgage Debt

Investing in mortgage debt and real estate notes is a unique option in the larger real estate investment market. Investing in mortgage debt and real estate notes enables people to be involved in the finance aspect of real estate transactions, unlike typical real estate investments that require direct ownership of buildings. This section will address the main features of this investment strategy, such as the characteristics of real estate notes, the benefits and factors to consider for investors, and the possible risks and returns connected to this course of action.

Comprehending Real Estate Notes and Mortgage Debt:

Real estate notes, often promissory notes or mortgage notes, are the debt incurred by borrowers who take out a mortgage loan to buy a property. A promissory note detailing the details of the loan, such as the principal amount, interest rate, repayment schedule, and any other pertinent conditions, is signed by the borrower when a mortgage is established. Investing in the debt side of real estate deals is made possible for investors by the ability to purchase and sell these notes as financial assets.

Types of Real Estate Notes:

These are loans for which the borrower is fulfilling the conditions of the agreement by making regular payments. An investor who purchases performing notes will consistently get interest payments. Compared to non performing notes, these notes are seen as having less risk.

These are loans for which the borrower needs to catch up on payments. Those who own non performing notes could negotiate a settlement with the borrower—for example, via loan modification or foreclosure—to get their money back and perhaps make more. Real estate notes may have a first or junior lien. First position notes offer additional security for the investor, who holds the principal claim over the property in the case of default. Junior liens, on the other hand, are seen to be riskier but may have a secondary claim and provide larger potential profits.

Benefits of Real Estate Note Investing:

Interest payments on performing notes are a regular source of revenue. Borrowers pay investors monthly or quarterly, giving them a steady stream of financial flow. Those looking for passive income may find this consistent source of income intriguing. Purchasing real estate notes often have fewer management duties than actual property ownership. The upkeep of real estate, managing tenants, and other operational duties are not the direct responsibility of investors.

Real estate notes provide a means of doing this. People may diversify their investment portfolios beyond standard equities and bonds by investing in mortgage debt, which may lower the portfolio's total risk. Non Performing notes may provide large rewards if properly settled. Investors may purchase non performing notes at a reduced cost and attempt to profitably resolve the situation via foreclosure, loan modification, or other tactics.

Things to Think About for Investing:

Before investing in non performing notes, it is essential to do extensive borrower due diligence. Investors may make better selections if they know the borrower's financial status, the property's state, and the local real estate market dynamics. Real estate note investors need to be aware of and abide by all applicable laws and regulations regarding debt investments. It is crucial to be knowledgeable about debt collection laws, foreclosure laws, and other pertinent legal issues. When determining an investment's risk and possible return, the underlying property's value is crucial. Investors need a trustworthy way to estimate the property's value and comprehend the state of the market.

Clearly defined risk management plans are essential for investors, particularly when handling non performing notes. Various tactics such as loan modifications, foreclosure, or other workout options might be used to optimize profits and minimize possible losses. The investor's degree of security is greatly impacted by the lien position. First-position notes provide more security since they have a larger claim to the assets in the event of default. Junior lien investors need to understand that their investment carries a higher risk.

Possible Hazards:

Borrower default is possible, particularly when involving non performing notes. Recovering the whole amount invested might be difficult for investors, especially if the property's value needs to be higher to pay off the mortgage. The performance of real estate notes might be impacted by real estate markets and prevailing economic conditions. The success of the investment may be impacted by market circumstances, falling property prices, or economic downturns.

Modifications to debt collection or foreclosure legislation, among other legal and regulatory developments, may affect an investor's capacity to uphold their legal rights. It's important to keep up with legal advancements. An important component of the investment's success is the state of the underlying property. If the property needs extensive renovations or the market negatively impacts its value, investors may need help.

Exit Strategies:

Working with the borrower to negotiate a loan modification is one possible exit strategy for non performing notes. This may include finding a consistent source of income for the investor and modifying the loan conditions to make them easier for the borrower to handle.This is possible if debtors cannot come to an arrangement or make payments. Investors should be informed of the expenses and legal procedures involved in foreclosure to recoup their investment cash. The property may be sold for that amount.

Resale of Notes:

Investees can sell their notes to other investors. This option offers liquidity and the chance to get out of the investment without having to go through a drawn-out foreclosure process or other drawn-out procedures.

Buying real estate notes and mortgage debt offers a special opportunity for those looking to diversify their investment portfolios and bring in a consistent income. It is essential to comprehend the intricacies of the debt side of real estate deals, regardless of whether one is investing in performing or non performing notes. Investors must handle risks well, conduct extensive due diligence, and have well-defined exit plans. People should approach real estate notes with a thorough grasp of the market, legal concerns, and the particular dangers involved with this investment strategy, even if the opportunity for regular income and portfolio diversity is enticing.

15.4 Understanding Real Estate Investment Trusts (REITs) and Their Benefits

An innovative and well-liked financial structure that lets people engage in the real estate market without actually owning any real estate is the Real Estate Financial Trust (REIT). Investors who want to diversify their holdings, benefit from consistent income, and participate in the possible growth of real estate assets must comprehend REITs and their advantages. In this part, we shall examine the main features of REITs, including their benefits, advantages, and investment concerns.

An overview of REITs, or real estate investment trusts:

An organization that owns, manages, or funds income-producing real estate in various markets, such as residential, commercial, industrial, and hospitality, is known as a Real Estate Investment Trust (REIT). The purpose of REITs is to provide investors with an alternative to direct property ownership when investing in real estate assets. They are accessible to a wide spectrum of investors and provide liquidity since they are traded on major stock exchanges.

Types of REITs:

These are the most prevalent kind, and they directly own and manage property that generates revenue. They get money via property appreciation and rentals. Particular property categories, such as commercial, industrial, or residential, might be the focus of equity REITs. Mortgage-backed securities or real estate mortgages are investments made by mortgage REITs (mREITs). Interest on loans or mortgage-backed securities is how they make money. mREITs operate as lenders in the real estate finance market rather than holding actual real estate.

These investment vehicles include aspects of mortgage and equity REITs. They could invest in mortgages or other real estate-related assets in addition to owning and managing properties.

Advantages related to Structure and Taxes:

Because REITs are set up as pass-through organizations, they are not subject to corporation taxes. Rather, they pay out dividends to shareholders equal to at least 90% of their taxable revenue. After that, shareholders are responsible for paying taxes on their received dividends.

Compared to other stock kinds, REITs often provide high dividend yields because of their tax structure. Because of this, they are appealing to investors seeking income, especially those nearing retirement or needing consistent cash flow.

Benefits of Putting Money Into REITs:

By exposing investors to a range of real estate industries, REITs provide a straightforward method of diversifying their portfolios. Comparing this diversity to buying individual homes may help lower risk. REITs are traded on major stock exchanges, in contrast to direct property ownership, which sometimes has less liquidity. Investors have flexibility in managing their investments and liquidity by being able to purchase or sell REIT shares at market prices.

REITs provide low entry barriers into the real estate market. Investors may acquire a diverse portfolio of real estate assets with very little initial investment. Teams of professionals with experience in real estate investing and management oversee REITs. The expertise and experience of these specialists help investors by lowering the need for direct participation in property management. REITs must deliver at least 90% of their taxable income to shareholders through dividends. Because of this, investors get a steady stream of income, which attracts income-focused investors to REITs.

As the value of the underlying real estate assets rises, REIT investors may also profit from potential capital appreciation in addition to dividends. The combined possibility for capital growth and income increases the total return profile of REIT investments.

Things to Think About for Investing:

The state of the market and the economy impact REITs as they do on any investment. Variables, including interest rates, economic growth, and movements in the real estate market, may impact the success of REITs. Variations in interest rates may impact REITs. REITs may see an increase in borrowing costs when interest rates rise, affecting their valuations and profitability.

Within the REIT market, different property sectors may have different risk profiles. For instance, housing trends may affect the performance of residential REITs, but office and retail market dynamics may impact the performance of commercial REITs. A REIT investment's performance is impacted by the caliber of its management group. When choosing an investment, investors should consider the management of the REIT's track record, expertise, and strategic vision. Investors should consider the dividend sustainability of REITs despite their reputation for having high dividend yields. A thorough examination of the REIT's occupancy rates, property revenue, and financial health might shed light on the probability of regular dividend payments.

A tempting option for people to engage in the real estate market, benefit from consistent income, and diversify their investment portfolios is investing in real estate investment trusts (REITs). Investors may choose the strategy that best suits their financial objectives and risk tolerance from various REIT types that cater to varying investing preferences. Both experienced investors and those new to real estate find REITs an appealing alternative because of their tax-efficient structure, liquidity, and expert management. However, making educated judgments and optimizing the returns on REIT investments requires rigorous evaluation of market circumstances, real estate markets, and management caliber—as with any investment.

15.5 Evaluating Niche Investments: Vacation Rentals, Co-Living Spaces, etc.

Analyzing investments in niche real estate, including co-living facilities and holiday rentals, requires a thorough grasp of the particular dynamics, dangers, and opportunities connected to these particular sectors. The main ideas of specialized real estate investing will be covered in this part, along with information on co-living facilities, holiday rentals, and other recent developments in the real estate market.

Holiday Homes for Rent:

The vacation rental market has changed dramatically due to websites like Airbnb, HomeAway, and Vrbo. Investors may buy homes built especially for short-term rentals, appealing to tourists looking for cheaper options than typical hotels.

More money for rent than long-term leases. Owners can rent out the property at other times and utilize it for their holidays. Vacation rentals provide an alternative to standard residential or commercial real estate investing in terms of diversity.

Things to Think About:

The possibility for revenue during off-peak times might be impacted by the extremely seasonal demand for holiday rentals. Local laws and zoning rules must be followed in some areas where short-term rentals are subject to stringent controls. Handling regular rotations, upkeep, and visitor interactions may take much time. Monitoring the occupancy rate of a property aids in assessing its general performance and level of popularity. ADR is a key metric for evaluating the financial success of the property as it represents the average rental revenue each night.

Co-living spaces:

Co-living spaces are shared housing arrangements in which people rent individual rooms or communal areas inside bigger properties. This trend is becoming more common, particularly among young professionals and millennials. Co-living may provide more economical housing choices than renting a flat.

Living in a community offers advantages such as social opportunities, shared conveniences, and belonging.

Co-living options sometimes provide flexible lease periods for short-term or month-to-month rentals. The success of co-living depends on the compatibility of the tenants, which makes tenant screening and selection essential. To handle tenant issues, oversee common areas, and guarantee a pleasant living environment, effective property management is crucial. The demand in a particular market and the inclinations of the target audience are key factors in determining the success of co-living spaces.

Monitoring these figures aids in determining the attractiveness of the property and the level of tenant satisfaction. Gathering tenant input might provide important details about the property's advantages and shortcomings.

New Developments in Niche Real Estate Investments:

As the population ages, there is a growing need for senior housing alternatives such as retirement communities, assisted living facilities, and age-restricted housing. The need for reasonably priced and student-friendly housing, especially in the vicinity of institutions, defines the niche market for student housing. As environmental awareness grows, eco-friendly or sustainable homes are becoming more popular among renters who share this concern. IoT gadgets and energy-saving systems in your home may increase value and draw in tech-savvy renters.

Investment Strategies for Specialized Properties:

Before making any investment judgments, it is important to comprehend the dynamics of the local market, the demand for specialized properties, and any possible regulatory obstacles.

Focusing marketing efforts on the target demographic of speciality properties may increase exposure and draw in the ideal renters.

Hiring a skilled property manager guarantees smooth operations and happy tenants, particularly for speciality properties with particular difficulties.

Because niche markets may be dynamic, adjusting to shifting consumer tastes and trends is important. It's critical to be flexible with property options and facilities.

Hazards and Countermeasures:

Be aware of the zoning rules, license requirements, and tenant limitations that apply to specialized properties in your area.

Demand in specialized markets may fluctuate. Investing in various property kinds and locales might help reduce the risks of investing in a particular market. High rates of tenant churn may affect both the cost of property management and rental revenue. Reducing turnover risk may be achieved by implementing tenant retention measures and providing favorable lease terms.

Different speciality markets may be impacted differently by economic downturns. Risk mitigation methods during hard economic times must include keeping cash on hand and adjusting plans. Investing in specialized real estate has particular possibilities as well as difficulties, whether it be in co-living facilities, holiday rentals, or developing trends. Thorough market research, a comprehensive awareness of the unique dynamics, and strategic approaches to investment and management are all necessary for success in these industries. Investors may benefit from niche possibilities as the real estate market changes by following market trends, welcoming innovation, and adjusting to the tenants' shifting demands in these specialized markets. In the fast-paced world of specialty real estate investing, careful evaluation of performance measures, risk factors, and mitigation techniques is necessary to maximize profits and make well-informed choices.

|16|

Environmental Sustainability in Real Estate

Going green is becoming more than just a trend in today's environmentally concerned world—it's a wise economic move. The vital role that environmental sustainability plays in real estate development is covered in detail in this chapter. We'll look at how adopting eco-friendly methods may help your business as well as the environment. We'll dissect green construction processes and certification schemes, examine the economic benefits of sustainable investments, and look at ways to include eco-friendly elements that raise property values. Lastly, we will talk about how the real estate industry is affected by climate change and the potential and threats it poses. So fasten your seatbelts and get ready to contribute to the answer for a sustainable real estate industry!

For the relevant case studies, worksheets and free resources you can visit: andonierealty.com

"The built environment has a significant impact on our natural environment, economy, health, and productivity."

- Rick Fedrizzi

16.1 Importance of Sustainability in Property Development

Sustainability in real estate development has developed from a trendy term to a vital sector component. The significance of sustainability in real estate development cannot be emphasized in a world that is changing quickly and where issues related to the environment, resource efficiency, and climate change have emerged as defining problems. This section explores the many aspects of sustainability in real estate development, including its importance, guiding principles, and industry-changing effects.

Sustainability's Importance in Real Estate Development

The effects of construction and operation on the environment are considered in sustainable property development. Incorporating sustainable methods minimizes the negative impacts on ecosystems, biodiversity, and the quality of air and water, as well as carbon footprints and resource depletion. Long-term economic viability is a common outcome of sustainable construction practices. The cost reductions throughout a sustainable property's life cycle, including energy and water efficiency, may provide significant financial rewards even if the initial expenditures are greater. Furthermore, renters prepared to pay more for environmentally friendly amenities are drawn to sustainable buildings, which often have higher market values.

Sustainability in real estate development favors community well-being and environmental and economic benefits. Green areas, social inclusion, and thoughtful design all help create healthier and more livable surroundings. The well-being of residents is given top priority in sustainable projects since this promotes a feeling of community and general well-being.

Fundamental Ideas of Ecological Real Estate Development

Sustainable buildings prioritize energy efficiency in technology, design, and building materials. This entails optimizing energy usage via smart building technology, energy-efficient HVAC systems, and incorporating renewable energy sources. Water-saving features like rainwater harvesting systems, low-flow fixtures, and effective irrigation techniques are all included in sustainable property construction. These innovations support water conservation and resilience in the face of growing water shortages by lowering water usage.

Regarding sustainable real estate development, selecting building materials is essential. Selecting locally produced, repurposed, or eco-friendly products reduces the environmental effect of resource extraction and transportation. Furthermore, sustainable building design often highlights recyclable materials and little waste production during construction. Smart urban planning is a component of sustainable development which goes beyond individual structures. This showcases developing walkable neighborhoods, mixed-use areas, and public transit as top priorities. Sustainable urban design improves environmental and social sustainability by lowering automobile reliance and fostering accessibility.

One of the main tenets of sustainability is integrating green areas and landscaping that supports biodiversity. This involves using native plants, establishing animal habitats, and building green walls or roofs. By doing this, sustainable projects improve the overall visual appeal of the surrounding area and support ecological equilibrium.

Revolutionary Effect on the Real Estate Sector:

As consumers' knowledge of environmental concerns has grown, there has been a sharp increase in demand for sustainable properties in recent years. Tenants and purchasers alike are increasingly looking for homes that reflect their values, and sustainable elements often play a role in this process.

Throughout the globe, authorities and localities are implementing guidelines and policies that require or reward sustainable construction methods. By following these guidelines, developers guarantee compliance, establish a positive reputation in the industry, and steer clear of any legal ramifications from antiquated methods. Investors who understand the durability and long-term worth of ecologically conscious projects are becoming more interested in sustainable property development. Sustainability in the real estate industry is further propelled by incorporating environmental, social, and governance (ESG) factors into the decision-making processes of institutional investors, in particular. Including sustainability in real estate development is a purposeful move for brand difference, not merely a reaction to market trends. Developers prioritizing sustainability set themselves out as socially aware businesses, enhancing their reputation and drawing in partners and customers who share their concerns.

Chances and Difficulties:

One of the main obstacles is the idea that sustainable real estate development would cost more upfront. Although eco-friendly features could need higher initial costs, sustainability is a wise and feasible investment due to its long-term economic advantages, market demand, and regulatory incentives.

Using cutting-edge building techniques and technology is often necessary to embrace sustainability. This might make it difficult to adjust to new procedures, but it also offers chances for industry innovation, teamwork, and the creation of ground-breaking solutions. Raising awareness and educating the sector is necessary to overcome opposition to sustainability in real estate development. To encourage wider adoption, developers, investors, and stakeholders must comprehend the many advantages of sustainable methods.

Outlook and Points to Remember:

One major trend in sustainable real estate development is the quest toward net-zero buildings, which produce as much energy as they use. This entails a thorough approach to energy integration, renewable energy, and, sometimes, carbon offset programs.

Using recyclable, reusable, or repurposed materials in architectural design is a key component of adopting circular economy concepts. Sustainability is enhanced by this move to a circular model, which reduces waste and lengthens the life cycle of resources.

As severe weather events occur more often, sustainable property construction is shifting toward designs that improve adaptation and resilience. This covers actions to deal with issues connected to climate change, such as rising sea levels and high temperatures. As a fundamental transformation that reflects the changing ideals of our society, sustainability in real estate development goes well beyond a fad. In addition to addressing urgent environmental issues, sustainable development is consistent with social justice, economic responsibility, and the long-term viability of the real estate sector.

As time passes, including sustainability in real estate construction will become more and more of a duty. Industry stakeholders, investors, and developers can influence how our built environment develops in the future. Adopting sustainable methods helps us build places with the least negative environmental effects while simultaneously promoting economic growth, healthier communities, and a legacy of responsible development for future generations. A vision of real estate development acting as a catalyst for good change and balancing human demands with the fragile balance of our planet's ecosystems is presented by the transformational path towards sustainability.

16.2 Green Building Practices and Certification Programs

Green building methods and certification schemes have become important drivers of change in the real estate and construction sectors, pushing them toward more ecologically friendly and sustainable operations. This section analyzes the importance of green building techniques, looks at some important tenets, and provides information on well-known certification schemes that have been vital in encouraging sustainability in the built environment.

Importance of Green Construction Methods:

At the core of green construction principles is environmental conservation. By using environmentally friendly building materials and techniques, these practices try to reduce the negative effects of conventional building methods on the environment. This entails reducing waste production, using fewer resources, and reducing the carbon impact of building projects. The focus on energy efficiency is fundamental to green construction techniques. Buildings are major energy users. Therefore, energy-efficient designs and technology are given priority in green practices. LoweringThis involves integrating energy-efficient appliances, lighting, insulation, and HVAC (heating, ventilation, and air conditioning) systems to lower total energy consumption.

By using sustainable materials and building methods, green building practices aim to maximize the use of resources. This entails selecting materials with less adverse effects on the environment, encouraging the use of recycled or locally obtained resources, and using building techniques that produce as little trash as possible. Green construction techniques emphasize the creation of healthier interior environments in addition to exterior environmental considerations. By lowering the risk of respiratory problems and boosting general health, improved indoor air quality—achieved via appropriate ventilation systems and non-toxic materials—contributes to building occupant wellbeing.

Fundamentals of Green Building Techniques:

Selecting locations for sustainable sites entails reducing their negative effects on the environment and encouraging wise land use. This covers things like being close to public transit, protecting natural areas, and staying away from areas very sensitive to the environment. Green building techniques include water-efficient technology and designs to reduce water use. This involves using drought-resistant landscaping, rainwater collecting systems, and low-flow fixtures to save water.

This cornerstone concept includes techniques like integrated renewable energy sources like wind turbines and solar panels, passive solar design, and optimal building orientation.

Material selection is essential in green construction. Choosing materials with a lower embodied energy, using recycled or recovered resources, and giving preference to those with the least environmental effects are all sustainable practices. Furthermore, green construction approaches often include recycling or reusing materials at the end of a building's life cycle.

By emphasizing indoor environmental quality, green building methods put occupant health and wellbeing first. This entails using non-toxic construction materials, getting enough ventilation, and avoiding items that release dangerous toxins.

Reputable Certification Courses:

Leadership in Energy and Environmental Design, or LEED, is one of the world's most well-known green construction certification schemes. Buildings are assessed using LEED, administered by the U.S. Green Building Council (USGBC), according to standards including indoor air quality, energy efficiency, water conservation, and sustainable site development. The certification levels—Certified, Silver, Gold, and Platinum—clearly show how sustainable a building is.

The Building Research Establishment Environmental Assessment Method, or BREEAM, is a popular certification scheme developed in the U.K. It evaluates a building's sustainability using materials, management practices, pollution, and energy and water usage. There are many levels of BREEAM certification, including Pass, Good, Very Good, Excellent, and Outstanding. This accreditation scheme uses an online questionnaire to assess a building's sustainability. The Green Building Initiative (GBI) created it, offering a flexible and affordable certification process that supports ongoing development. One to four globes are awarded for achieving a Green Globes certification; four globes indicate the greatest sustainability.

This U.S. Environmental Protection Agency (EPA) certification program focuses on energy-efficient goods and buildings. Although it has nothing to do with construction, a building's ENERGY STAR certification satisfies stringent energy performance requirements, lowering energy expenses and greenhouse gas emissions.

Chances and Difficulties:

The idea that green construction techniques would cost more upfront is one of the drawbacks of the practice. Even while the initial expenditures may be higher, they are often outweighed in the long run by the savings on energy bills, the appreciation of the property, and the possibility of receiving government subsidies. The real estate and construction sectors need to be educated and aware of green building principles to be successfully implemented. For professionals to successfully incorporate green ideas into their projects, they must thoroughly understand sustainable building processes, materials, and technology.

Regulatory frameworks greatly aid the broad adoption of green construction techniques. In some areas, incorporating sustainable practices may be hindered by the absence of uniform legislation or incentives. In contrast, areas with strong legislative backing often see a quicker uptake of green construction practices.

Outlook and Points to Remember:

The idea of net-zero buildings—generating as much energy as they use—is becoming increasingly popular. Net-zero buildings may be realized by combining energy-efficient building designs and advancements in renewable energy sources. A key component of green architecture is incorporating circular economy concepts, which call for materials to be made for reuse and recycling. This move to a circular model aims to increase the life cycle of construction materials and reduce waste. Using smart building technology improves a property's sustainability. Smart technologies improve resource utilization and increase overall energy efficiency. These technologies include energy management systems, intelligent lighting, and HVAC controls.

To sum up, green construction methods and certification schemes are at the forefront of a revolutionary movement that will make the built environment more ecologically sensitive and sustainable. Adopting these methods is now a strategic need for the real estate and construction sectors, not just a niche activity. It is impossible to overestimate the significance of sustainable building in light of the urgent environmental issues facing the globe. The tenets of green building, which are based on occupant well-being, energy efficiency, and environmental stewardship, provide a path forward for a more accountable and resilient future. Programs for certification like ENERGY STAR, Green Globes, BREEAM, and LEED provide concrete standards that let project participants measure and share their sustainability accomplishments.

A rising market of environmentally aware customers is expecting more from businesses, and adopting green construction principles positions stakeholders as responsible contributors to global sustainability objectives as the sector continues to change. The long-term advantages in terms of cost savings, market competitiveness, and favorable effects on the environment and human health exceed the difficulties related to upfront expenses and industry education. The combination of net-zero building concepts, circular economy ideas, and smart building technology will shape the next stage of sustainable building. The quest for a more environmentally friendly built environment is dynamic, ever-changing, and motivated by our shared need to design environments that balance the needs of the natural world with the needs of the future.

16.3 Financial Benefits of Sustainable Real Estate Investments

Sustainable real estate investments have grown in popularity due to their favorable effects on the environment and the strong financial returns they provide investors. This section delves into the financial benefits of sustainable real estate investments, elucidating how incorporating environmental, social, and governance (ESG) factors may foster sustained financial prosperity.

The possibility of increasing property value is one of the main financial advantages of sustainable real estate investments. Sustainable features, including eco-friendly designs, green certifications, and energy-efficient technologies, often increase a property's appeal to prospective renters or purchasers. Research demonstrates that homes with green certifications, such as ENERGY STAR or LEED, fetch better market values and rentals. The perceived value of features that are energy-efficient and ecologically conscientious is reflected in this premium.

Energy-efficient technology and practices are incorporated into sustainable real estate investments to minimize energy usage. In addition to aligning with environmental objectives, this also results in substantial financial savings for property owners. Lower utility costs are a common feature of energy-efficient buildings, which boosts net operating income (NOI) and enhances cash flow.

The consistency and predictability of operating expenses in sustainable buildings become a desirable financial asset if energy prices remain volatile.

Access to green financing alternatives and a range of incentives are among the financial advantages of sustainable real estate. Lending institutions increasingly provide loans with favorable terms and rates for sustainable projects. In addition, governments and municipalities often offer tax credits, rebates, and grants as incentives for sustainable development. These financial benefits improve the project's financial sustainability while lowering the total cost of capital.

Renters who value environmental responsibility are often drawn to sustainable real estate investments. These renters could be prepared to pay more for space in buildings that have energy-saving measures or green certifications. Property owners benefit from a steady and consistent revenue stream when they can draw in and keep environmentally conscientious renters. Furthermore, renters who prioritize sustainability might be more likely to sign longer-term leases, providing landlords with financial security and lowering the chance of vacancy.

Purchasing sustainable real estate may help reduce risk, especially in light of the legislative changes and growing concerns associated with climate change. Properties that use sustainable and resilient design features are better equipped to resist the effects of climate change, including rising sea levels and intense weather. This resilience reduces the possibility of expensive losses and interruptions, which helps the investment maintain long-term financial stability. Including sustainability in real estate investments aligns with larger CSR objectives for corporate entities and institutional investors. Sustainable real estate aligns with the ESG elements many investors prioritize when making decisions.

In addition to improving the organization's image, this alignment may draw funding from ethically conscious investors who actively look for ventures that fit their principles.

Regulations are changing to encourage or require green construction methods as governments across the globe place a greater emphasis on environmental sustainability. Putting money into sustainable real estate puts investors in a better position to handle regulatory changes. Investors future-proof their homes by proactively adding sustainable features, ensuring compliance with changing environmental regulations and preventing prospective retrofitting expenditures.

Sustainable real estate investments influence Brand and market competitiveness. Properties with energy-efficient features and green certifications make a statement in an environment where sustainability is becoming a differentiator more and more. This unique selling point may draw in a larger group of prospective renters or purchasers, accelerating the lease-up or sale process and increasing profits.

Green building certifications such as LEED or BREEAM may favorably impact financial results.

These certificates provide investors, renters, and other stakeholders with transparent standards for a property's sustainability. The legitimacy of these certificates may increase the property's marketability and worth, which can lead to financial success. As a result of a growing number of people expressing a desire for eco-friendly and sustainable living and working environments, consumer tastes are changing. Investing in sustainable real estate shows that one is aware of and adaptable to shifting consumer tastes. Sustainable homes are well-positioned to maintain their appeal and long-term financial success as these preferences continue to affect the real estate market. Innovative technologies and building techniques are often integrated into sustainable real estate ventures. This dedication to innovation puts Investors at the forefront of industry trends. Additionally, keeping up with technology developments may result in cost savings, improved property performance, and operational efficiency that support financial success.

Sustainable real estate investments provide chances for social impact in addition to environmental benefits. Investments that support social inclusion, strengthen local communities, and put tenants' needs first align with larger societal objectives. Investments with a social impact not only meet corporate responsibility requirements but may also have a good effect on investors and customers, which boosts financial performance. Investing in sustainable real estate has many more financial advantages than just being environmentally conscious. Including sustainability in real estate plans has several financial benefits, such as higher property values, lower expenses, easier access to green finance, and a competitive advantage. Adopting sustainable methods helps investors and developers present themselves as astute financial decision-makers aware of the changing real estate investment environment and contribute to a more sustainable future. Sustainability is becoming a crucial part of smart real estate investment plans because of the growing demand for sustainable homes and the significant financial benefits that come with them.

16.4 Implementing Eco-Friendly Features for Property Value Enhancement

Adding environmentally friendly amenities to real estate has emerged as a key tactic for raising property values and satisfying the public's rising desire for sustainable living. This section looks at the several eco-friendly elements that may be included in real estate developments. It investigates how these characteristics raise the value of the property. An essential component of environmentally responsible real estate construction is including energy-efficient systems. This covers installing HVAC (heating, ventilation, and air conditioning) systems, lights, and appliances that use less energy. In addition to lowering energy consumption, energy-efficient buildings reduce utility bills for their tenants, improving the property's allure.

Including renewable energy sources in a property's design, such as solar or wind turbines, is an excellent environmentally responsible touch that may greatly raise its value. Renewable energy-equipped buildings appeal to environmentally aware renters and purchasers since they support environmental sustainability and may result in lower power costs. Water conservation technology is another essential component of environmentally friendly real estate. This covers using smart irrigation technology, rainwater harvesting systems, and low-flow fixtures. These elements help save water and provide the impression that the house is ecologically conscious, which appeals to those who value sustainable living.

Using sustainable materials and techniques is essential to environmentally responsible real estate development. Using locally sourced or recycled materials and building techniques that reduce waste output may enhance an eco-friendly profile. Sustainable building materials may improve a property's longevity and aesthetic appeal, having a good environmental effect and increasing its total worth. One concrete approach to highlight a property's eco-friendly aspects is to pursue and get green certifications, such as BREEAM (Building Research Establishment Environmental Assessment Method) or LEED (Leadership in Energy and Environmental Design). These certifications may greatly increase the property's marketability and value by offering a recognized standard for sustainable construction techniques.

Including eco-friendly features such as smart home technology is becoming increasingly common. Smart home technologies improve overall resource management by making it possible to regulate and monitor water and energy use efficiently. These innovations raise the attractiveness and value of the house by appealing to tech-savvy purchasers and being environmentally friendly.

These techniques include integrating plants into the architecture of buildings. These elements enhance air quality, energy efficiency, and insulation. Green walls and roofs have advantages for the environment. Still, they may also improve a property's aesthetic appeal and contribute to its total worth by creating a distinctive and beautiful atmosphere. An essential component of eco-friendly real estate is landscaping. Using drought-tolerant native plants and environmentally friendly landscaping techniques helps save water resources and promotes biodiversity in the area. Landscapes that are thoughtfully planned and kept up improve the property's curb appeal and raise its perceived worth.

Energy-efficient fixtures and technology added to a well-planned lighting design increase the home's value and make it more environmentally friendly. For instance, LED lighting saves energy, has a long lifespan, and has many adjustable choices, improving the property's overall lighting aesthetics.

Including recycling and trash reduction initiatives in real estate projects demonstrates a developer's dedication to sustainability. The property's value is further increased by implementing effective waste management systems, encouraging recycling, and fostering a sustainable culture, all of which have a beneficial environmental impact.Improving indoor air quality directly affects occupants' health and is an environmentally beneficial feature. Low-emission finishes, non-toxic construction materials, and ventilation systems facilitate healthy interior environments. In addition to improving occupant comfort and health, a home with excellent indoor air quality attracts more buyers' attention in the real estate market. A property's eco-friendly profile is influenced by its location and proximity to green areas. The property's overall appeal is increased, and sustainable living concepts are aligned with accessibility to parks, natural reserves, and recreational places. The occupants' quality of life is enhanced by this closeness, which also raises property prices.

Sustainable transportation choices are often considered when developing eco-friendly real estate. Access to electric vehicle charging stations, bike-sharing programs, and public transit all help people live more ecologically friendly and lower their carbon footprints. These characteristics increase the property's total market value and attract eco-aware purchasers. The resort's overall eco-friendly reputation is enhanced by educational efforts and community engagement activities supporting the property's sustainability. The property's value and attractiveness may be increased by implementing green projects, holding seminars, and encouraging a feeling of Community around sustainability.

Two strategies that support environmentally responsible real estate practices are the adaptive reuse of existing structures and the preservation of historic buildings. Repurposing old buildings gives the property a distinctive identity while lowering the environmental effect of new development. In addition to increasing the historical and cultural significance of the property, preservation initiatives may also lead to tax benefits. Including eco-friendly elements in real estate is a comprehensive approach that extends beyond environmental stewardship—it directly influences property value and attraction to buyers. Property is positioned as an attractive and progressive investment when energy-efficient systems, renewable energy sources, sustainable materials, and certifications are integrated. These actions also support global sustainability objectives.

To appeal to a wide range of potential renters and purchasers, real estate developers and investors that emphasize eco-friendly amenities are positioning themselves to benefit from the growing demand for eco-friendly living. In the changing real estate development scenario, integrating eco-friendly elements is a strategic and financially feasible decision due to the tax advantages linked to increased property prices, energy savings, and market competitiveness. In addition to helping create a healthy world, the real estate sector benefits from encouraging sustainable practices in a market where buyers increasingly prioritize eco-friendliness.

16.5 Addressing Climate Change Risks and Opportunities in Real Estate

A key component of sustainable and progressive real estate development is addressing the possibilities and hazards of climate change in the real estate industry. This section examines how climate change affects the real estate industry, the dangers that come with it, and the possibilities for developing resilient, sustainable properties.

Effects of Climate Change on Real Estate:

Properties along the coast are especially susceptible to rising sea levels brought on by climate change. Infrastructure, property prices, and the general sustainability of coastal real estate are all at risk from rising sea levels. Developers and investors need to evaluate and address these risks by implementing strategies like raised building, effective stormwater management, and, in some situations, a calculated withdrawal from high-risk regions.

Real estate is significantly in danger from the rising frequency and severity of severe weather events, such as hurricanes, floods, and wildfires. Properties in areas vulnerable to these kinds of occurrences could sustain harm, resulting in monetary losses. Enhancing building rules, planning for disasters, and using climate-resilient design can reduce these risks and safeguard property values. Increasing temperatures and the growth of urban heat islands may affect a property's desirability and worth. To combat this and improve the appeal of houses, real estate developers may include cool roofing materials, green areas, and sustainable urban design to lessen the impacts of intense heat.

Regulatory and Policy Landscape:

In response to climate change, governments all over the globe are modifying building laws and regulations. Developers and property owners must be up-to-date with the latest regulations and guidelines concerning energy efficiency, carbon emissions, and resilience. Complying with or surpassing these requirements may improve a property's long-term value and marketability. Many governments provide financial aid for developing real estate that is both climate-resilient and sustainable. Projects emphasizing energy efficiency, renewable energy integration, and climate resilience include tax benefits, subsidies, and accelerated permits. Taking advantage of these incentives has financial advantages and encourages ecologically friendly behavior.

Prospects for Real Estate Resilient to Climate Change:

Including rain gardens, green roofs, and porous surfaces increases a property's ability to withstand climate change. By maximizing energy efficiency, lowering water use, and creating healthier living spaces, sustainable design techniques may raise the value of real estate.

Using renewable energy sources, including wind turbines and solar panels, gives real estate developers a chance to raise the value of their properties. In addition to lowering dependency on conventional energy sources, properties with on-site renewable energy systems can increase revenue by selling extra energy back to the grid. This refers to creating buildings resilient to the effects of climate change via design and construction. Elevated foundations, durable materials, and cutting-edge construction technologies may be examples. Climate-adaptive properties are more likely to retain their value and usefulness in the face of climatic effects.

Accessibility and Sustainable Transit:

Encouraging Sustainable mobility: Real estate developers may help create climate resilience by endorsing sustainable mobility alternatives. This might include building real estate close to hubs for public transit, adding bike-sharing services, and providing infrastructure for electric vehicles. Having access to eco-friendly transportation raises the value and appeal of a home. Building bike and pedestrian-friendly neighborhoods supports sustainability objectives and mitigates hazards associated with climate change. Properties in pedestrian-friendly, well-designed areas are more resistant to severe weather-related interruptions in transit. Property prices tend to rise in walkable areas because they are more attractive.

Sustainable Land Use and Conservation:

Real estate developers may help create a more resilient climate by combining conservation techniques and protecting natural habitats. This might include preserving wetlands, green areas, and natural buffers that provide ecosystem services and lessen the susceptibility of properties to the effects of climate change. This kind of urban planning considers climate hazards when making choices about land use. This entails steering clear of high-risk regions, encouraging mixed-use construction, and establishing green corridors. A property's long-term worth may be increased by proactive urban design techniques that reduce vulnerability to climate-related risks.

Disclosures and Transparency Concerning Climate:

Owners and developers of real estate are realizing the value of open and honest communication about strategies and risks associated with climate change. Encouraging prospective buyers, stakeholders, and investors with details on a property's sustainable practices and climate resilience measures may boost trust and favor property prices. A property's dedication to sustainability and climate resilience may be shown by its pursuit and acquisition of green certifications, such as BREEAM or LEED. These certificates raise the value of properties by offering an established and acknowledged norm for ecologically conscious real estate development.

Community Involvement and Social Resilience:

Social resilience is a climate and structural resilience component. Real estate developers might interact with communities to comprehend local climate risks and possibilities. Building community resilience and promoting social cohesiveness enhance a property's attractiveness and value.

Giving communities a voice in creating adaptation plans increases their sense of ownership over programs promoting climate resilience. In addition to promoting climate resilience, community-based strategies like participatory planning and educational initiatives also favor the perceived value of real estate in such places. Managing climate change opportunities and risks in real estate is essential for resilient, sustainable, and value-added property development. Real estate professionals must proactively identify and mitigate climate-related risks to build homes that not only endure the effects of climate change but also contribute to environmental sustainability and community well-being.

Real estate developers may effectively traverse the constantly changing terrain of climate-related concerns by integrating climate-resilient design, sustainable technology, and community participation. In the end, this results in a real estate portfolio that not only withstands environmental shifts but also meets the demands of a market that is becoming more and more concerned with sustainability, which raises long-term property values.

Conclusion

We have traveled over the complex terrain of property acquisition, financial methods, investment methodology, and the ever-changing real estate market in the chapters of this extensive book on real estate investing. The goal has been to provide investors with the information, resources, and understanding required to successfully negotiate the intricacies of real estate and forge a route toward accumulating wealth and financial success.

The adventure started with exploring the basic mathematics of real estate investing, grasping the nuances of Capitalization Rates (Cap Rates), Return on Investment (ROI), and Cash Flow. These fundamental ideas provided the framework for assessing an investment's profitability, enabling investors to make well-informed choices based on financial indicators. The guide clarified the many methods for optimizing returns on borrowed cash as we dug further into leveraging tactics. Investors were presented with various alternatives for maximizing their capital structure, ranging from conventional mortgages to innovative financing methods. However, the handbook also stresses how crucial it is to control financial risks, minimize any drawbacks, and ensure that investing methods are sustainable. A key component of the guide's content is comprehending the tax ramifications of real estate investments. Investors acquired insights into the complex world of taxes, from credits and deductions to investing for the best tax results. The handbook emphasized strategic tax planning as a crucial real estate portfolio financial optimization component.

Spreading assets over various property kinds and markets is important, and portfolio diversity has become a major subject. Investors were recommended to take a comprehensive approach to financial planning and match their real estate pursuits with more general wealth management objectives. A focus point was the development of criteria for choosing lucrative properties, which let investors assess possible investments based on factors such as property attributes, location dynamics, and market trends. Extensive approaches for due diligence were examined, highlighting the need for careful investigation and evaluation before entering into any real estate deal. By guiding readers through the complexities of comparing prospective value to market value, the handbook gave them the resources they needed to spot profitable possibilities. Methods for evaluating the depreciation and appreciation of real estate were disclosed, providing a strategic perspective for estimating the prospective return on investment over time.

Investors could maximize their financing plans by investigating mortgage alternatives and loan arrangements. Creative financing strategies, including partnerships and crowdfunding, were offered as cutting-edge answers for individuals looking for alternative capital sources and cooperative investment models. Using financial measures to reduce risks, including various asset protection methods, has emerged as a key issue. Developing techniques for the best cash flow management and comprehending debt-to-income ratios were essential to the risk reduction conversation. The book gave investors a thorough grasp of the many techniques accessible by navigating buy-and-hold tactics, property flipping, and hybrid approaches. Investors were armed with the information to match their tactics with their financial objectives, whether long-term wealth-building or short-term profit maximization.

The field of Real Estate Investment Trusts (REITs) and syndication was further explored, providing a window into the potential for passive income and collective investment strategies. Developing individualized investment plans became a prominent topic, urging investors to modify their methods to their financial goals. Ethical considerations and successful negotiating strategies were covered in the handbook. These strategies create win-win scenarios that benefit both buyers and sellers. Techniques for obtaining homes in advantageous conditions were shown, underscoring the need to establish and preserve moral connections within the real estate sector.

Property Management and Sustainability:

- It was noted that a key component of the investment process is effective property management for return on investment.
- The adoption of sustainable and environmentally friendly procedures for preserving property value.

The pros and disadvantages of employing property managers vs self-management.

Renovations, Upgrades, and Legal Compliance: Increasing the value of real estate via upgrades and renovations have turned into a strategic element that provides information on maximizing profits through well-considered adjustments. Being a responsible property owner required knowing local and federal real estate regulations, navigating the legal system, and ensuring everything was in conformity.

Adapting to Innovation and Market Dynamics: The handbook discussed the significance of developing strategies for remaining ahead in a dynamic market, embracing technology, and adjusting to changing market trends. The ability of an investor to recognize favorable times for investing became contingent upon their capacity to analyze and anticipate market patterns and cycles.

Portfolio Expansion and Wealth Creation: The last portions of the handbook examined methods for increasing and diversifying assets, balancing risk and growth, and using scaling approaches for long-term development. Creating long-term value via portfolio expansion techniques and efficiently managing many properties were important aspects of the wealth-building conversation.

Generational Wealth and Ethical Practices: The guide's conclusion discussed the importance of creating generational wealth via real estate, including estate planning and succession plans. The importance of philanthropy and community service was highlighted as a way to use real estate prosperity for good.

Global Markets and Future Trends: The last few chapters covered foreign investment methods, the global real estate markets, and the possible advantages of investing outside one's country. The book examined digital advancements such as big data analytics, blockchain applications, and smart home technologies transforming the real estate sector.

Crowdfunding and Niche Investments: The conversation about platforms for real estate crowdfunding, the investigation of opportunity zones for tax advantages, and the purchase of real estate notes and mortgage debt all contributed to the expansion of the investment environment. Assessing specialized assets, including holiday rentals and co-living spaces, gave investors information about new trends and other ways to diversify their portfolios.

To sum up, the goal of this book was to provide investors with a comprehensive grasp of real estate investing. Covering everything from basic ideas to sophisticated tactics, the handbook addressed every angle necessary for success in the ever-changing real estate industry. The significance of information, flexibility, moral concerns, and long-term planning characterizes the trip. Readers need to understand that real estate success involves more than simply making money; it also involves building sustainable wealth, giving back to communities, and leaving enduring legacies. This is especially true when they start their real estate venture. Based on sound financial judgment, strategic planning, and moral behavior, the tenets presented in this book operate as a guide for investors as they negotiate the complex real estate market.

Ultimately, the real estate industry is dynamic and full of chances and problems. Investors who maintain awareness, welcome change, and incorporate morality will be well-positioned to prosper in the current market and leave a lasting legacy based on ethical and significant real estate activities that transcend just financial gain. With this book ending, we encourage readers to go out with renewed knowledge, self-assurance, and a dedication to the values that characterize ethical and successful real estate investing.

BiblioGraphy

- PapersOwl. (2024, April 29). *The Wealth of the Medici Family: a Historical Examination*. PapersOwl.com. https://papersowl.com/examples/the-wealth-of-the-medici-family-a-historical-examination/
- *Mortgage Interest Rate Fundamentals*. (n.d.). https://www.mortgageretirementprofessor.com/A%20-%20Interest%20Rates/interest_rate_fundamentals.htm
- *The one chart you need to understand how income is distributed in the US*. (2022, July 12). World Economic Forum. https://www.weforum.org/agenda/2022/07/ho

usehold-income-distribution-wealth-inequality-united-states/

- Statista. (2024, April 19). *U.S. inflation rate versus wage growth 2020-2024.* https://www.statista.com/statistics/1351276/wage-growth-vs-inflation-us/
- Lamacchia Property Management. (2023, January 11). *7 features of a profitable rental property.* https://lamacchiapm.com/7-features-of-a-profitable-rental-property/
- *Creative financing for personal projects | Top 7 methods.* (n.d.). HeroX. https://www.herox.com/blog/1083-7-ways-to-fund-a-personal-project

- Khan, F. A., Pal, N., & Saeed, S. H. (2021). Stand-alone hybrid system of solar photovoltaics/wind energy resources: an eco-friendly sustainable approach. In *Elsevier eBooks* (pp. 687–705). https://doi.org/10.1016/b978-0-12-820004-9.00030-9
- *How can you build and maintain trust with investors?* (2023, September 18). https://www.linkedin.com/advice/0/how-can-you-build-maintain-trust-investors
- Better Homes LLC. (n.d.). *How upgrades and renovation can boost your property Market Value*. Betterhomes. https://www.bhomes.com/en/blog/betterinfor

med/how-upgrades-and-renovation-can-boost-your-property-market-value

- *real estate transactions*. (n.d.). LII / Legal Information Institute. https://www.law.cornell.edu/wex/real_estate_transactions
- Leads, A. (2024, March 9). *The role of community involvement in real estate*. ALL THE LEADS. https://www.alltheleads.com/the-role-of-community-involvement-in-real-estate
- Nguyen, J. (2023, July 20). *The 3 big risks faced by international investors*. Investopedia. https://www.investopedia.com/articles/basics/11/biggest-risks-international-investing.asp

- *How do you keep up with the changing trends and demands of the real estate development industry?* (2024, March 9). www.linkedin.com. https://www.linkedin.com/advice/0/how-do-you-keep-up-changing-trends-demands-1f
- Davis, C. (2024, April 23). *4 Best Real estate crowdfunding Investment Platforms of June 2024 - NerdWallet*. NerdWallet. https://www.nerdwallet.com/best/investing/real-estate-crowdfunding-platforms
- 국제 S. (2024, May 4). 호텔 시장 조사. SIS 국제 시장 조사. https://www.sisinternational.com/ko/expertise/industries/hotel-market-research/

- *Green Business Certification Inc.* (n.d.). Green Business Certification Inc. https://www.gbci.org/
- Admin. (2024, March 14). *Top 11 green building certifications that can increase your property's marketability*. SharpLaunch. https://www.sharplaunch.com/blog/green-building-certifications/
- *Managing transition risk in real estate: Aligning to the Paris Climate Accord*. (n.d.). https://www.unepfi.org/themes/climate-change/managing-transition-risk-in-real-estate-aligning-to-the-paris-climate-accord/

www.ingramcontent.com/pod-product-compliance
Lightning Source LLC
LaVergne TN
LVHW052210200926
848481LV00001B/67

9798330253340